Special

Special

The untold story of Australia's Holden

JOHN M. WRIGHT

ALLEN&UNWIN

First published in 2008

Allen & Unwin
83 Alexander Street
Crows Nest NSW 2065
Australia
Phone: (61 2) 8425 0100
Fax: (61 2) 9906 2218
Email: info@allenandunwin.com
Web: www.allenandunwin.com

National Library of Australia
Cataloguing-in-Publication entry:

Wright, John M., 1950–
Special : the untold story of Australia's Holden / John M. Wright.
Crow's Nest, N.S.W. : Allen & Unwin, 2008.

ISBN 9 781 74175 172 7 (pbk.)

Includes index.
Bibliography.

General Motors-Holden's Automotive Ltd.—History.
Holden automobiles—History.
Automobiles—Australia.

629.2220994

Set in 11/16 pt Sabon by Midland Typesetters, Australia
Printed in Australia by Ligare Book Printer

10 9 8 7 6 5 4 3 2 1

Contents

Introduction

Until now the true genealogy of the Holden car has never been told, despite the fact that many accounts have been written. So this book amounts to a revision of Holden history. The original 1948 Holden car is generally accepted as an Australian icon. It paved the way for such dominance of the local market that the release of a new model was front-page news through the 1950s. In 1959 one of the British weekly motoring magazines, *The Motor*, observed in the course of its November 1959 road test of the FC model, that 'it was hard to find a counterpart anywhere else in the world' for the Holden's dominance of its home market. But, while the Holden's locally iconic status has been understood overseas, the nature of the car's international automotive significance has not been grasped.

This is principally because the historical narratives concerning the origin and development of the Holden have been nationally rather than internationally focused. To understand how the Holden came into existence, we need to consider events that occurred in Detroit and Berlin, as well as those that took place at Fishermans Bend in Melbourne. It was at Fishermans Bend that General Motors-Holden's, the Australian subsidiary of General Motors Corporation, introduced the first model on 29 November 1948 at a gala function where Prime Minister Ben Chifley addressed the

1100 guests. (Significantly, a key message in Chifley's speech was the prospect of a third World War.)

While it is well known that the original Holden, the 48-215, owed its existence to an American experimental car (195-Y-15) built in the late 1930s and then discarded, the significance of this connection has never been fully analysed. Perhaps in the desire to cherish the Holden as a national symbol, as indeed a kind of symbol of Australia's coming of industrial age in the aftermath of World War II, local historians have felt little need to examine the more distant question of where the experimental car came from in the first place? If the Holden butterfly emerged from the chrysalis of a 1938 experiment, what had inspired the experiment? What was it based on? What can we learn from it about General Motors' global thinking? Nothing comes from nothing, as King Lear told Cordelia.

If the Holden butterfly emerged from the chrysalis of a 1938 experiment, what had inspired the experiment?

Equally, US-based historians of General Motors have shown no interest in this subject, perhaps because the car that eventually came to market finished up being an Australian Holden and not an American Chevrolet, and then not until 1948, by which time Detroit had found a whole new postwar focus in the guise of creating larger cars with new high compression V8 engines.

The history of General Motors itself has been well covered, mainly by US historians. There is near unanimity on the pivotal role of the management policies of Alfred P. Sloan Jr, who became president and chairman of the executive committee on 10 May 1923, served as president until 1949 and was chairman until 1956. How Sloan drove General Motors with its un-coordinated management and chaotic assortment of more and less successful products from a very distant second place behind Ford to a position of utter market dominance within a decade is well documented. This work has been done mostly by historians whose principal interest is either business/economics or business management. For American economic and political historians Sloan has been a rich source. But the Australian Car Program which was initiated in November 1944 has, unsurprisingly, mostly eluded their notice. Many pay scant attention to GM's overseas manufacturing programs and, compared with Opel in Germany, for example, Holden's revenue contribution to General Motors has been modest, which has doubtless further discouraged interest in the corporation's role in Australia. There is a persistent US-centricity in the work of virtually all historians working in this field.

General Motors itself had an international perspective of a kind from 1911 when it organised the General Motors Export Company to sell its products overseas. The name was changed in 1938 to General Motors Overseas Operations. This reflected the shift from exporting either whole vehicles or chassis (to be fitted with locally manufactured bodies, as for example in Australia) from the US to the local manufacture in England and Germany of cars specifically developed to suit European markets. By 1962, 14.26 per cent of all GM vehicles were manufactured outside the US. This statistic alone—from a standing start in 1926 when Vauxhall produced 1513 cars and trucks—implies the parochialism of the US automotive and economic historians researching General Motors.

For most of the American writers, except those specifically concerned with the evolution of the Detroit-based automotive industry and for motoring journalists focused on product, motor vehicles are peripheral to their studies of Sloan. This perhaps should be surprising, especially when comparison is made with histories of Henry Ford where the Model T inevitably receives significant analysis. It is surprising, too, because Sloan's product policy was at the heart of General Motors' international as well as its American success. So if Chevrolets, Pontiacs, Oldsmobiles, Buicks and Cadillacs are barely discussed by these historians, what hope is there for the humble Holden, which is not even sold in the US? And how about the German Opels and English Vauxhalls? It is effectively an isolationist reading of history, as if General Motors overseas business were at best peripheral to the corporation's international dominance.

The history of GM's German subsidiary, Opel, during the twelve years of the Thousand Year Reich, was largely neglected by historians until Henry A. Turner's 2005 study *General Motors and the Nazis*. It was indeed the success of Opel almost as much as the Detroit manufacturers that consolidated GM as far and away the world's pre-eminent automotive manufacturer heading towards World War II (by which time its ownership of Opel was at risk). But the German company thriving under its new US know-how (which included mass production techniques, advanced new engines, and radical lightweight monocoque, or one-piece, body construction) had grown to the stage where it could become the leading supplier of the land-based weapons of destruction for the Nazis. Even proud Daimler-Benz was compelled against its inclination to build Opel trucks under licence in the final years of the war. It seems clear to me that without the efforts of Opel, Hitler could not have triggered World War II as early as 1939. Also never analysed has been the nexus between the ferocious growth of Opel in the 1930s and the Australian Car Program.

Without Hitler, there may never have been an Australian car for two separate reasons.

Without Hitler, there may never have been an Australian car for two separate reasons. General Motors learnt lessons at Opel that it could apply to cars made for other markets in the postwar years. And the Australian government's preoccupation with national defence provided the imperative to manufacture cars in Australia; thus the socialist-inclined Labor government happily leapt into bed with multinational General Motors. (This explains Chifley's preoccupation with war when launching Australia's first mass-produced passenger car.)

As for Australian writers, they have their own preoccupations. It is fair to say that the mythology surrounding the man often referred to as the 'father of the Holden', Sir Laurence John ('Larry') Hartnett, has deflected more questions than it has answered. By and large, Hartnett's account of events has been swallowed whole by the automotive industry, although it has been shown by historian Joe Rich in *Hartnett: Portrait of an Industrial Tycoon* to be wrong in many elements (and more will be uncovered here). The Hartnett myth reads: the Australian car was his idea, he fought the good fight against Sloan and the Americans, and he was never fully appreciated by GM which was all too ready to let him go before the car had even made its debut. It is a nice Australian story which minimises US cultural imperialism in bringing the Holden to fruition.

And so the American writers tell their history with only the briefest passing reference to Australia. The Australians mention the experimental car that might have been destined to be a Chevrolet but was rescued and transformed into the rugged Holden. The emphasis is on how significantly reworked the experimental vehicle was for its transformative role, which is certainly true. In Australian automotive history, the line between history and GMH's own advertising is a fine one: the slogan 'Australia's Own Car's is too easily appropriated as a descriptor. All of this amounts to a failure of history which results from the blinkered vision of historians tackling the huge subject of a multinational corporation from a national rather than international perspective.

An international reading of the Holden history actually renders that first 48-215 model more important in the automotive world than the purely local reading does. Some historians, and most notably Don Loffler, who has written three books on the subject, have understood the thoroughness with which the first Holden was engineered, but until now this process has not found its full international context. Loffler compares the Holden with its peers on the Australian market, but how would it have shaped up against the best cars available overseas at the time?

The Holden 48-215 deserves to be included among the half dozen most important vehicles produced by General Motors anywhere ever, even though in sales terms it barely amounted to a pimple on the General's huge, well-fed face. (In 1962 General Motors produced 5,238,601 cars and trucks internationally with Holden accounting for just 133,325 of these.) That is because the Holden was probably the first car since Henry Ford's Model T developed to a thorough agenda to suit a carefully defined and most demanding market. Only General Motors could have done this because only General Motors was a truly global player by 1945 (despite Ford's best efforts). A minor but relevant point is that General Motors led the way in testing its own products under arduous conditions at a dedicated proving ground (a Sloan innovation).

So the Holden is more important than has been realised and its significance is international in meaning even though its sales have been, for the most part, principally local. This century, Holden ships Pontiacs to the United States and Chevrolets to the Middle East, so its place in the international automotive world is self-evident. But the first Holden provides another key piece of evidence, missed by all General Motors scholars until now, of the genius of Alfred Sloan and his role in shaping the global economy.

To tell this story it will be necessary to review some well established history, notably of how Sloan reshaped General Motors both domestically in Detroit and internationally. It will also be necessary to analyse the qualities of the Holden car itself—to 'read' it as one might a text. One of my conclusions is that the early models were not just ideally suited to Australian conditions but they were for a few years the best cars made anywhere in the world when judged against the unique criteria of Australian motorists in the late 1940s and early 1950s. Obviously millions of words have been written about the car but until now I believe full justice has never been done to the place of this ostensibly parochial and quintessentially Australian product in the international automotive world.

Prologue

EFIJY, and why only Holden has Australia's automotive pulse

It is 17 July 2006 and, in a moment of corporate open-heartedness, Holden is hosting the motoring media inside its highly secure technical centre at Fishermans Bend in Melbourne. The occasion is the launch of the fourth-generation Commodore, Australia's top-selling car for most of the past 28 years and for the past ten in succession. This VE range is, Holden's American chairman and managing director, Denny Mooney, insists, the most Australian Holden ever. This new Commodore has been designed, says design director Tony Stolfo, not just from a clean sheet of paper but an entire roll.

The journalists, of whom I am one, are escorted through the highly secure building to various studios where detailed briefings are held. Security guards quietly watch the corridors. If ever Holden's design culture is on display, this is the occasion. Naturally, all talk is of the brand new model range, the years of planning and research involved, why the VE looks the way it does, has the features it has, and why these proud designers believe the latest Commodore range is such a fantastic achievement. At times the mood and detail are too intense. We feel like voyeurs. There is obsession in the air. These designers get off on talking about 'Holden DNA'.

As can be found in every automotive design centre throughout the world, the walls are adorned with framed futuristic sketches. Here in Holden's Technical Centre most depict the VE Commodore as the stylists had conceived it in 1999, 2002, 2003, but one particular three-dimensional object delivers a more concentrated dose of what can indeed be termed Holden DNA. No one mentions it. Outside the main studio for exterior design there is a beautiful purple clay model in 30 per cent scale. But this is not the new Commodore. It is the EFIJY show car of 2005, the masterpiece of Richard Ferlazzo, who also happens to be the chief exterior designer of the new Commodore. EFIJY, lifesize in glittering metal and absolutely drivable (although it will turn out that very few people outside Holden's innermost sanctum ever will drive it), was the undisputed star of the 2005 Australian International Motor Show at Sydney's Darling Harbour. In 2006 the US magazine *Hot Rod* named it Hot Rod of the Year. In 2007 EFIJY won the North American Concept Car of the Year. How universal is its appeal? In the December 2007 edition of *Wheels* magazine, a reader wrote: '. . . when we stopped to take a photo of a typical "outback" settlement in western Mongolia the only sign in the town was a photo of the Holden EFIJY.'

EFIJY is an artistic reinvention of the 1953 FJ Holden Special. Here is a work of high automotive art morphed out of 1950s popular culture, a show car that seemed to cause a deep intake of breath from all present that day at Darling Harbour when it was first unveiled, but more so perhaps from those among us who are grizzled around the edges from carrying the responsibility of being baby boomers. We are the ones whose parents drove Holdens, who learnt to drive in Holdens, who slipped into the back seats of Holdens at suburban drive-ins, who later bought and hotted up Holdens that might have been owned by our parents or grandparents. For us, and perhaps particularly the males of the species, the Australian landscape was defined almost as much by these early Holdens taking Australians about their business as it was by eucalypts, Vegemite or Gwen Meredith's long-running radio serial *Blue Hills*.

EFIJY is a baby boomer's cry from the heart. Deep purple ('Soprano Purple'), it packs a high-powered supercharged V8 engine out of Harrop Engineering, an engine which could power a contemporary V8 Supercar. You look inside, at the steering wheel, the dashboard, the view through the windscreen—this is time warped backwards to the future. Richard Ferlazzo has taken a cultural memory of the early 1950s and morphed it into a car for a new century. Even the uninitiated can see the cues taken from the FJ: the badging, the grille, even the hub caps. Here is a profound metamorphosis: green frog into purple-robed prince. Nobody but the copywriters ever described the FJ Holden Special as 'beautiful', but now we can see where the beauty lurked, waiting to be freed by an artist's vision. Had this coupe suddenly appeared outside a suburban milk bar in Northcote or Newtown in 1955, someone would have had a heart attack. You. Or me. Or both of us. All of us.

EFIJY is a baby boomer's cry from the heart.

EFIJY was to the 2005 Australian International Motor Show what the Commodore Coupe—which became the Monaro—was to the 1998 event. But unlike the 1998 showpiece this one is highly unlikely ever to make it to production. To someone unfamiliar with the unique position of the early Holdens in Australian postwar life, this reincarnation of a 1953 car is harder to explain than the '98 Commodore Coupe. It is easy enough to see how a slinky Commodore-based two-door would win hearts. It took the still new 1997 VT Commodore's styling and drove it further into eternal streamline. But a hot rod FJ Special in 2005, half a century beyond bodgies and blue heaven milkshakes? Surely the connection is more difficult, more limited? And didn't anyone worry that it might backfire, that someone might ask why Holden is looking back 50 years rather than forwards? (This has been said of Jaguar, after all.)

In fact EFIJY is nothing less than Australian Graffiti, drawing entirely on local memory, aimed like Cupid's arrow at baby boomer hearts, and seductive, too, of much younger people. Not just car enthusiasts, but just about everyone who has lived in Australia long enough to have any sense of what Holden is and was, what the brand means, has meant, and will continue to mean. EFIJY is, in a sense, the poetic metaphor for the brand: it *is* Holden.

The ubiquity of the FJ from its debut through until well into the 1970s meant that young car enthusiasts grew familiar with it when their parents or grandparents bought one. Those poor old Holdens! Having served a hard and worthy life as the family car, they then found themselves sprayed Midnight Blue or Candy Apple Red, fitted with wide wheels, lowering kits, noisy exhausts and expected to go and handle much better than their maker had ever intended. I still remember how feeble my mechanically standard (except for the lowering blocks in the rear suspension and the Speco-Thomas floorshift conversion) 1954 Mosman Blue FJ seemed after I had been taken for a ride in a friend's 'FX' with its full race engine. My car valve-bounced in second as the speedo brushed 50 miles per hour, but the modified car could reach 70 in its intermediate ratio and a true 105 in top.

And thus has the FJ reverberated through the generations. Men who were twenty or 25 in the mid 1950s and perhaps unable to afford a new FJ waited until they were retired before buying one and lovingly restoring it. So in a sense many of them have taken over the role of their own grandparents, but the FJ has, if anything, even more meaning to them now than it did when new.

Arguably, the FJ is even more famous than

> And thus has the FJ reverberated through the generations. Men who were twenty or 25 in the mid 1950s and maybe unable to afford a new FJ waited until they were retired before buying one and lovingly restoring it.

the original 48–215 (popularly known as 'FX') model on which it was based. With the first new model in the five years since 1948, a Special variant was added to the FJ for just that hint of fifties flashiness, meaning there were minimal chrome fins and options which included Elascofab upholstery and two-tone paintwork; the Special edition of the FJ certainly was for 1953. In the end, however, the two models 'FX' and FJ merge in our cultural memory as truly 'Australia's Own Car'.

The early Holdens have now acquired too much respectability to become victim to the homegrown hot-rodder's art. Besides, who would spend a fortune trying to make a 1955 model go hard, corner crisply without falling over, and stop on a florin when you could open your street-machine account with a Commodore V8 instead? So the generations move on. The FJs are polished up for slow cruises and concours, while the Holden petrolheads are happy with their HSVs. And this is where the EFIJY show car purples our picture. Here, Chiko Roll and blue suede shoes memories meet the new century.

Imagine the self-made boomers queuing to splurge $250K on an EFIJY, ready for a long cruise down Nostalgia Boulevarde through eternal autumn and no more broken dreams . . . Real money has been offered many times and sometimes by rock stars for whom price is no object, but this dream is not for sale, it seems. Except to anyone with a camera and memory bank.

There's nothing gratuitous, gimmicky or overdone with EFIJY. It is integrated in the way only the very best designs are. The cultural and marketing message embedded here amounts to this priceless catchline: *only Holden has Australia's automotive pulse*. Only Holden could display a hot rod interpretation of a 1953 model to out-star the latest Ferraris, Porsches, Rolls-Royces, Bentleys, Maybachs and all others. This is a more lustful, expansive style of retro than we see in, say, the Volkswagen New Beetle or even the MINI Cooper S. EFIJY is streamlined dreamery on huge wheels, much more George Barris than Alec Issigonis. Its greatness goes beyond one market, as the award from *Hot Rod* magazine attests.

EFIJY would have been inconceivable in 1948, even by George Barris, the master of custom car design, or Harley Earl, chief stylist at General Motors in Detroit (although Earl did create the fabulous Buick Y-Job of 1938). But, without the background of the early Holden emanating from its every stylistic element, whatever considerable beauty and artistry EFIJY embodies would be greatly reduced. Would this be similar to the difference between a grand piano standing in the corner of a room and that same instrument with Vladimir Ashkenazy playing Rachmaninoff's Second Piano Concerto? EFIJY is completely modern. You could drive it over the Sydney Harbour Bridge or around the speed bowl at Holden's Lang Lang proving ground. But EFIJY was not created to pound over corrugated creek crossings in the way that the early Holdens were and nor could it come close to equalling the amazing fuel miserliness that so endeared those cars to buyers in the fag-end 1940s, when petrol was still being rationed.

Can it be coincidence that the man who created EFIJY, Richard Ferlazzo, is the man in charge of the team who will deliver the fourth generation Holden Commodore less than a year later? Surely not. Ferlazzo, you see, *knows* what Holden means and how, in 2006, the core elements can still be related to those of 1948.

'How does Holden keep doing it?' people asked that morning at Darling Harbour. 'How do they manage to steal the show with a car that no-one has been able to imagine?' 'Why couldn't Ford do something like this?'

The obvious answer is that Ford simply doesn't have the depth and breadth of cultural footprint that Holden does, despite the immense fame of the Falcon GTHO Phase III and its siblings. When the FJ Holden was sweet-talking buyers, Ford's bestseller in this country was the English Zephyr, a car far too low slung for Australia's corrugated roads. It was not until 1960 that the company finally followed its arch-rival into full Australian manufacture, the car of choice being the Falcon.

Ford Australia's early experience with the Falcon set it on a conservative road from which it has never been able to deviate, at least with the mainstream Falcon. In 2000, I was working as a consultant to the marketing department at Ford Australia and an anecdote from that time might illustrate one particular aspect of Ford's conservatism. A senior marketing person asked me if I could convince the engineers (she had a less polite phrase on her lips, there traditionally being intense rivalry in automotive companies between those who design the cars and those who have to sell them) to lower the ride height of the Falcon, to make it sit closer to the ground like the then current VX Commodore. The AU Falcon sat up like Jacky and there was a huge amount of blank space between the tops of the front tyres and the guards. This problem was indeed addressed with the AU II, but not in the way the marketing executive had envisaged. The ride height wasn't changed, but a larger 16-inch wheel/tyre combination solved the visual issue. Simply, it was part of Ford Australia's engineering doctrine that a certain level of ground clearance be preserved, despite the fact that comparatively few Falcons were ever driven into country where such conservatism might be appreciated.

Holden, being less hidebound, had another solution to the same problem. Buyers who wished to use their Commodores on unforgiving roads just had to order the optional country pack suspension with higher ride height. Of course, by the time the change of century was drawing close, neither a Ford Falcon nor a Holden Commodore was the vehicle of choice for most Australians living in the bush; the Toyota Landcruiser and Nissan Patrol had long taken over this role.

Why, then, did Ford Australia's engineers insist on the higher ride height? Corporate memory can be short, but I would suggest that it was the company's experience in the very early 1960s that dictated policy. The first Falcons produced at Broadmeadows, north of Melbourne, were mechanically identical to their US counterparts, except for their right-hand drive. The front suspension was not rugged enough for Australian conditions. Ball joints failed. For different reasons, clutches failed. The US engineers expressed

So even as late as 1960, it seems that Ford's grasp of just why the early Holdens had been so successful was, at best, weak. As were the cars themselves.

bewilderment, having seen no such issues in North America. So even as late as 1960, it seems that Ford's grasp of just why the early Holdens had been so successful was, at best, weak. As were the cars themselves. Ford Australia learnt the hard way, almost having to abandon its Falcon program as late as 1965. Motoring in this country, then and even now, differs from the North American or European experience, and it's mostly tougher. But Australia still calls Holden home, as it were.

This book intends to take a long look at the past half-century or more before EFIJY—at the time before Holden manufactured cars in Australia, and at the processes that enabled multinational General Motors to do a deal with the socialistically inclined government of Australia to bring the Holden to market.

Why was the Holden the kind of car it was? Was it really so special? And how did it come into being in the first place? From under which cabbage did the Holden emerge to change Australia's automotive culture forever? Was 'Australia's Own Car' some kind of weird historical fluke? Was it actually Australian, was it even our own? And where did it fit into the huge and often unforgiving corporate world of General Motors? Who did the thinking? What was the name of the senior stylist in Detroit who drew its shape, and why has this never been told in Australia before? Were there any precedents for a car of this type? Perhaps there is an even bigger question to ask, beyond mere motoring and the love of cars: what is the true context of the Holden 48–215 in twentieth-century history? Can its status be compared with other motoring icons such as Henry Ford's Model T, Hitler's Volkswagen, the Citroën *Diesse* or the Mini-Minor? Is the Holden really 'Australia's Own Car'?

> **From under which cabbage did the Holden emerge to change Australia's automotive culture forever? Was 'Australia's Own Car' some kind of weird historical fluke? Was it actually Australian, was it even our own?**

Chapter 1

Australia not on wheels

By nine that night, the bush telegraph had summoned from far and near, those others who had or had not seen a thylacine alive. For miles the roads were blocked—phaetons, gigs, traps, buggies, jinkers and spring drays, hacks and bicycles and almost as wonderous [sic] as the tiger, there was a motor car.

—Anonymous, Meunna, Tasmania, 1916

Nineteen sixteen, the year after Australian troops hurled themselves into enemy gunfire at Gallipoli, looks like another country now. From 3 July 1916, the Battle of the Somme would change Europe forever. Billy Hughes was prime minister of Australia. Singer Nellie Melba was building her career. Thylacines were not yet extinct and had only just become a rarer sight than a motor car to residents in remote parts of Australia such as Meunna, Tasmania. Henry Ford's Model T had been putting American families on wheels since 1909 (508,000 were sold in 1915), but Australia was slower to embrace the horseless carriage. Before the 1880s, while the moneyed took comfort in carriages pulled by teams of horses in finest Jane Austen tradition, Shanks Pony had been mainstream transport.

The long period between the 1880s and 1945 is often called the era of public transport, which does not explain much because public transport varied enormously throughout Australia and was effectively non-existent in many areas. The bicycle, invented only a handful of years before the car, was also a favoured means for transcending pedestrianism. As late as the mid 1930s car ownership was only taken for granted by the wealthier groups in Australian society. The silent majority got by as best it could, as it always does, rarely dreaming of cars, and the description 'phaetons, gigs, traps, buggies, jinkers and spring drays, hacks and bicycles' is an evocative summary for much of rural Australia in 1916.

War is often a phenomenal catalyst for industry and this was the case for Australia on three separate occasions last century, with the Holden name to the fore on all three. The Boer War boosted the fortunes of companies such as Holden & Frost, which made saddles and leather goods, all needed by the cavalry sent from Australia to fight in South Africa. James Holden had started his saddles and leather goods business at 46 King William Street, Adelaide, in 1857. By the 1870s he had diversified into carriage manufacture. In 1879 his eldest son Henry James Holden was made a partner and effectively took over the business, taking on Henry Frost as a partner in 1885. By the early years of the new century Holden & Frost was the federal government's largest supplier of military saddles. But diversification continued and in 1916 the company built its first custom motor body as a replacement for a Hotchkiss car belonging to an Adelaide publican, and more orders followed.

The economic isolation forced upon Australia during World War I drove the development of what would become a thriving homegrown automotive industry. Let's jump forward one year from our thylacine sighting at Meunna to a parliamentary gazette of 10 August 1917. In response to danger posed by German U-boats, the government introduced a somewhat curiously named Luxuries Restriction. Shipping space was placed at a premium and the government decided it could no longer be wasted on the import of 'luxuries', a catch-all term for a motley lot including 'Ale and other beer ... biscuits, confectionery, eggs (in shell or otherwise), fur apparel, perfumery ... bodies for motor vehicles, whether imported separately or forming part of a complete vehicle'.

The economic isolation forced upon Australia during World War I drove the development of what would become a thriving homegrown automotive industry.

If only the chassis could be imported, then bodies would have to be manufactured locally or there would be no cars. And so from a trickle of bespoke bodies supplied by Holden & Frost and others came the stream of mass production. Even when the prohibition was lifted, a heavy tariff regime remained. The die was cast: the overwhelming majority of cars sold throughout the 1920s and 1930s would combine a fully imported chassis with an Australian body.

Under the government's regulation, the 'chassis' could be imported with bonnet, scuttle, dash, mudguards and running boards included. Under these rules Holden Motor Body Builders, a new company formed by the Holden family, was able to supply a fully painted Dodge body for £57.10/– delivered to any port in Australia—much less than some dealers had been expecting.

There was immediate strong demand, with Holden Motor Body Builders in the thick of the action. The ready availability of competitively priced local bodies contributed to a dramatically increased demand for cars. At the end of 1921, four years before Ford commenced its operations in Geelong, there were 24 cars per 1000 people in South Australia compared with sixteen in Victoria, fifteen in New South Wales, thirteen in Tasmania, twelve in Western Australia and just eight in Queensland. As in the United States, employment within a locally based industry encouraged participation via ownership. The fledgling body building industry was focused in South Australia, which by 1928 had 140.7 vehicles per 1000 people. This was significantly more than any other state, and only the tiny, more densely populated and predominantly middle-class Australian Capital Territory outstripped the South Australian rate of ownership with 163.5 per 1000, with many of these vehicles being government-owned.

A fivefold increase in motorisation from 1921 to 1928 was indeed dramatic but not sufficient to redefine Australia as a car-oriented society in the US style. Contemporary photographs show that traffic discipline was yet to apply even in the main streets of Sydney and Melbourne, where pedestrians jaywalked and cars were sometimes left unattended in the middle of the road. Reasonably high unemployment levels doubtless helped dampen the demand for new cars. In the years between 1915 and 1928 male unemployment ranged between 5 and 9 per cent, but in the financial year 1928–29 there was a spike to 11.5 per cent. By 1929, however, everything was at risk as the Great Depression spread like influenza from Wall Street to the rest of the world. Male unemployment jumped to 17.2 per cent in 1929–30, to 26.6 per cent in 1930–31 and peaked at 30.6 per cent in 1931–32. It was not until 1935–36 that the figure dipped below 20 per cent (16.8), and by the start of World War II it was still 13.6 per cent.

On the eve of the Great Depression, Australian motorisation was more widespread than in any European country but, like any numbers, these can be misinterpreted. However, American automotive historian James J. Flink, noting that in the first six months of 1927 81.4 per cent of Australian new car sales went to US brands, has claimed:

> . . . the automobile cultures developing in 1920s Canada, Australia, and New Zealand were tightly integrated with the American car culture, through both manufacturing and marketing . . . [There was a] shared set of material conditions that permitted Americans, Australians, Canadians, and New Zealanders to actualise the possibilities of mass personal automobility a generation ahead of the Europeans.

Flink's assertion that Australian automobility (for want of a more stylish term) followed the US blueprint is partly right. The motor body industry quickly developed a high skill level, having to create bodies to fit a wide variety of chassis. Eighty per cent of these chassis came from the United

States in the first half of 1927 while the rest came from Britain. But the above begs the question of what precisely—or even approximately—constitutes 'mass personal automobility'. The ratio of people to cars in 1927 was one to 5.3 in the United States, one to 10.5 in New Zealand, one to 10.7 in Canada, and one to sixteen in Australia. In both France and Great Britain there was one car for every 44 people and in Germany there was just one for every 196. But while Australian vehicle ownership was obviously greater than in Europe, it does not amount to 'mass personal automobility' even by purely numerical criteria. A rate of one car per sixteen people meant that only about one Australian family in four owned a car—not high enough to justify the claim that this country enjoyed mass personal automobility. (Let's call it 'motorisation'.)

Car ownership in Australia was still unusual, although not rare, as late as 1920. Farmers tended to own cars by then, as did doctors and those whose work required access to private and flexible transport. Wealthier people often owned cars, but public transport served for the majority. By the time cars began to trickle into Australia the government-run train and tram services were well established.

The United States, by contrast, could be said almost to have achieved mass motorisation (with exceptions for poorer groups, such as the majority of African Americans) by the time of its engagement in World War I in 1917. In 1915 the total number of vehicles registered passed two million, but in that year alone 660,000 new passenger cars had been sold: growth was exponential. Los Angeles led the world. The city already had 141,000 cars in 1919 and 777,000 by 1929, which was 50 per cent more than Australia's total.

Economies of scale combined with the highest standard of living in the world to give Americans the wherewithal to buy this second most expensive of all consumer items many years

Los Angeles led the world. The city already had 141,000 cars in 1919 and 777,000 by 1929, which was 50 per cent more than Australia's total.

before most other countries arrived at a similar stage of material development. Hire purchase was prevalent in United States, where the advance of capitalism was probably at least a quarter of a century ahead of everywhere else. General Motors' own finance company, General Motors Acceptance Corporation (GMAC), was founded in 1919. This was one factor that helped General Motors to overhaul Ford during the 1920s, with Henry Ford refusing to endorse hire purchase while General Motors chairman and president Alfred P. Sloan was actively encouraging it. In Australia, the buying of motor cars on hire purchase was not introduced until the 1920s and was not commonplace until after World War II. And it was a big factor in booming British motorisation during the 1920s and 1930s, although many buyers shopped at a distance from home so their succumbing to usury would remain secret from their social set.

Certainly Australia had plenty in common with the United States, as did, in their different ways, Canada and New Zealand. Outside the major cities roads were appalling and the stylish European vehicles had trouble traversing them. But the differences between Australia and the United States outweigh the similarities. In the first quarter of the twentieth century an overwhelming majority of the population already lived in the coastal capital cities, making Australia one of the most urbanised nations in the world, while the United States had a plethora of hinterland settlements inaccessible except by private transport. In Australia public transport was government-owned and run, and policy favoured it wherever possible. By contrast, private companies ran the railroads in the United States, and by the 1920s the construction of good roads was a priority; indeed, several federal Acts were passed which metaphorically paved the way for effective highways in all states. By 1925 the Lincoln Highway issued its invitation to motorisation via a strip of bitumen from one side of the United States to the other. Cars had been deemed 'democratic' and were subsidised by governments. Rail services declined. Cars drove the growth of US industry.

Motoring historian Richard Burns Carson demonstrates the connection between the democratisation of motoring and the rise of a new class of luxury cars in the United States. By 1925 riding in a car was 'an everyday event'. So 'more specialized pleasure' was required. This was the same thinking that drove General Motors' product planning in the mid 1920s, as we shall see in the next chapter. With motoring no longer an adventure, Ford's Model T became merely quaint and outmoded. While the rich sought new-style luxury cars, middle-class motorists and an increasing number of blue-collar workers wanted something low slung, sleek and speedy. So by 1925 US motoring had already diverged strongly from the Australian experience.

The land mass of Australia was similar to that of the United States but its population density was dramatically less, which made the cost of developing an adequate road system far more expensive per capita. In 1920 the census showed Australia's population (excluding 'full-blood aborigines') to be 5,472,318 with a density of 1.84 people per square mile, while the United States had 105,253,300 people at a density of 35.39 per square mile. Given the dramatically higher rate of car ownership in the United States, the density of cars per square mile across the two countries would have borne no comparison.

One major reason for the rapid spread of motoring in the United States was the size and strength of the domestic automotive industry centred in Detroit, a city whose population swelled from 300,000 in 1900 to 1.8 million by 1930. Living at the heart of the new industry provided people with a great incentive to participate in the culture by buying their own cars. Ford, General Motors and Chrysler were the biggest among numerous automotive companies. Many of those who didn't work in the industry themselves had a brother, sister, son, daughter, uncle or aunt who did. By 1913 there were a million cars in the United States, much more than half of which were Model T Fords, and many had been bought by the men who built them on the world's first automotive assembly line. It had been a policy of Henry Ford's from the start to encourage his workers to buy cars and in 1914 he raised the minimum daily wage from $2.30 to $5. Australia would not have a million cars on its roads until 1948.

Ford understood that, if his company were to continue to thrive, working-class people would have to be able to afford cars. In 1914 a Model T runabout cost US$575, which represented 115 days of work for a Ford employee. In 1915 the price of a new Ford in Australia was £210, which represented almost 500 days of work. So in real terms cars were almost five times as expensive in the country Americans have always loved to call 'Down Under'—and in 1915 this was true in both geographic and economic terms, when it came to the ownership of motor vehicles.

The state of Australian 'roads'

By 1906, when sightings of *any* car were still occasional in Australian capital cities, congestion in the Chicago central business district was already severe enough to provide the catalyst for a 'Plan of Chicago'. The United States would soon enjoy a modern freeway system on a scale not seen anywhere else in the world, and in 1929 Carpenter's drive-in restaurant was opened in Los Angeles, which was well on the way to becoming 'an auto-mobilised city' like no other. Increasingly, the lack of access to a car would represent a severe curtailment of social possibilities for Los Angeles residents. An automobilised city has supermarkets, for example, and these only become viable when sufficient numbers of people drive rather than walk or catch public transport. In the days of the local shop, people bought only what they could carry or wheel home in a buggy.

Australian motorists did not enjoy anything like the same quality of roads as had long been taken for granted in the United States. At the start of World War II Victoria, the most densely populated state of Australia, had just 5000 miles (8000 kilometres) of bitumen out of a total road distance of 9900 (which did not include dirt tracks), and even in 1947 tarred roads were by no means to be taken for granted, comprising as they did just 5700 miles (9173 kilometres) of the total 13,200 (21,240). Nevertheless, this was a huge increase on the 1400 miles (2253 kilometres) in 1928, and it suggests that the Country Roads Board had some political clout in Victoria.

An oblique reference in the Country Roads Board's 1946–47 annual report implies how far Victoria was behind the United States when it came to the quality and style of roads. The 'spectacular' was not on the menu:

In general, the available funds and resources in this State are sufficient to deal only with the urgently-needed road facilities of a less spectacular type . . . [and] 'clover-leaf intersections, multi-lane divided highways . . . [the] lighting [of] rural roads for their full length . . . [is] only warranted in densely-populated areas.

The same report lists total mileage of 'black surfaces' at just 1931 miles (3108 kilometres) for state highways, 3747 (6030) for main roads and 95 (153) for tourists and forest roads. 'Black surfaces', then, were hardly to be taken for granted even on significant thoroughfares in 1947.

The situation in New South Wales was worse. Of 124,443 miles (200,300 kilometres) of roads in 1946, only 377 (607) were 'cement concrete', 212 (341) 'asphaltic concrete' and 2701 (4347) 'tar or bituminous macadam', meaning just 3290 miles (5295 kilometres) were tarmac. (Fifteen years after the Victorian CRB claimed 3842 miles of 'black surface', New South Wales had not reached this number despite its vastly greater area.) 'Gravel/crushed rock' accounted for 30,316 miles (48,790 kilometres), while 83,288 (134,000) were either 'formed only' (26,114 miles, or 42,030 kilometres) or 'cleared/natural surface only' (57,174 miles, or 92,010 kilometres). But 'the spectacular', in the guise of clover-leaf intersections and multi-laned highways, was already taken for granted in some areas of the United States as early as 1930.

Paradoxically, some of Australia's most famous scenic roads were created during the 1930s when unemployment relief schemes provided work for able-bodied men. Notable among these were sections of Victoria's Great Ocean Road and the construction of the Mount Panorama tourist road (and sometime race circuit) at Bathurst, in western New South Wales. But apart from such projects there was little improvement in Australia's rural road networks during the 1930s.

Car ownership peaked in Australia in 1927–28 and would not return to that level until after the introduction of the Australian-manufactured Holden twenty years later. New vehicle registrations in Australia, as in the United States, slowed in 1929 and again in 1930. Sales of new vehicles plummeted from about 104,000 per annum in 1927–28 to 13,921 in 1932. Used car prices also fell, while turn-of-the-century vehicles were pressed back into service. Unemployment remained high throughout this two-decade period from 1928 to 1948. During the war severe petrol rationing was imposed with the consequence that many substitute fuels were used, including 'producer gas', which entailed passing an inflammable mix of carbon monoxide and nitrogen over hot charcoal. Some cars carried the gas in a balloon on the roof, while others had a small generator on the rear of the car or towed in a trailer.

The Great Depression concentrated the minds of businessmen wonderfully and forced the closure of many once thriving operations. By 1931 Holden Motor Body Builders, which had built its business rapidly from 1917 to the mid 1920s, was facing difficulties due to declining demand for motor bodies. General Motors, through its Overseas Operations division, seized the opportunity to form a merger with the Adelaide firm and General Motors-Holden's (GMH) was created. But the cultures of the two companies produced conflict. Interestingly, though, the parent company had readily conceded to the Australian government's insistence that Holden be allowed to continue to supply bodies for other manufacturers in order to keep the local industry viable.

The bodies being built by GMH were mostly for mounting on the lower-slung US-style chassis for Chevrolets and Pontiacs, and absorbed a terrible pounding from Australian roads. But they were more robust than those built by Fisher Body for GM cars in the United States because they needed to be. If one takes a big picture view, it is possible to argue that the 1930s saw a clash between the needs of a culture already imbued with mass motorisation and one that wasn't. The chassis imported from the United States for marriage to locally manufactured bodies were designed for the modern era of smooth roads and effortless travel, and were thus post-mass-motorisation items. But GMH's engineers had to build into its bodies as much pre-mass-automobility ruggedness as possible. Hence the observation by the unnamed GMH brochure writer, ghosting for pivotal Holden boss Larry Hartnett, that Australia must solve its own problems.

It was also the case that GMH's contracts with companies other than its parent occasionally introduced the Australian engineers to new technology. Hartnett, an Englishman who came to Australia to take over the Holden reins, cites one particularly interesting example.

> *The following year, 1938, GM went to all-steel and I had a cable from New York, followed by a letter which said, 'Now with the advent of the all-steel body with a turret top the Australian Government should realize it will no longer be practical to make bodies locally in Australia.' I sent back a perky cable saying we had been making all-steel bodies for Chrysler for the past twelve months. I could imagine the reaction that cable would have provoked in New York. They wouldn't have believed it at first. And I wouldn't have blamed them, because we were doing things in Australia at that time that I wouldn't have believed were possible until I came to Australia and saw for myself.*

Hartnett's recollection of the actual years here is inaccurate, but the point itself is well made. Like some others, the GMH boss looked forward to a time when the whole car, suited to the local conditions, would be manufactured in Australia, but he shared the general view that the time was not yet right. His view was echoed by the Chamber of Automotive Industries, of which he was a prominent member, in July 1936. 'The production of a complete Australian chassis is economically impractical at this time.'

1948–60: Off the sheep's back and into the car

In the case of both world wars, Australia's island-nation isolation forced a new emphasis on resourcefulness and self-sufficiency, with direct consequences for secondary industry. Just as shipping constraints in World War I fostered the rapid growth of the motor body building business in Australia, so too would World War II provide the impetus (including General Motors' so-called 'basic conditions') that would lead to the commencement of local manufacture of the entire car in 1948.

While Australian motorisation lagged far behind that of the United States, there was still a higher per capita level of car ownership in Australia than in countries such as Great Britain, where they were relatively more expensive to buy due largely to poor economies of scale. In Britain cars were also far more expensive to run, thanks to dearer petrol and a taxing regime (based on 'RAC horsepower', effectively a measure of engine size rather than power) that was punitive on vehicles with engines larger than about 1.5 litres.

Before 1945, indeed before 1948 and the advent of the Holden, Australian cities were in no way predicated upon car ownership. How people got to and from work illustrates this. Almost as many people walked or cycled as drove, but more than double the combined number of walkers, cyclists and drivers caught a tram or train in 1945—the last year when the Victorian railways were profitable. Some of these rail-bound commuters doubtless owned a car but were discouraged by petrol rationing from using it.

Entering the 1950s, the Australian public was still queuing to buy Holdens, and by the end of 1951 some 160,000 names were down for cars to be supplied as the waiting list gradually shortened. There were already more than 53,000 Holdens colouring the traffic and GMH headed the new car sales charts by a steadily increasing margin. Australians were buying cars in unprecedented numbers and their first choice was generally the Holden. But the first Holden off the assembly line in November 1948 had not just driven out of nowhere. Its history is inextricably bound with that of General Motors Corporation, and specifically to the vision of its greatest president, Alfred P. Sloan Jr. With this in mind it is therefore necessary to take an extended look at General Motors as it grew to dominate first the domestic US market and later the global car manufacturing industry.

With mass motorisation, driven mainly by the Holden, at hand in Australia, public interest in the subject reached a new high and various political debates centred on the rights of motorists. On 8 February 1950 the newly elected Liberal government kept its election promise to end rationing, but government ownership of the railways and many other elements of the public transport system meant that overhauling Australia's rudimentary road network remained a low priority. Concern about the poor condition of roads grew as more drivers ventured upon them and—with petrol readily available for the first time since 1940—as heavy trucks increasingly competed with rail for long-distance freight haulage.

An editorial in GMH's in-house magazine, *People*, in August 1953 viewed 'with concern the increasing restrictions by State Governments on the use of road transport for the haulage of goods of all kinds'. Commentary on the condition of the roads followed:

> *Equally important are highway modernisation, and rehabilitation. Australia is a country where the motor vehicle plays an important role. With one motor vehicle to six people, it ranks fourth in the world, and its commercial vehicle density of one to 15 people is higher than any other country. Yet each day our highways and roads are becoming less adequate to handle the ever-increasing traffic. They are not only becoming more and more obsolete, but are deteriorating faster than they are being repaired, and road congestion and road accidents are steadily increasing.*

Conversely, railway authorities were often forthright in appealing to parliament for protection from the encroaching challenge presented by trucks for freight and buses for passengers.

> *In the suburban area, railways revenue continues to be adversely affected by the extension of competitive omnibus services to which reference was made in our last report. The services authorized between Footscray and Williamstown, which closely parallel the existing railway, were responsible for particularly heavy losses of railway revenue. We feel strongly that there is no justification whatever for the existence of these services, and we urge that authority for their operation should not be renewed upon expiration of the current licences.*

Nineteen forty-eight was the first year when the rate of car ownership in Australia exceeded that of twenty years earlier, thanks to both the Great Depression and World War II. But a million cars (including taxis, police cars, etc.) for seven million people suggests that a motor vehicle in the family was no more to be taken for granted than a telephone.

Australia's social geography in the immediate postwar years was barely different from 1930 or even 1920. Social historian Graeme Davison says that in 1945 Melbourne was 'still a recognisable child . . . of the land boom of 1888', while Geoffrey Blainey has likened the development of Australian cities to a cartwheel 'with compact settlement in the hub and with ribbons of settlement following the spokes of the wheel'. The spaces between the 'fingers' or the 'spokes' began to be filled in with the rapid growth of car ownership in the 1950s and dependence on public transport declined. By 1953 the ratio of cars was one per five people, and the new outer suburban developments occurring in all Australian capital cities from the middle of the 1950s were essentially dependent on private car ownership. And if one car was borderline essential, two were highly desirable. However, ownership of even one car (not necessarily either a Holden or new) encouraged prospective home buyers to shop for property in the subdivisions such as Melbourne's Glen Waverley and Sydney's Baulkham Hills.

Economic historian Greg Whitwell has argued the contrary, namely that the growth of outer suburbia was not a consequence of dramatically increased motorisation, but rather it 'forced' Australians into car ownership. Whichever is the case, it was burgeoning automobility which began with the introduction of the Holden in 1948 and proceeded apace throughout the 1950s and 1960s that permitted, if not *invited*, the in-filling between the older suburbs following the train and tram lines. Cars fuelled the well-documented Australian dream of home ownership in a 'nice' suburb.

Davison charts the arrival of what historian Reyner Banham has termed 'autopia'—the culture of the car. Davison's study centres on Melbourne, but much the same pattern applied in other Australian cities. Melbourne got its first drive-in theatre (a concept pioneered in 1933 in New Jersey) in

Burwood in 1954. That same year, the ES&A opened a drive-in bank in Camberwell; I remember accompanying my mother and sister there in the late 1950s, in our already anachronistic and faintly quaint 1950 Armstrong Siddeley. The Chadstone shopping centre of 1960 was Melbourne's first American-style regional drive-in complex, which significantly provided its own parking in a new confirmation of (impending) mass automobility and the two-car family. But US-style (indeed US-owned) fast-food outlets with dedicated car parking would not appear in Australian capital cities for another decade, by which time large outer suburban drive-in bottle shops were also beginning to proliferate. Before the suburban race had gathered its full momentum—the cream brick veneer of the 1950s and 1960s colouring towards the clinker brick of the early 1970s—Australia's changing social geography was already evident and much of it was clearly autopian.

Meanwhile, the quality of roads was still poor. My family's Armstrong Siddeley prematurely wore out its suspension and grew cracks in its body while traversing potholed suburban roads. Other English cars such as Austins and Morrises did not fare much better, although the Redex-winning Peugeot 203 and the Volkswagen Beetle were two exceptions to this rule. The 1955 annual report of the Country Roads Board suggests how bad things were. Under the heading of 'Bituminous Surfacing', we find:

This type of work is becoming increasingly important in the Board's programme . . . While work of this nature is, of course, governed by financial considerations as is the case of other aspects of the Board's work, the average rate of extension of seal over 10 years of 234 miles per annum leaves much to be desired.

Much effort was being made just to keep the existing roads in passable order, aside from building much-needed new ones:

> It would be sound transport policy to adopt a much more rapid programme of both sealing extension and pavement reconstruction, but the Board has not been able to afford the effort and must, in fact, waste money in patching worn-out and obsolete assets.

The quality of suburban roads varied from city to city, but unquestionably Sydney's were generally worse than Melbourne's at this time.

Well into the 1950s long stretches of the Hume Highway linking Melbourne and Sydney remained in poor condition to discourage road freight from competing with the rail. Significantly, the inaugural issue of *Wheels* magazine, published in April 1953 (and dated May 1953, presumably to buy some extra newsstand freshness), included a story on the poor roads, especially the Hume Highway.

What difference does the car make?

This is not just a question of numbers and statistics; it is about the way a society organises itself and how it expresses itself culturally. The degree of private car ownership influences how and where real estate developers can proceed, where schools and hospitals will be built, what kind of businesses will flourish where, and so on. Once the widespread assumption is made that new residential and business developments should not necessarily be located in reasonable proximity to a railway line, tram line or bus service, then mass motorisation has become the status quo; the car has moved from the realm of leisure/luxury into the category of near-essential. Architects must envisage space for the car when designing houses, town planners and developers must consider parking, and trams will be threatened with extinction—Sydney's last ran in 1959.

The evolution of Australian culture is often said to follow a similar pattern to that of the United States, but this assertion obscures more than it illuminates. At first sight it is difficult to comprehend why there were just fifteen cars per 100,000 Australian residents at the end of 1921 when the US market would by 1925 reach 'saturation point' (the point at which most new cars are replacement rather than new or 'conquest' sales to people who did not previously own one). Australians were at something more like car-starvation point when the first Holden drove into town on 29 November 1948, and saturation was a destiny to be dreamed of somewhere beyond the summer of the seventeenth doll.

- **8 July 1901** Speed limit for cars in French towns set at 6 miles per hour.

- **16 June 1903** Formation of the Ford Motor Company in Dearborn, Michigan.

- **2 February 1927** Malcolm Campbell sets a world speed record of 174.224 miles per hour (280.4 km/h) on the Pendine Sands in Wales.

- **3 September 1935** Sir Malcolm Campbell breaks his own world record to smash the 300 miles per hour (482.8 km/h) mark with a speed of 301.337.

- **29 November 1948** Prime Minister Ben Chifley launches the Holden car.

- **19 March 1932** The Sydney Harbour Bridge opens.

Chapter 2

The Sloan ranger takes on the world, 1920–33

Let me assure you that our prime objective is to develop our activities at Opel in such a way that its character as a German company is upheld. We shall use German material, produced by German workers, to the greatest possible extent.
—Alfred P. Sloan Jr addressing Opel employees, 18 October 1930

In 1920 the Ford Model T still rode proud and mighty over the high-crowned roads of North America and had established a strong presence in overseas markets including Australia. Fifty per cent of the world's cars were Model Ts. The following year Ford commanded a 59 per cent share of the US car market. But a challenge was looming. After a decade, an element of familiarity breeding contempt for 'Tin Lizzie' was just beginning to appear, and there was evidence from within Henry Ford's mailbag that some consumers were expecting more from their vehicles.

What no one was expecting as the 1920s opened, however, was the introduction by General Motors Corporation (GM) of a whole new way of doing car business, under the brilliant presidency and chairmanship of Alfred P. Sloan Jr. The Ford Motor Company's greatest rival heading into the Roaring Twenties was indeed General Motors, but the contest was in no way close. In 1920 General Motors was almost broke for the second time. In 1921 Ford held 55.7 per cent of the domestic market while General Motors' share of 12.73 per cent (193,000 vehicles) was down more to good luck than good management. Ten different model lines were produced by seven divisions—Chevrolet, Buick, Cadillac, Oldsmobile, Sheridan, Scripp-Booth and Oakland. All these brands operated individually in the market with no corporate policy for synergies or to reduce what would today be called 'cannibalisation'. At least two, Sheridan and Scripp-Booth, were no longer viable. Much of the remaining 35-plus per cent of the US automotive market went to mainly very low volume domestic brands because US tariffs on imported cars were 40 per cent.

Sloan knew how to take the challenge to Ford, and before he was invited to take his place behind the corporate steering wheel in 1923 he had already recommended a radical product policy of 'a car for every purse and purpose'. This was also the year when the car industry would become the largest American business in terms of sales. Under Sloan's custodianship, GM became the world's most successful and influential carmaker.

Sloan knew that the principles he was bringing to bear on the US market would work equally well overseas. Within the first five to six years of his presidency Sloan would guide GM to domestic dominance while positioning it adroitly as a local player in three major overseas markets—Britain, Germany and Australia. 'Think global, act local' was a late twentieth-century catchphrase, but Sloan understood that for

'Think global, act local' was a late twentieth-century catchphrase, but Sloan understood that for business it was better to act global by thinking local. Had he taken GM into Italy, he would have done what the Romans do, but better.

Sloan drove all GM's major policy decisions until World War II, many of which were in place at the onset of the Great Depression, including the introduction of styling as a crucial element in the product design process.

business it was better to act global by thinking local. Had he taken GM into Italy, he would have done what the Romans do, but better.

Sloan drove all GM's major policy decisions until World War II, many of which were in place at the onset of the Great Depression, including the introduction of styling as a crucial element in the product design process. In mid 1921 he introduced the company's product policy—the world's first systematic approach to brand integration within a corporation. Where Henry Ford's product philosophy is often encapsulated in the phrase 'any colour as long as it's black', Sloan understood that long-term success would depend on competing across a broad spectrum of market segments and developing a range of brands to encourage consumers to aspire to more expensive and better equipped cars. Sloan knew what the 'want factor' meant years before this became a buzz phrase in marketing circles. He knew that the want factor required constant renewal. You had to make people a little unsettled with the car they already owned, so they would go out and buy a new one. Here was the origin of 'planned obsolescence', the policy that dare not speak its name, right back in 1921.

Although a considerable amount of research has focused on Sloan in particular and General Motors in general, virtually none of it apart from Sloan's autobiographical *My Years with General Motors* deals closely with how General Motors' policy led to radical changes in the corporation's overseas markets. David Farber's *Sloan Rules* is an outstanding biography and generally acknowledged by scholarly reviewers to be far and away the most comprehensive as well as the most recent study of the man's life and attitudes. But Farber's emphasis is political, his essential concern being about how what is often termed 'rational management' relates to personal moral convictions. The automotive industry itself is peripheral to Farber's concerns.

Numerous historians have examined how General Motors, guided by Sloan and his new range of management policies, achieved market dominance in the 1920s and 1930s. Arthur Kuhn's work is perhaps the most comprehensive such study, but it is strongly focused on the United States and he provides only a broad brush treatment of General Motors' activities in overseas markets. Kuhn's work, along with Chandler's, is a common starting point for scholars interested in the corporate history of General Motors. But almost without exception, these writers have minimal interest in engineering issues or in evaluating GM as a creator of motor vehicles within an international context. How well were the corporation's cars conceived and designed? How did they compare with those of other manufacturers? How did the cars developed for overseas markets differ from those of Detroit? How well did General Motors, under Sloan, apply its corporate intelligence internationally? How far did it advance what might be called the *art* of the motor car?

As for *My Years with General Motors*, it is best read in company with John McDonald's *A Ghost's Memoir*. McDonald was the true author of *My Years with General Motors*, and his recollections, published posthumously, of 'ghosting' Sloan's story and General Motors' attempts to suppress publication give more context to *My Years*. McDonald's work serves to authenticate the account given by Sloan, much of which was sourced from committee reports, correspondence and policy documents. McDonald's work also lends support for some of the conclusions reached in this book about the decline of aspects of the General Motors way of doing business once Sloan vacated the driver's seat—adecline which was clearly evident by the time the ill-fated Chevrolet Corvair 'compact' came to market in 1959.

Curiously, Sloan pays scant attention to the corporation's Australian subsidiary, General Motors-Holden's (GMH), and the Holden car is mentioned by name only in the tables at the end of the book.

Sloan defined the Ford policy as 'basic transportation at a low dollar price' and GM's as the 'mass-class market with increasing diversity'. Inherent in the Sloan approach was the recognition that 'different things appeal to different people'. In contrast to the one basic Ford model (still the T at this stage), General Motors would offer buyers in ascending price order the Chevrolet, Oakland, Oldsmobile, Buick and Cadillac. 'Mass-class' is a neat phrase which makes best sense when understood in the context for which Sloan coined it. The first phase of motoring was pre-T, the 'class' market where only the wealthy participated. Ford created the 'mass' demand. Under Sloan, General Motors then seized the dialectic opportunity. This consisted in offering prospective Model T buyers two General Motors alternatives—a new Chevrolet for a little more money or a used one for the same or somewhat less. The new Chevrolet, positioned slightly above the Ford, would have obvious advantages in equipment, contemporary design and more power. Sloan saw the late model used Chevrolet as the Model T's *direct* competition. Another key idea was that General Motors' less expensive models would compete on quality (against Ford, Dodge, etc.), while its high-quality cars such as Cadillac would compete on price against rivals, specifically Packard. Interestingly, there seems to have been no explicit statement by Sloan of the marketing advantage the less expensive General Motors models would inevitably derive from association with the premium brand Cadillac, and to a lesser extent Buick and even Oldsmobile.

Morality versus capitalism

At the heart of Sloan's thinking was a recognition that had escaped Henry Ford. There was no such thing as the ideal, one-size-fits-all car that would continue to serve the market more or less un-changed for years. Where Ford was in some ways socialistic in his thinking, Sloan was the quint-essential capitalist. It was not a matter of a car for everyone, a *volkswagen*, but a new car for everyone *every few years*, a car that looked differ-ent and packed more features.

To keep selling new cars to people who had already owned at least one new car, Sloan knew he had to turn 'new' into 'new . . . and better'.

The GM product policy was backed by new emphases on advertising and instalment purchase. Glamour had to be sold; much money would need to be borrowed by purchasers, preferably at the point of sale. Sloan knew that by the mid 1920s the US car market would be nearing 'saturation point'. Here was the sweet kernel: why would a customer who had bought a brand new Model T in, say, 1916 want to replace it with an almost unchanged vehicle six or seven years later? To keep selling new cars to people who had already owned at least one new car, Sloan knew he had to turn 'new' into 'new . . . and better'. And with General Motors Acceptance Corporation (founded in 1919) on hand at the point of sale to provide instal-ment finance, those few extra dollars for a new GM car could be absorbed over a period of time. Henry Ford, by contrast, was an outspoken opponent of hire purchase. His morality would at times work against his business, where for Sloan, business was just business and he did not view himself as a moralist.

Sloan's special planning genius was immediately evident in how he planned to make the Chevrolet more competitive against the high-volume Model T, while simultaneously offering a broader spread of models in the low-to-medium price range. He noted a 'dangerous gap between the Chev-rolet and the Olds', and introduced an additional car line, Pontiac, to fill it. The Pontiac would share componentry with the less expensive Chevrolet while having an identity of its own 'to share Chevrolet's economies, and vice versa'. It would use a six-cylinder engine instead of the Chevrolet's four. This car would be produced by the Oakland division in Pontiac (Michigan)—hence the name. This was the first time in the world that a car had been 'designed to fit a market slot and [was] designed to use parts from a sister car'. At about the same time he also conceived a less expensive variant of the Cadillac known as the La Salle.

Improved economies of scale, resulting from the product policy, unleashed new synergies for General Motors. The fact that the Pontiac and Chevrolet were priced so closely that they could steal sales from each other posed no problem for Sloan; this was a better outcome than losing sales to an outside rival. Sloan had added a new sophistication to the Fordist mass-production concept, demonstrating that 'mass production of automobiles could be reconciled with variety in product'. Pontiac and La Salle, both of which were successful in the market, together proved an important point, as Sloan discusses in *My Years with General Motors*:

> For General Motors, with its five basic price classes by car makes and several subclasses of models, the implication of the Pontiac idea was very great for the whole line. If the cars in the higher-price classes could benefit from the volume economies of the lower-price classes, the advantages of mass production could be extended to the whole car line.

Whereas Ford believed that customers would continue to be satisfied with utility, Sloan planned to sell them style. After all, by the 1920s a high degree of utility was already a given and cars were generally reliable; in the United States the pioneering days had passed. Sloan observed in 1924 that sales success was closely connected with the promotion of style and even what we now call lifestyle. It was in that year Eddie S. Jordan's famous 'Somewhere West of Laramie' advertisement was published in the *Saturday Evening Post*, depicting the Jordan car as a means of accessing a more colourful life. This was at the opposite end of the spectrum from Ford's advertisement of the T's utility. By 1924 General Motors bought more magazine advertising space than any other company, and although the themes were less extravagant than Jordan's Laramie creation there was a strong emphasis on how the right car could deliver newfound personal status.

Although Sloan had his plans in place, he was stuck for the present with some outdated models, and in the recession of 1924 he watched as GM performed worse than its rivals, largely because of the unloved Chevrolet model that year. GM's share of the passenger car market fell from 20 per cent to 17, while Ford's climbed from 50 to 55. This serves to show just how remarkable the turnaround from 1925 to 1927 would be. Sloan noted ruefully the contrast between his policy of 1921 and the sales performance of the 1924 Chevrolet. The revamped 1925 model, though 'far from being a radically new car', brought a 64 per cent gain in sales.

Alfred too fast for Henry

In 1926, and already too late, Henry Ford threw down his gauntlet, as Farber quotes in his book *Sloan Rules*:

> *The stability of the substantial bulk of the American people is most definitely evidenced by the continued leadership of Ford. Despite confusion in the minds of many, of extravagance with progress, a vast majority cling to the old-fashioned view of living within their incomes. From these come and are coming the millions of Ford owners . . . They possess or are buying efficient, satisfactory transportation.*

However, Ford's homespun messianism did nothing to halt buyers' desertion of Ford in favour of General Motors brands, especially Chevrolet (up from 68,080 units in 1921 to 940,277 in 1927). In 1927 General Motors passed Ford, achieving sales of more than 1.8 million vehicles, to become not just the biggest manufacturer in the United States but the entire world. The Model A was due to succeed the Model T the following year, but Sloan's policies had already won out in the market over Ford's. Historian of the marque, Robert Lacey, has observed that while Ford achieved a new car in the 1920s 'with great travail', General Motors invented 'the modern corporation'.

As for the new Ford which grew out of that travail, Sloan damned it with impressively faint praise in *My Years with General Motors*:

Anyway, his Model A, which he brought out in 1928, as fine a little car as it was in its time, it seems to me was another expression of his concept of a static-model utility car.

The allure of the new, dismissed by Ford, was in keeping with the spirit of the Roaring Twenties. As for the trusty Model T, automotive historian James Flink has described it as 'a farmer's car for a nation of farmers'. By the 1920s growing urban prosperity shifted the automotive imperative towards the cities, with the ready availability of borrowed money a further incentive for buyers to embrace the latest models. In 1922, 73 per cent of all new cars sold in the United States were bought on borrowed money. Roland Marchand writes in *Advertising the American Dream* that consumers were voting for 'style, beauty, "extravagance", and the instalment plan . . . [and] against automobiles defined simply as "satisfactory transportation"'.

It was almost as if Ford had written his own marketing epitaph in that drab phrase 'satisfactory transportation'. Sloan, with the benefit of decades' hindsight, observed in *My Years* that 'the old master (Henry Ford) had failed to master *change*'.

Mr Ford failed to realise that it was not necessary for new cars to meet the need for basic transportation. On this basis alone Mr Ford's concept of the American market did not adequately fit the realities after 1923. The basic-transportation market in the United States (unlike Europe) since then has been met mainly by the used car. When first-car buyers returned to the market for the second round, with the old car as a first payment on the new car, they were selling basic transportation and demanding something more than that in the new car. Middle-income buyers, assisted by the trade-in and installment financing, created the demand, not for basic transportation, but for progress in new cars, for comfort, convenience, power, and style. This was the actual trend of American life and those who adapted to it prospered.

. . . the four elements . . . installment selling, the used-car trade-in, the closed-car body, and the annual model, interacted in the 1920s to transform the market.

Sloan identified 'a rising curve of used-car trade-ins', and this probably inspired the policy of an annual model change. The GM chairman and president expressed his theory in 1941 in *Adventures of a White-Collar Man*:

> *. . . we want to make you dissatisfied with your current car so you will buy a new one—you who can afford it . . . And you who can afford it perform—probably unconsciously—a very important economic service. You pass on to the used-car market your old car at a value in transportation with which no new car could possibly compete.*

'Sloanism', as it has been termed, defeated 'Fordism', and for the first time, GM offered its customers something that went beyond mere utility to symbolise the customer's hopes and aspirations. Henry Ford was a marketing genius, but that genius was in the time capsule of the first quarter of the twentieth century, the first motoring century. His Model T has been widely proclaimed as the Car of the Century, and that's because, essentially, it defined the early possibilities of motoring. Sloan, by contrast, took a long view. The fact that his policies brought General Motors from well behind Ford at the start of the 1920s to well clear of it ten years later is less a measure of Henry's old-fashioned outlook or any other failing than a clear indication of Sloan's brilliance. This was shown not just in terms of product and marketing but also in the financial system which he masterminded. Arthur J. Kuhn in *GM Passes Ford, 1918–1938* goes so far as to argue that Henry Ford deliberately repudiated planning and adopted 'anti-planning' as his dominant strategy.

In contrast to Henry Ford, Alfred Sloan worked through committees, relying on intellectual synergy. By the time Sloan's first book, *Adventures of a White-collar Man*, was being written, Hitler's dictatorship was already

His Model T has been widely proclaimed as the Car of the Century, and that's because, essentially, it defined the early possibilities of motoring. Sloan, by contrast, took a long view.

poised to launch World War II. This might have encouraged the following formulation:

> *In bringing General Motors into existence, Mr. Durant had operated as a dictator. But such an institution could not grow into a successful organization under a dictatorship. Dictatorship is the most effective way of administration, provided the dictator knows the complete answers to all questions. But he never does and never will. That is why dictatorships eventually fail. If General Motors were to capitalize its wonderful opportunity, it would have to be guided by an organization of intellects. A great industrial organization requires the best of many minds. Yet Mr. Durant had no more sincere admirer than I.*

The parallels between Henry Ford and Adolf Hitler have been touched on by many authors. Both were unwilling to take advice or to operate through committees. Hitler owed his *volkswagen* concept—a generic term long before it became an actual car—to Henry Ford. And the relationship between the Model T, the Volkswagen and the new types of cars which emerged in the postwar era will be dealt with later in this book.

GM's pursuit of economies of scale

To realise his vision, Sloan needed to find considerable economies of scale. Obviously, if a company makes just one type of car—the Model T, say— these are easy to achieve. Sloan's product policy, entailing as it did immense variety, would require an underlying commonality of componentry to achieve cost savings. General Motors had a 60 per cent stake in the Fisher Body Corporation heading into the 1920s, and this provided an excellent starting point for sharing body components among the various GM brands. Sloan saw that inexpensive and minor variations on the one theme could be exploited to great effect, especially when styling had been developed as part of the design process. Here is a kind of manufacturing utilitarianism, reminiscent of John Stuart Mill's axiom of the greatest good for the greatest number of people.

By 1927 General Motors had not only moved past Ford but it was easily the most successful automotive manufacturer in the world, and this outcome was clearly a result of Sloan's finely elaborated strategies. Sloan's personal wealth was so great by this time that he was added to a very small group afforded 'extraordinary stock market opportunities', courtesy of the Morgan Bank. The contrast between Sloan and Ford may not have been reflected in their fortunes, for both were extremely rich, but the fortunes of the world's two largest automotive companies were directly consequent upon their respective presidents.

Even before Henry Ford introduced his new Model A, General Motors had, in 1927, opened the automotive industry's first styling department in Detroit, under the title Art and Color Section, probably for want of any more formal or recognised term; *styling* as a concept had not previously existed in the mass-production automotive industry, although the term was already in use in other contexts. As with every other major General Motors initiative of the 1920s, this was a product of Sloan's visionary thinking. In July 1926, he had written to H.H. (Harry) Bassett, general manager of GM's Buick division (second in status to Cadillac): 'I am sure we all realise . . . how much appearance has to do with sales; with all cars fairly good mechanically, it is a dominating proposition and in a product such as ours where the individual appeal is so great, it means a tremendous influence on our future prosperity.'

Early in 1926 Lawrence P. Fisher, general manager of the Cadillac division, was already thinking on similar lines. Cadillac was losing market share to Packard, and Fisher commissioned Harley Earl, a 'Californian body-customizer', to bring new interest to the Cadillac's appearance and also to design a less expensive model (to plug the enormous gap between the

By 1927 General Motors had not only moved past Ford but it was easily the most successful automotive manufacturer in the world, and this outcome was clearly a result of Sloan's finely elaborated strategies.

Buick and the Cadillac), which would be released as the La Salle of 1927. The La Salle made the contemporaneous Cadillac look 'dull', as Sloan noted. Sloan, pleased with Earl's work, then decided to ask Earl to apply his talents to other General Motor divisions. His work was to be across the entire corporation and he would report directly to Sloan, which gave him 'a degree of responsibility for design unique in American industry then and now'. Harley Earl, whose influence on General Motors would continue for more than 30 years and would affect more than 50 million cars from the late 1920s to 1960, was given a staff of 50 people for his 'beauty shop', as Art and Color was described internally. Sloan knew there would be misgivings among some of his executives. One or two might even have shared Henry Ford's well-publicised view that automotive ornamentation of any kind could be summed up derisively as 'knicknacks'. Sloan wrote to William Fisher, Lawrence's more conservative brother who was president of the Fisher Body Corporation:

> To sum up, I think that the future of General Motors will be measured by the attractiveness that we put in the bodies from the standpoint of luxury of appointment, the degree to which they please the eye, both in contour and in color scheme, also the degree to which we are able to make them different from the competition.

But, the La Salle excepted, it would take until 1933 for Earl's brew of ideas to trickle down from the Cadillac division in the upper echelon of the General Motors range to the basic Chevrolet. The 1933 model Chevrolet, with its new A series body, was, says Sloan, 'the first manufactured expression of Harley Earl's philosophy of automotive form'. The term 'Styling' officially replaced 'Art and Color' in 1937.

Harley Earl's styling philosophy involved lowering and lengthening the car, and he once wrote that his sense of proportion told him that oblongs are more attractive than squares. Earl's approach would eventually drive the entire US industry, but it would also have an impact on overseas markets—detrimentally in the case of Australia with its poor-quality roads. So while such low-slung cars fared well in US conditions, they would be less than ideal for Australian roads and Holden's Motor Body Builders went to great lengths to build stronger bodies than were seen in the United States. Harley Earl's desire to lower the car would therefore be less happily received in Australia than in most other markets where, in general, roads, though imperfect, were more likely to be of bitumen construction. The notorious Australian corrugations were virtually unknown. Fashion and high cruising speeds would not become significant factors in Australian motoring tastes until after World War II.

Even further than Laramie . . .

As early as 1911 General Motors had begun to look beyond North America. General Motors Export Company had been formed in that year and cars were shipped to various countries, including Australia. But by 1919 there was a growing sense that a more direct kind of involvement in export markets was needed. Europe became the first focus of what could be described as GM's move towards multinationalism. An early foray disappointed, and in 1923 Sloan announced a new plan to establish assembly plants around the world where knocked down bodies exported from Detroit could be 'assembled, painted and finished so they can be dropped directly on to the chassis'.

The Australian case was rather different and demanded a unique strategy. Two Export Company executives—James D. Mooney, who had been appointed general manager of the General Motors Export Company the previous year, and his second-in-charge, Edward C. Riley—crossed the Pacific in 1923 to have a look for themselves. Their initial idea had been to set up General Motors' own body building business. General Motors Export Company was Holden's biggest customer, but by 1921 Holden's had also supplied bodies to suit Oakland, Bean, Essex, Overland and Ford chassis, among others. Frank Daley, a long-time GMH employee and unpublished historian, has written:

In 1917–18, the first years of Holden's Motor Body Builders Pty Ltd, just a few hundred bodies were built, but by 1926 to 1927 the industry-wide total was 100,552, of which 36,171 were being produced by Holden. (Holden's output for GM that year was 22,000.) Holden and other firms were getting blueprints and drawings from the United States and working so quickly that they could often release a new fully bodied car onto the local market at the same time as it was being launched in the United States.

The problem for the GM Export Company was that demand for Holden's bodies exceeded supply. Daley notes:

Since 1918 the [Export Company] company had had to compete with Dodge, Ford and others for its share of what could be acquired from local manufacturers. From the local body-builders' perspective the demand must have been gratifying. But there was a problem having to produce the variety expected by the automotive companies. Within the year Holden's Motor Body Builders developed, built and delivered 65 different body designs.

Evidently, Jim Mooney and Ed Riley liked what they saw of the Holden's operation and a deal was struck that Holden's planned new manufacturing facility at Woodville in South Australia would be devoted entirely to General Motors business. In exchange for this exclusivity, Holden's would receive technical assistance from General Motors as well as a supply of skilled personnel from the United States. The company could continue to produce bodies for other makers in its existing King William Street plant. The General Motors bodies would be shipped to assembly plants around Australia. No additional capital was supplied by GM for the Woodville plant. Frank Daley writes:

It is interesting to dwell for a moment on the outstanding initiative of General Motors Export Company in this matter, for the agreement cited was probably among the first documents of its kind in Australian industrial history. It offered the country continuous technical development, unlimited recourse to 'know how' and managerial help. This was in striking contrast to many other overseas manufacturers of the time, who continued to see Australia purely as a primary producer. One leading British motoring manufacturer is reported to have said: '. . . and they should leave secondary industry to those who really understand it, and remember that there is wheat to be sown and sheep to be shorn'.

General Motors was not alone in courting Holden's. Just six weeks after the deal between the companies had been made, Riley learnt that Ford had been considering a similar proposal for Holden's but had been beaten by GM. The Woodville deal gave impetus to Ford's eventual decision to set up its own body-building and assembly operation at Geelong in 1925.

Meanwhile, Holden's gained fantastic momentum. In 1923 the corporation's share of the Australian new car market was 16.9 per cent and two years later it had almost doubled to 31.4 per cent. Daley attributes much of the improvement to GM's bringing in of numerous specialists in the fields of 'merchandising, distribution, supply, servicing, and also men to reinforce the financial and commercial phases'. Before the end of the 1920s the Chevrolet would be Australia's top-selling car. In November 1929, 858 new Chevrolets were registered for the month compared with 580 Fords. The biggest selling English brand was Austin on 251.

Two years after the Woodville deal had been made, the Export Company renewed its efforts to gain a foothold in Europe. A deal was almost struck to purchase the English Austin company, but with disagreement over asset value Sloan and Mooney turned to Vauxhall instead. The push into Europe was driven by the recognition that the export of American cars into overseas markets was, as Sloan put it, being 'threatened by economic nationalism'. Mooney favoured European production, although the executive committee of which Sloan was chairman remained doubtful about moving into production overseas.

The British market not only had a 'formidable tariff barrier to all foreign vehicles', but its system of basing registration fees on the RAC horsepower system made the annual expense of running most large-engined cars prohibitive. According to Sloan, the standing charges in Britain for a Chevrolet were about $250 per year compared with $138 or so for an Austin. This was before taking into account either the much higher purchase price of the American car or its heavier fuel consumption. On the negative side of the equation for the British manufacturers was the absence of the economies of scale that prevailed in the United States, where the Fordist production system predominated across the motor industry.

From the start, Mooney wanted to produce a smaller Vauxhall. At the time of the takeover Vauxhall was making just one car that was similar in size to the Buick and was quite expensive, Vauxhall not being a mass manufacturer. Something with mass appeal would be necessary. In the autumn of 1930 Vauxhall introduced its small car, the Cadet. Just two years later, when an upgraded Cadet became only the third car in the world after Cadillac and Buick with a synchromesh gearbox, the synergy became evident. Here was Sloan's product policy profoundly at play. General Motors was the world's first truly multinational automotive corporation.

Germany was a rather different case from Britain. The German industry was effectively still in its infancy, comparable in 1929 to the US market of 1911. Sloan and Mooney saw great potential there, and General Motors was already assembling Chevrolets in its Berlin plant. But while the president was keen to link up with a German manufacturer, Mooney wanted to expand the existing GM operation.

It was at this time that the idea of designing a smaller Chevrolet suitable for overseas markets originated. But despite enthusiasm from Sloan and presumably a significant number of his colleagues, nothing remotely along these lines would eventuate for the better part of a decade. Sloan's recollection of this process casts interesting light on an experimental project of 1937–38, which will be examined later:

> I was interested in a suggestion that we create in the United States an organization
> to design a modified 'small-bore' Chevrolet—a car that would escape the heavy
> horsepower tax in England and Germany. I felt that if this were done, it might prove

unnecessary to develop a new small car at Vauxhall or to go into production in Germany; or, if it should become necessary to produce such a car abroad, we would at least have a design available.

And so the analysis continued. James Mooney remained keen both to produce a smaller Vauxhall and to manufacture a similarly sized vehicle in Germany. Sloan felt that, in the German case, it would be better to deal directly with local car company Opel. In October 1928 Sloan and two fellow executives toured Europe, during which time an option to purchase Opel was negotiated. The option gave the GM team six months to look into the operation. The deal was concluded on 18 January 1929. By acquiring the country's largest motoring manufacturer, Adam Opel AG, General Motors could 'acquire a "German background", instead of having to operate as foreigners', as Sloan put it.

On 18 October 1929, Wilhelm von Opel had a special guest to introduce to the assembled Opel dealers at a presentation of the 1930 models. Alfred P. Sloan Jr was by this time effectively in control of Opel and was keen to convey his views on the company's future in the custody of the world's first truly multinational automotive corporation. Sloan outlined General Motors' international policy of expansion: 'I observed to them that, while Germany was a highly industrialized country, its automobile production was very low by American standards, and that I anticipated Opel production might one day run as high as 150,000 vehicles per year.' Only the year before, Opel had produced about 43,000 vehicles per year. The dealers laughed. 'I was viewed as another impractical, visionary American', says Sloan. Just a few days later the New York stock market crashed and this would only have reinforced the dealers' initial scepticism.

In the fall of 1930, as the Great Depression deepened, James Mooney, general manager of the General Motors Export Company, visited the Soviet Union with a view to selling the corporation's vehicles there. Mooney's attitude to national politics was absolutely pragmatic and seemingly untainted by ideology. He wrote to Sloan:

I confined my official observations very definitely . . . to the economic considerations in which, as a businessman, I am exclusively interested . . . [and] involved only one [question] which touched upon the political aspect of things in any way, and that was the question that we have to ask ourselves in any market—including the United States—where we contemplate doing business; the question simply as to whether or not the government is stable.

Sloan grew interested in dealing with the Soviets following Mooney's trip and hoped to sell used GM vehicles to Russian customers. This plan, had it come to fruition, would have provided a much needed stimulus to the US car market.

Taking over down-under

The Great Depression, like both world wars, had a huge impact on the automotive industry, but General Motors took advantage of this to consolidate its position in Australia. One of the many local corporate victims of the 1929 Wall Street crash was Holden's Motor Body Builders. This had serious implications for General Motors because Holden's built all the bodies for the cars GM sold in Australia and the Chevrolet had been the top-selling make in the second half of the 1920s. 'We established close business relationships with this company', writes Sloan, 'and obtained almost its entire output during the latter part of the twenties'. So there was a compelling business case for a GM buyout of its Australian body supplier. In 1931 GM bought Holden's outright; it was merged with General Motors (Australia) and became General Motors-Holden's Ltd (GMH). But according to Holden's Motor Body Builders chairman at the time, Edward ('Ted') Holden, some 30 per cent of the firm's business had been with companies other than General Motors, and it was a federal government condition for allowing the merger that the new company would not become a monopoly for General Motors to the detriment of other automotive companies. This meant that GMH would make bodies not just for General Motors cars but also for rival companies including Dodge. Ted Holden may have believed that 'General Motors . . . have always recognised a moral responsibility towards us', but the merger represented a further illustration of the corporation's far-sighted international strategy.

Hartnett takes the lead in Australia

In 1934 General Motors sent one of its up-and-coming executives to run its Australian subsidiary—Laurence John ('Larry') Hartnett—and, significantly as it would prove, he was an Englishman rather than an American. Prior to this, in its first three years of operation General Motors-Holden's had joint managing directors, Ted Holden from the old Adelaide company and Gus Lawrence, who had had been sent out from the United States some years earlier to be managing director of General Motors Pty Ltd in Australia. There was a measure of rivalry between the two men and a significant clash of corporate cultures. The choice of Hartnett, who had run Vauxhall's export company for several years, to supersede both men must have seemed like an inspired solution to many. Holden continued as chairman and Lawrence was recalled to the United States.

Thirty years later Hartnett published his memoirs under the title *Big Wheels and Little Wheels*, and it is one of very few primary-source documents that deals with GMH in the 1930s. Unfortunately, as will be seen, it is in many respects, to borrow Clive James' brilliant title, a most unreliable memoir. Hartnett, by his own confession, was prone to exaggerate and he was often careless when it came to detail. According to Hartnett, he was appointed to the job by GM Overseas Operations boss Graeme Howard with the instruction to make GMH work or to close it down:

> He [Graeme Howard] said, 'you'd be managing director of this GMH company. I've told you it's a sorry mess. The two fellows we've got out there, Ted Holden, the head of the Holden Company, and Gus Lawrence, the fellow we had as managing director of General Motors Pty. Ltd., are trying to operate in double harness as joint managing directors, and it's not working out at all well. You'd take over from both of them. You'd either wind it up and we would get out, or straighten it out and turn it around into something worth-while.'

Hartnett may have been one of the first overseas-born industrialists to identify the resourcefulness that has always been evident in Australian culture.

Hartnett also says that Jim Mooney himself entreated him to accept the challenge of solving the 'Australian problem': 'This Australian problem has got the whole outfit across a barrel, Larry. Unless we can do something about it, the Overseas Division will get a long and lasting black eye.' Hartnett may have believed he personally saved General Motors-Holden's, however the company was already emerging from the Depression when Hartnett sailed into Sydney Harbour.

Despite the profusion of errors and omissions in Hartnett's account of how the Australian car came into being, there can be no doubt that he did a great job of building up GMH during the 1930s. And he may have been one of the first overseas-born industrialists to identify the resourcefulness that has always been evident in Australian culture. He could see that sometimes the Holden way was more efficient than the standard General Motors approach. It is clear that Holden differed greatly from the other overseas operations, excepting Vauxhall and Opel which manufactured entire cars, rather than fitting bodies to American chassis, as Hartnett writes:

> In countries except Australia, the GM assembly operation worked to a very smooth pattern. The overseas plants were like glorified Meccano sets. A shipload of cases arrived from America and inside them were all the bits and pieces of the cars. When the pieces were put together, each part having its number, and its sequence in the assembly line, you had the car, complete down to such parts as the door-handles and the dashboard knobs, the glass, the trim and even the paint included.
>
> In charge of these plants GM had a breed of men who were pure assemblers. They were not engineers, in the true sense. They followed the book of instructions to the letter . . .
>
> When men with this background were transferred to Australia, they invariably struck trouble. They, or most of them, made the mistake of insisting that the

Australian bodies should be made exactly to the design and specifications of the bodies made in Detroit.

Hartnett's enthusiasm for the job he had initially rejected was matched by his response to living in Australia and becoming a local. 'From the moment I arrived I liked Australia, and her people', he writes. 'And conceitedly, I had the feeling Australia needed me.' Hartnett could not have known in 1934 that this very enthusiasm would eventually lead to his departure from General Motors.

Sloan and his fellow overseas travellers did not just choose Vauxhall out of the blue. Before acquiring the Luton-based company they had eyed off first Citroën and then Austin. The French operation was dismissed in a late-night meeting at the Hotel Crillon when the GM men decided that too much money would be needed to fix the production facilities and install a new management team. One proposal had been that either Sloan himself or Walter P. Chrysler (the pair's friendship dated back to when they were fellow GM executives) should move to France to take on the top job, but Sloan 'was personally not interested in this proposition'. That was in 1919. The notion of buying Austin was considered in 1924–25, but Sloan and his team of rangers reckoned Herbert Austin was placing too high a value on his assets.

No proposition was ever advanced to acquire Hispano-Suiza, but Harley Earl recognised style when he saw it. According to Frank Hershey, who was employed in Art and Color in 1928, the first La Salle was pure Hispano-Suiza in style. 'If you ever put the two together, you couldn't tell the difference.'

Chapter 3

General Motors and the Third Reich, 1934–45

General Motors emerged less scathed from the Great Depression than any other automotive company and, under Sloan's direction, was better equipped than its rivals to deal with the new demands of the 1930s. Increasingly, these rivals were perceived by Sloan as international in nature. By 1931 the corporation had wholly owned subsidiaries in Great Britain (Vauxhall from 1925), Germany (Opel from 1929) and Australia (General Motors-Holden's from 1931). But while this decade saw the sales success of GM products eclipsing all rivals (with the exception of Vauxhall, which was a smallish fish in the biggish British automotive pond), the very success of the corporation and the drive for ever improved efficiency began to undermine some aspects of Sloan's product policy, particularly in the United States.

The General comfortable on home territory

In every single year of the Depression General Motors made profits and paid dividends. Increased centralisation removed much autonomy from the individual car divisions but it made GM more cost-efficient than its competitors.

Sloan's 'high-variety marketing plan' promoted flexibility. When luxury car sales recovered in 1939–41, GM had the right brands to take advantage of changed conditions and great scope to differentiate a Cadillac from a Buick and a Buick from an Oldsmobile; it was an ingrained habit.

By the end of the 1930s, Ford was teetering on the verge of collapse and placed third in sales behind GM and the Chrysler Corporation, while numerous smaller companies had disappeared altogether. Between them, the 'Big Three', as they were becoming known, held 90 per cent of the market in 1939, compared with 75 per cent ten years earlier. Even Studebaker had almost gone bankrupt in 1931. Sloan's great friend, Walter P. Chrysler, was the only automotive industry chief executive to adopt the key elements in Sloan's product policy. The Chrysler Corporation added Plymouth to its armoury as a Chevrolet and Ford rival, while De Soto shaped up to Pontiac and Oldsmobile. Few besides Walter Chrysler, it seems, had analysed the role of Sloan's *organisation* of GM in that corporation's increasing dominance of the automotive market.

> Studebaker introduced a smaller, less expensive car under a new brand name, Rockne, after an Indiana football hero of the time. It was to be sold in Europe as well as North America, but failed on both sides of the Atlantic. Doubtless the footballer's death before the car's launch could not have helped the Rockne's fortunes, but here was some evidence of how hard the independent makers would find the contest against the Big Three after 1930.
>
> Among producers of medium-priced and luxury cars to go out of business during the 1930s were Durant Motors, Reo, Auburn and Hupp. By 1940 Paige-Graham was broke and Willys would only be saved by its contract with the US government to build Jeeps for World War II.

Despite the financial strength and sales dominance of General Motors there were a number of negatives evident in the corporation's approach to blanketing the market. It could be argued that in Sloan's early years as chief executive he had placed a greater emphasis on engineering than finance in directing the business, but there was a gradual shift in favour of counting 'beans'. Throughout the 1920s the pace of engineering development was swift and largely driven by General Motors, whose breakthrough inventions included the synchromesh gearbox and, more laterally, the proving ground. GM's engineering was superior to its rivals and, generally, the cars represented better value for money. Arguably the Depression ushered in an even more rigorous approach by Sloan to managing the corporation's resources, and this ultimately had implications for engineering excellence. The capacity of individual divisions to develop bold engineering solutions was undermined. Major decisions were centralised and expertise was concentrated at head office.

The precedent created by the appointment of Harley Earl as stylist across the range of GM cars was increasingly reflected in engineering and product planning through the 1930s. From Sloan's point of view, economies of scale had dictated a policy of increasing centralisation, despite much rhetoric to the contrary. General Motors' corporate wealth meant that it could invest the necessary funds to develop competitive models using its engineering and design expertise, but most of this occurred at head-office level. 'The more you co-ordinate, the more questions you draw up into the policy area', said Sloan. The car divisions, having lost the right to style their own vehicles, soon found that they had to share much mechanical componentry as well. Initially this had been confined to 'bolts, nuts, screws, washers, pins, keys, and other small articles of hardware [which did not play a role in] the individuality of design of the different cars'. But when it was seen how easily inexpensive changes could be used to make, say, a Pontiac look different from a Chevrolet, the temptation to reduce the mechanical differences between the wide range of cars must have become irresistible to Sloan and his management team, all of whom had large shareholdings in the corporation; profits lay in rationalisation.

Beyond styling, another way of differentiating the more expensive cars was to incorporate the latest technology. So, in 1939, Oldsmobile offered the world's first automatic transmission, but Chevrolet did not follow suit until after the war.

By the very early 1930s, the product policy which had helped GM to market dominance in the second half of the 1920s was already unravelling in the United States. At the end of 1929, GM manufactured in the United States 'a total of 137 styles and body types, ranging in price from $495 to $9,700'. This product variety was spread fairly evenly from the bottom to the top of the 'price stairway', suggesting that GM did indeed provide the 'car for every purse and purpose' of Sloan's famous edict. With the most expensive car costing twenty times as much as the least expensive, the contrast between GM's product range and Ford's could hardly have been greater. Clearly, a V16-powered Cadillac (with even its engine bay styled by Harley Earl to reflect the brand's status) was not in any way to be confused with a Chevrolet.

In 1926 the low-price group, which included Chevrolet and Ford, had 52 per cent of total sales but by 1933 it supplied 73 per cent of the total market. This meant that the more expensive four (Pontiac, Oldsmobile, Buick and La Salle) of GM's six domestic brands competed within a band of just 27 per cent, while Chevrolet had to cover the rest. Demand for luxury models fell but at the same time buyers were more determined than ever to obtain maximum value for their automotive dollar. Sloan's response was to reduce prices on all models. Rationalisation of componentry watered down brand identity, with the La Salle, for example, using the Oldsmobile straight eight engine. When the La Salle brand was discontinued, Cadillac dropped further in price to fill the gap it left; the remaining five US brands drew closer.

As for GM's price leader, the Chevrolet, as early as 1928 it had ceased to be a truly small car and was powered by a six-cylinder engine in contrast to its new rival from Ford, the Model A. The Chevrolet's price tag of $585 put the squeeze on the medium-priced market, including Pontiac and Oldsmobile. Mostly, the independent manufacturers such as Studebaker, Packard and Hudson operated in the $750 to $1500 sector, and all found they needed new strategies. But in fact the seeds of the demise of these three (and many others before them) had been sown with Sloan's product policy.

Even before the stock market crash in 1929, there was evidence that the economies of scale available only to GM, Ford and the Chrysler Corporation were giving them leverage over the smaller independent manufacturers. The concertina effect on the market brought short-term losses for some GM divisions while threatening ruin for smaller companies. There may have been more brands operating in the medium-priced sector but it was the cheaper Fords, Chevrolets and Plymouths that were gaining the most sales.

But this double effect of concertina and consolidation was in its infancy, a marked tendency rather than the ineluctable trend it was to become in the 1950s. While Sloan remained on deck and at the helm, there was an inherent check on any temptation to steer off course. Brands preserved much of their individual identity. Nevertheless, as *Fortune* magazine reported in 1938, the price difference of 'about $300 from the cheapest Chevrolet to the cheapest Buick, and less than $130 from the most expensive Chevrolet to the cheapest Buick' spelled the end of 'a car for every purse and purpose'.

Even so, Sloan's mastery of the entire corporation moved General Motors even further ahead of its US rivals during the interwar years, particularly in sales but also in the introduction of new technology. Although increased centralisation removed much autonomy from GM's individual car divisions, it contributed to the company's superior cost efficiency via economies of scale at almost every level. Sloan's 'high-variety marketing plan' promoted flexibility. When luxury car sales recovered in 1939–41, GM had the right brands to take advantage of changed conditions and great scope to differentiate a Cadillac from a Buick and a Buick from an Oldsmobile, even if in their fundamentals all the brands were much closer than they had been, with six-cylinder engines the common factor, except for Cadillac.

Significantly, as the General Motors brands moved closer to one another the physical sizes of the cars largely converged, significantly towards the Cadillac end of the spectrum. Although a mid 1930s Cadillac was not only grander than a Chevrolet but also longer, wider, taller and heavier, the differences had nevertheless contracted.

Opel presented Adolf Hitler with an expensive birthday present on 26 April 1938, an Admiral limousine.

The 1939 Opel Kapitan played a small role in the development of the 48-215 Holden, although Russ Begg had better ideas by then.

Heading straight for the Southern Cross, the sky was no limit for Australia's Own.

An artist cleverly e-l-o-n-g-a-t-e-d the FJ's humpy lines to make it look just that little bit more modern. And a seaside context always helps.

Two-toning and miniscule tailfins brought '50s glamour to the FJ Special.

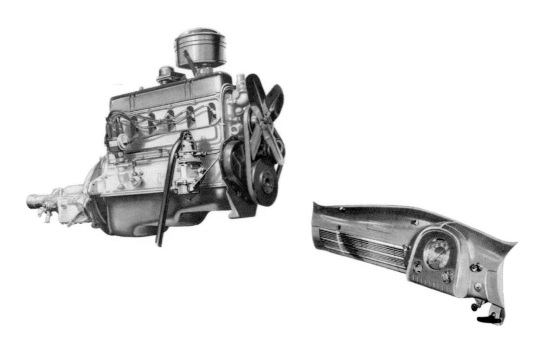

(Left) The Holden's straight six engine worked magnificently in this lightweight car. (Right) A plain but functional dashboard capable of inspiring nostalgia six decades down the bitumen.

The **NEW** Armstrong Siddeley

Sapphire 234

100 m.p.h. saloon

Even an artist's generous re-interpretation of the 1955 Armstrong Siddeley Sapphire 234 cannot hide its high roofline. At least senior executives could wear their Homburgs in the rear seat. By the mid-1950s, most makers had gone for the Detroit-driven three-box theme but Armstrong Siddeley, utterly British, would be out of business within five years. In 1956 GMH introduced the thoroughly modern FE.

Introduced in July 1956, the FE was the first completely new Holden since the 48-215 of November 1948.

The FC Special is one of the classic models and was the best car of its type in the world in 1958 by the criteria Australian buyers held dear—performance, economy, space, durability. Beneath the ornate chromework and creative colour schemes lay a simple car.

It took until January 1960 for some of the key elements of the 1955 Chevrolet to appear on a Holden.

Oh dear, some strange two-tone combinations were offered on the FB Special.

This publicity shot of the EH Premier reminds us how far architecture has moved since 1963. But the white picket fence is a charming touch.

The one millionth Holden, a bronze EJ Premier sedan, makes its way down the production line in October 1962.

1965 HD Special sets off the Sydney Harbour Bridge, or is it vice versa?

See how easily the VE Commodore could be transformed into a Pontiac G8? This is a one-off show car. Harley Earl would have loved it.

More than a hotrodded twenty-first century FJ Special, EFIJY drives straight to the centre of Holden DNA.

(Left) This detail spells FJ Holden. Designer Richard Ferlazzo dug into the Australian psyche to make 1953 live again, and this time in the fast lane. (Right) One of the myriad clever details is the chrome stone guard. But you couldn't drive this car on the dirt roads of 1953.

Did we never grasp the potential of that centre tail light?

Remarkably, a grille design dating back to 1953 looks ultra modern on Woodward Avenue, Detroit.

EFIJY has attracted rapturous attention all around the world, including in Dubai and Mongolia, as a letter to *Wheels* magazine attested.

The photographers tell this story. Holden has refused offers of A$1 million for this unique concept car.

Car as art.

Unlike some concept cars, EFIJY cries out for the road where its HSV engine fulfils the promise of that gorgeous streamline.

The 1935 Opel Olympia was GM's first ever monocoque, pioneering some crucial technology for the Holden.

Dr Ferdinand Porsche was the genius Hitler needed to bring his *Volkswagen* dream to reality. Porsche used design elements from his sleek, oversteering Auto-Union Formula One racer.

Yes, Mr Hitler, you see I have placed the engine in the rear, just like in my Auto-Union Formula One racing car.

GMH management gave employees and suppliers a preview of the Holden at the Woodville plant in August 1947.

Reflecting on the Australian Car's performance at the Milford Proving Ground.

Plenty of loving hands-on work for the Holden grille.

'She's a beauty,' says Prime Minister Chifley who looks rather like a proud father. But he had more on his mind than a simple utility car. On 29 November 1948 he spoke of the risks of another world war. For Chifley and his colleagues, a strong manufacturing industry meant military capacity and superior defence.

(Left) Harold Bettle was charged with bringing the Australian car into production and GMH back into line with head office policy. (Right) By the time this photograph was taken, Larry Hartnett was being treated as a celebrity by Holden management. Charles (Chuck) Chapman offered the olive branch, which Sir Laurence was delighted to grasp.

In 1953 a new radiator grille proved sufficient to refresh the appeal of Australia's Own Car. Compare this image with the EFIJY fascia and count the shared (if transformed) details.

The 1953 FJ Special added some Detroit-style pizzaz to help the old shape last almost three more years. GMH could not afford the luxury of the famed GM annual model change.

The FJ's interior was neat but far from luxurious. Nevertheless, these themes inspired the heavenly EFIJY concept car.

Nothing posed about this delightfully dated publicity shot of the original matching Holden sedan coupe utility (with matching husband, wife and labourer)!

This may be the most iconic photograph of an Australian ute. The setting is somewhere in Leongatha, Victoria.

The FE was a seriously stylish and practical ute for 1956 and beyond. Australia's suburban sprawl helped the sales of one of the country's great inventions, the coupe utility.

The Citroën DS of 1955 set a trend which few followed, but it did make everything else look suddenly old.

Citroën DS19 GBW 25/9/97 – March 2008

The 1955 Citroën DS19. Sketch by Geoff Webber, March 2008.

The 1958 FC Standard utility poised to drive forwards into history.

Well before World War II the new pattern for Detroit had been set by Sloan, with simple Model T-style cars a thing of the past, and each successive new model was likely to be physically bigger. Recently, an historian specialising in American studies asked me about a framed photograph on his office wall. It showed a long line-up of late 1930s cars in the main street of a town. 'Most of these cars were owned by Nebraskan farmers', he said, 'but in 1938 times were tough. How could they afford to buy such large cars?' The answer to his question goes to the heart of US 'automobility'. Well before 1938 such cars were typical and no longer viewed as large but 'regular'. Henry Ford's one-size-fits-all *Volkswagen*-style car had been replaced by Sloan's vision, but this in itself had metamorphosed from a car for every purse and purpose to a larger car to suit most purses and many purposes. Simply, in the late 1930s, few small cars were in evidence on North American roads.

There was no room in Sloan's view for physically smaller cars of the type common in Europe because it cost almost as much to make a medium-sized model as a larger one. But larger cars can support a higher profit margin. Sloan was first to enact this large-car policy, and during the 1930s it became conventional Detroit wisdom. The generous size of the American cars of the 1930s and their ubiquity even, for example, in depressed rural Nebraska, indicates the extent to which US 'automobility' was unique in the world, driven by the early start and the fact that Fordist production methods and inexpensive fuel made the cost of motoring far cheaper than anywhere else.

Larger cars can support a higher profit margin. Sloan was first to enact this large-car policy, and during the 1930s it became conventional Detroit wisdom.

That Nebraskan street photographed in 1938 invites discussion of the people's car concept as it was seen in various markets. Henry Ford produced what must be defined as the first *Volkswagen*. Following Sloan's thinking, the true US successor to the Model T was a two- or three-year-old used Chevrolet. But the idea of a people's car was gaining strength in Europe, and especially Germany during the 1920s.

The General buys into Germany

Mass motorisation, Fordist production methods and the interchangeability of spare parts had not arrived in Germany by the time GM bought the Opel company. This acquisition gave Sloan an opportunity to apply his theories in a foreign theatre. Vauxhall, purchased back in 1925, did not afford the scope of Opel because the specialist British company was much smaller. Despite the Depression, Sloan's optimistic predictions for Opel were fulfilled during the 1930s, providing in the process a blueprint for the successful creation of GM cars to suit overseas markets rather than trying to sell American Chevrolets, mostly with little success. By introducing American methods, General Motors would bring superior quality and significant economies of scale to Opel. The company's engineers would learn from their US counterparts.

The benefits of being owned by General Motors were evident surprisingly early. In November 1930 Opel showed its dealers the revised 1931 model line-up, the highlight of which was a 1.8-litre model. This car used the smallest six-cylinder unit in the world, which had been developed in the United States specifically for Opel. Its body bore more than a superficial resemblance to a scaled-down Cadillac. At 2700 Reichsmarks it was a bargain and the smooth six-cylinder engine offered a high cruising speed of 90 kilometres per hour.

Here was a new and distinct advantage for Opel. Sloan's team had decided to give the 1928 Chevrolet a 'six' to extend its advantages over its rival, the four-cylinder Ford. The additional cylinders meant smoother running and more refinement, giving an impression of luxury. This same thinking was extended to Opel, albeit in downsized form. And smooth, effortless six-cylinder engines would be ideal for Hitler's high-speed *auto-*

bahnen. In a pure product sense, this is about the point where the seeds of Holden design were sown.

In June 1931 Fritz von Opel proudly announced that his products made up 77.6 per cent of all Germany's car exports. By that time the Great Depression was receding but Germany had its own economic woes. In July of that year both the Darmstadt and the National Bank collapsed. Many of the smaller German manufacturers went out of business. Even Opel had to shut down its plant for a period, but General Motors was undeterred. Strong export markets meant, at least in theory, that GM dealers worldwide could sell Opels. Australia provided the exception to prove this rule.

The German economic crisis actually advanced General Motors' multinational planning with this full-scale export program justifying the cost of expanding the Rüsselsheim operation. Even so, it is difficult to see how even that entrepreneurial genius, Alfred P. Sloan Jr, could have predicted the enormity of General Motors' success with Opel in the 1930s.

Hitler changes (almost) everything

In 1929 it was by no means inevitable that Hitler's National Socialist Party would form a government. While the problems that beset the German economy helped General Motors to expand its Opel operation, they helped Adolf Hitler and his National Socialist Party even more. The former lance corporal became chancellor of the Reich on 30 January 1933, largely on a promise to restore Germany as a great power. But there was little chance of achieving world dominance without first rebuilding the domestic economy.

The Nazis' apparently mutually opposed goals of bringing mass motorisation to Germany and reducing the influence of foreign-owned companies in the national economy could not have been foreseen. As it happened, Hitler's rise to power contributed mightily to the growth of Opel and thus to GM's expertise in overseas operations. GM brought American mass-production technology to Opel just as the Nazis provoked an industry boom; this amounted to a telling synergy between GM overseas planning

Lessons learnt at Opel in the hothouse of the Third Reich would endure; without the Third Reich, it would have taken the corporation many more years to develop the technology that would subsequently be used in the Holden.

and Nazi industrial policy. Germany became the automotive industrial crucible out of which GM's product planners and engineers conceived a whole new approach to creating cars, and consequently the 1930s Opels were different in major respects from the typical 1930s North American models. Lessons learnt at Opel in the hothouse of the Third Reich would endure; without the Third Reich, it would have taken the corporation many more years to develop the technology that would subsequently be used in the Holden.

On 11 February 1933, less than a fortnight after his accession to power, Hitler presided over the opening of the 1933 Berlin Motor Show, his first important public function in his new role. Hitler's speech was devoted to the need for inexpensive mass-produced cars, first-class roads and an international motor competition to showcase the technological competence of the German nation. He said it was his intention to support the production of a *Deutschen Volkswagen*.

At first sight and certainly from a General Motors perspective, the logical choice of company to bring this dream of a people's car to Germany was Opel, which had been the country's largest manufacturer of small cars since 1923. According to Opel's official history, the company 'had every hope of being awarded this glittering prize, particularly since it already possessed suitable production facilities'.

But the contract was instead eventually awarded to Dr Ferdinand Porsche, whom Hitler first met at a motor sport meeting in 1925 or 1926. Ferdinand Porsche had, says historian Henry Ashby Turner, 'stirred Hitler's fancy with his design for a radically different vehicle with swooping, aerodynamic lines and a compact air-cooled rear engine', which made the Opel P–4 appear 'hopelessly antiquated'.

Given Hitler's obsession with Germany's future, the Porsche design must have held obvious appeal. But it is unlikely that this was the sole reason Opel was apparently never seriously considered for the Volkswagen contract.

Why was Opel's proposal rejected? Probably for a combination of reasons, in particular Hitler's obsession with what the industry in general, and Opel in particular, regarded as a totally unrealistic selling price of 1000 Reichsmarks. Ferdinand Porsche never quibbled about the price. It is also likely that the National Socialists were unwilling to commission a People's Car from a foreign-owned company. But perhaps this unwillingness might have been overcome. Certainly, the Nazi regime threw itself upon Opel expertise when it came to the production of trucks and tanks for World War II, rejecting the old favourite Daimler-Benz in the process.

There is no evidence that Opel ever designed a dedicated car to meet Hitler's requirements. Given the choice between Ferdinand Porsche's modernistic creation, which could be seen as symbolic of the Third Reich's narcissistic self-image (streamlined, futuristic, ascetic, universal), and a dated, boxy model at a higher price to be supplied by a foreign-owned company, the choice must have been clear. Even so, Opel could still have won the contract to manufacture Porsche's *Volkswagen* and had even gone to the trouble of building a new factory which would be dedicated to its manufacture.

History is jam-packed with happenstance. Hitler, obsessed with cars, appears to have felt something close to hero worship for Ferdinand Porsche. It was no coincidence that the discussion of a German *Volkswagen*, the new road system and success in international motor racing were, for Hitler, three closely linked elements. Design similarities between the awesome Auto-Union Formula One racing cars designed by Porsche and the humble but equally radical Volkswagen were probably decisive in Hitler's choice of Porsche as the car's designer; both had a streamlined aesthetic and rear engine.

Had there been no Ferdinand Porsche, Hitler would almost certainly have chosen Opel not only to produce his people's car but also to design it.

This counterfactual is perhaps best supported by the evidence that Hitler's experts rejected indigenous Daimler-Benz's truck proposals in favour of Opel's during World War II.

Opel showed little imagination in responding to Hitler's demands for his people's car. If the Ford Model T as the world's first *Volkswagen* had not needed any special grace or style to justify its role, the German context of 1933 was very different and Hitler would expect his *Volkswagen* to embody Nazi ideological rhetoric. Style was a major element in Nazi ideology, from the depiction of the Aryan soldier to the wirelesses which transmitted propaganda into German parlours. Porsche's simple, glamorous design met this requirement, while the dowdy little Opel P–4 looked backwards to the lumpy, upright cars of the 1920s rather than forwards to the Aryan supremacist future of the Fuehrer's obscene fantasy; it was more Austin Seven than, say, Citroën *Diesse*.

Because the Third Reich was dependent on Opel for much needed export sales to pay for the imports it required, the decision was taken to leave the company largely alone. Hitler's removal of sales tax on new cars and his plan to build a national network of *autobahnen* further augmented General Motors' plans for Opel. GM's corporate wealth allowed the investment necessary to develop competitive new models. Lower selling prices ensured a larger market, not just for Opel but for all German automotive manufacturers, and especially Daimler-Benz, but more on this later. Opel was transformed within a very few years as GM engineering and marketing expertise was applied to the company. Because it specialised in low-priced cars and could utilise GM manufacturing technology, Opel was the greatest beneficiary of the Third Reich's automotive policy. The indigenous German manufacturers had no access to Fordist methods and thus could not realise the almost exponential growth which Opel experienced in the period. From production of 20,914 vehicles in 1932, the figures for the next four years respectively were 39,295, 71,665, 102,765 and 120,397. While sales of Mercedes-Benz cars increased significantly every year from 1933 to 1938, its share of the market declined.

From the Olympia to World War II

With its expanded range of GM-designed cars in the mid 1930s, Opel brought more foreign currency into the country than any other German company. Opel had even negotiated with Larry Hartnett to export the Olympia model to Australia but the minister for trade, Sir Henry Gullett, would not permit this plan to proceed on the grounds that it would offend the British manufacturers whose vehicles accounted for an increasing share of the Australian market. Significantly, Gullett also thought the Olympia was too small.

The Olympia was the most significant car created by General Motors since the six-cylinder Chevrolet of 1927, and in terms of the Holden story its relevance can hardly be overestimated. This was a four-cylinder model with better performance and fuel economy than its direct rivals, thanks mainly to a radical engineering approach which would bring great weight savings. By European standards the Olympia was a medium-sized vehicle but, as we have seen, the US perspective was that Chevrolet-size was typical.

Remarkably, Sloan makes no specific mention of the Opel Olympia in *My Years with General Motors* despite it being the most radical new model the corporation developed in the 1930s. The design of the new Olympia probably started early in 1934, with a prototype on display at the Berlin Motor Show in February 1935 and production beginning the following year. It was much bigger (and more expensive) than the P–4, which would have been Opel's *Volkswagen*, but this did not prevent the company from making reference to that project. On the occasion of the Olympia's debut, Opel issued a press release which made passing reference to the People's Car as 'this gap on the German market [which] has still not been filled', while extolling the special qualities of the Olympia, especially its radical new load-bearing, all-steel bodyshell.

> *Opel has always striven to supply large sections of the population with full-sized cars at popular prices. With the Olympia it is giving a decided impetus to mass motoring in Germany at a time when this gap on the German market has still not been filled. The new car dispenses with the previous separate chassis and body. The body framework can be compared with a steel bridge, which weighs very little yet is capable of effortlessly withstanding the most severe loads. This framework consists of sectional steel members linked together by the methods used in the construction of metal bodied aircraft.*

At just 835 kilograms the Olympia was remarkably light for its size, which in the European context was accurately described as 'full'. (The Volkswagen, known initially as the 'Strength Through Joy' car, was notably smaller and lighter again.) Not only would the Olympia escape the punitive high-horsepower tax regime, but it would also use less fuel than other similarly sized vehicles. General Motors' first European car, then, was of novel design and proved hugely popular. By April 1936, it was being produced in volume and total production of Opel cars and trucks for that year was 120,397. Sloan's prediction was on the way to coming true.

The fact that the Olympia was created so soon after the General Motors takeover of Opel shows how keen Sloan and his fellow executives were to cater to what they saw in general as European needs, and specifically those of the German domestic market. In styling, the new Opel had a general resemblance to a scaled-down Chevrolet but utilised monocoque (literally: one-piece) construction. Instead of having a separate chassis to which a body would be attached in the standard fashion, the Olympia's body and chassis were integrated into one unit. It was the first car of this type ever to be designed within GM and the first to be produced in Germany. The Olympia was shown just a year or so after the Citroën Traction Avant, which was the French marque's first monocoque, so it was in the vanguard of automotive engineering. Lancia had been first in 1925 (the Lambda, designed by Vittorio Jano), but the Citroën and Opel were the first mass-produced examples.

> Opel had close links with Ambi-Budd, a company at the forefront of all-steel body design. (Ambi-Budd was the German division of Budd, which was based in the United States.) The monocoque was a logical consequence of using steel alone instead of a combination of steel and wood. In this respect the European automotive industry was somewhat ahead of Detroit. But Budd had produced a curvaceous all-steel vehicle in 1923; General Motors' body division, Fisher, did not introduce a steel turret top until the fall of 1935 when the 1936 models made their debut.

The fundamental engineering decisions were made by American engineers, a fact acknowledged in the official history of Opel: 'Opel's engineers would be able to profit in full measure from their American colleagues' knowhow and it was planned to pass on research findings from the USA to Rüsselsheim. American manufacturers were quite clearly well ahead of German and other European competitors at this time.'

The most significant of these American engineers was Russell ('Russ') Begg. He seems to have been involved with Opel from 1934 and took up the position of assistant chief engineer two years later. Begg's significance to our story will emerge in subsequent chapters, but at this stage it might help to mention that he was the chief engineer of the first Holden and had worked as chief engineer at a number of automotive companies before taking up his post at Opel. He had also worked for Budd and probably played a key role in the decision to employ monocoque construction for the Olympia.

By the mid 1930s Opel had clear technological advantages over its rivals. Not only was it at the forefront in the adoption of unitary construction, but it also produced more six-cylinder cars than any other non-US manufacturer. This second factor constituted a major reversal as in 1930 the company had ceased manufacture of large six-cylinder models due to slow sales. But the following year saw the small 1.8-litre six-cylinder engine fitted to the small Cadillac-style model mentioned earlier. Six-cylinder engines became an Opel speciality under General Motors and the company's rise to become the biggest manufacturer of cars outside the United States was clearly a result of the Sloan management approach—a remarkable achievement in the context of a mostly, and increasingly, hostile German government.

By 1938 Opel's line-up reflected Sloan's product policy. Two new six-cylinder models were introduced at the 1937 Berlin Motor Show. The Super Six used a 2.5-litre engine and the luxurious Admiral had a powerful 3.6-litre unit. Demand for both was strong. The case of the Admiral is especially interesting. According to Opel's official history, it 'was not expected to sell in large quantities' and 'Opel mainly intended it as a demonstration that it could design and build state-of-the art cars. Be that as it may, 6404 examples were delivered between 1937 and 1939, a sign that although times were not easy, there was a definite market for luxury cars'.

The Admiral was Opel's interpretation of what would these days be termed state of the art. This new flagship was proclaimed in its brochure to be 'Acknowledged by all: the most beautiful car I have ever seen'. The Admiral's styling, signed off like every other design produced within GM by Harley Earl, was certainly more avant-garde than GM had dared with any of its American cars. It seems possible that the Admiral's streamlined appearance represented an *en passant* tribute to Ferdinand Porsche's Volkswagen, which was by this time a matter of public record if not consumption. An example was presented by Opel to Chancellor Hitler on 20 April 1938 as a birthday present. Unfortunately, history has left us to guess whether or not Hitler regarded this gift as the most beautiful car *he* had ever seen!

By the late 1930s, it was becoming difficult to import vehicles into Germany and the Admiral filled out the top end of General Motors' range in Europe, simultaneously serving notice to Daimler-Benz that Opel intended to participate in the luxury car market.

Evidence of a new American/European dialectic was already evident in Opel product planning. The Admiral was one case and the Super Six another. As stated in the sales brochure for the Super Six:

> . . . *for the first time in the history of the automotive industry, a car was introduced [sic] which does actually incorporate the often praised combination of best European tradition in taste and craftsmanship with the last word in American-like performance.*

Perhaps Larry Hartnett drew inspiration for the first Holden from the Opel example, although there does not seem to be any record of his saying so. Nevertheless, his ideal of an Australian car that would be between the 'two types' (American and European) reflects this kind of thinking.

Late in 1938 Opel introduced the monocoque Kapitän six-cylinder sedan to replace the Super Six, giving General Motors perhaps the most comprehensive range of cars on offer in Europe, some of which were also among the more advanced (although the Citroën Traction Avant of 1934, with its pioneering use of front-wheel drive as well as monocoque construction, represented the cutting edge of automotive technology). The Kapitän was the first General Motors car to combine a six-cylinder engine with monocoque construction, and was in this respect the true predecessor to the Holden, which in 1949 would be the only car of this new type on the Australian market. So the work done by GM at Opel during the Third Reich contributed significantly to the DNA of the Holden, specifically via Russ Begg.

The Kapitän was the first General Motors car to combine a six-cylinder engine with monocoque construction, and was in this respect the true predecessor to the Holden, which in 1949 would be the only car of this new type on the Australian market. So the work done by GM at Opel during the Third Reich contributed significantly to the DNA of the Holden, specifically via Russ Begg.

The biggest negative for General Motors in the 1930s and early 1940s was the prospective total loss of its successful Opel operation to the Nazis. Government interference in Opel's operations continued to increase as Germany re-armed and preparations for war gathered pace. On 6 October 1936 Jim Mooney reported to Sloan that 'Practically nothing can be done for operating the business without government sanction' and Graeme Howard's view was that 'Opel, among other duties to the State, has a duty to provide whatever the Army requires'. Opel was at risk of being appropriated by the Third Reich by the time the Admiral came to market. James Mooney and his executives faced the challenge of retaining control of Europe's largest carmaker as Hitler's government relied increasingly on Germany's factories to produce weapons of war, which included Opel Blitz trucks. The government ultimatum finally came in June 1940: all Opel production must be turned over to armaments. This put at risk the company's position as one of the more advanced automotive manufacturers in Europe and a jewel in the General Motors crown. The corporation was faced with a possibly permanent loss of what was by this time its highly valuable German asset.

The profits earned by Opel continued to soar throughout the war years even though the factories were turned over to military production. By 1941 it looked as if the capital assets would never be repatriated to the corporation, and for the 1942 taxation year GM claimed its entire German capital investment as a one-off loss against income.

As David Farber demonstrates in *Sloan Rules*, it was business first, second and last with Alfred Sloan in the case of Opel. The coming to power of the National Socialist government was not in itself identified as a problem for General Motors; indeed, in the early years the Nazi regime helped the company to achieve Sloan's forecasts as Hitler's removal of taxes on cars led to a sales boom. Like other German companies, Opel conformed to the requirements of the government, albeit less enthusiastically than Daimler-Benz. As late as April 1939, Sloan was justifying the corporation's activities in Germany to shareholders. He argued that it was not GM's business 'to police . . . political sympathies'. In December 1941 the German government placed control of Opel in the hands of the Reich's minister for the treatment of enemy property. Between 1936 and the end of 1939, under US ownership, Opel had produced more than half a million vehicles; it would now become a resource for the German war effort. Interestingly, General Motors-owned companies produced more road vehicles for World War II than any other, and these were used by both sides. With war having broken out in Europe and the future of its German subsidiary in doubt, General Motors recalled Begg and other American executives working at Opel to the United States in September 1939.

Sloan looks to the postwar future

It is clear that, while Sloan dreaded any kind of government interference whether from the left or right wings of politics, Hartnett, by contrast, could not leap into the political fray quickly or publicly enough. While the Anglo-Australian had been politically active for some years before the war in

As early as 1941, prescient Sloan could see enormous potential in the aftermath. There would, he believed, be unprecedented demand for consumer goods of all types, not just in the United States but in overseas markets such as Australia.

advocating the Australian government prepare itself for that likelihood, Sloan's professional focus, as ever, was almost entirely on General Motors and its profits: his life's work. But even before turning over Opel's factories for the production of the materials of war, and in fact before the United States had even declared war on Germany and Japan, the GM chairman was looking beyond the cataclysm to a reconfigured postwar world. As early as 1941, prescient Sloan could see enormous potential in the aftermath. There would, he believed, be unprecedented demand for consumer goods of all types, not just in the United States but in overseas markets such as Australia.

Sloan's vision and the corporation's great success with Opel between 1929 and 1940 would underpin the creation of a unique car for the Australian market. His may not quite have been the sole voice crying out in the wartime wilderness, but his view of postwar plenty was certainly an extreme one. In 1944, when many economists were predicting recession and unemployment, Sloan was convinced boom times lay just down the road, using phrases such as 'this tremendous aggregation of purchasing power'.

Amazingly, three days *before* Pearl Harbor, Sloan recommended a 40 to 50 per cent expansion in US production. General Motors would lead the United States and maybe the world into the brave new postwar world of consumer demand. It is easy to see how Sloan had already incorporated into his intellectual armoury the view expressed some years later by Charles Wilson, his hand-picked successor as chairman: 'I thought what was good for our country was good for GM—and vice versa. The difference did not exist.' And it is difficult to disagree with Sloan's suggestion that General Motors' thinking would provide 'a positive inducement to other business-men to plan for growth'.

The entire history of the North American automotive market was largely driven by Sloan's initiatives from the early 1920s through to the

> **The entire history of the North American automotive market was largely driven by Sloan's initiatives from the early 1920s through to the late 1950s.**

late 1950s. By the time he gave his December 1941 speech, Sloan's GM Overseas Operations executives had already applied similar thinking to Australia. A June 1943 report under the chairmanship of Albert Bradley dealt with the 'corporation's plans for expansion abroad', specifically the possibility of moving from partial to full manufacture in Australia. So when Larry Hartnett and his team came to New York in September 1944 to argue the case for local manufacture, a favourable corporate mindset, *pace* Hartnett, was already in place. The evidence suggests that the only impediments were Sloan's misgivings about the Australian political situation, heightened perhaps by the corporation's dire experience with Opel, and almost certainly Sloan's 'low regard' for Hartnett himself.

General Motors was taking a global view more than a decade before Marshall McLuhan coined the term 'global village'. It is impossible, then, to understand the significance of the Holden car simply by studying it on a national basis. Above all, the Australian car was not solely the result of Larry Hartnett's vision. Hartnett was more of a pawn in GM's chess game than even he realised, either at the time or later.

After 1942, Daimler-Benz grudgingly conceded to a government demand to build the Blitz under licence from Opel. This required a massive reorganisation, but there were three positive outcomes. First, it kept Daimler in the truck business; second, it gave the manufacturer close instruction in General Motors mass-production methods; and third, it provided a vehicle to build in the immediate aftermath of the war.

Without GM engineering, Germany would almost certainly have lost World War II sooner. Of course, the Allies used GM trucks and tanks as well; GM and Ford provided the majority of trucks for both sides. Imagine the surprise of the Allied soldiers landing in Normandy in June 1944 to see that the enemy was driving GM and Ford trucks. So, who emerged most strongly from the war? Certainly big automotive business was a huge winner, and especially the world market leader, General Motors.

Chapter 4

'This, our first car'

We cannot afford, however to risk going into production on our first model in Australia on the basis of a design which is the product of an untried and untested engineering department. I'll be glad at any time to review models which you could develop in Australia and consider them for production in Australia for future programs. I am not willing, however, to plunk down our blue chips on the production of this, our first car, on the basis of such design . . . I just cannot put our money on your crowd for this first job.

—Edward C. Riley to Laurence J. Hartnett, 7 August 1945

Let's step into a time-travel machine and go back to August 1944 to a warehouse deep within General Motors' Central Engineering division at its Detroit headquarters. Among a collection of experimental prototypes are two outwardly identical black cars, labelled 195-Y-13 and 195-Y-15. The vehicles have gathered some dust and it may well be that few people have been in here for a while. We will take a long, close look at the one described as 195-Y-15. Catchy name, eh? But despite the lack of a more evocative one—Cadet, say, or Velox—this humpy-shaped vehicle constitutes one of the largest single pieces in our big-picture Holden jigsaw puzzle. Any day now, a couple of senior engineers are going to march into this room and change the course of Australian history.

Until now, the true antecedents of the Australian car program (labelled 195Y25) have never been identified. In this chapter I intend to reveal them. Much evidence has been destroyed. General Motors was not 'an "archive" company', as John McDonald discovered when he ghosted Sloan's *My Years with General Motors*. '"We don't believe in archives," he [Sloan] said . . . "GM's way, you lose some good things and get rid of some bad."' General Motors claims to hold no GMH-related archival records in the United States, but the GMH archive, housed in the Mortlock Library in the Library of South Australia, contains some material which has never before been fully explored.

It was here I located vital documents which reveal a decision was taken that the experimental light car 195-Y-15 was of no further interest to GM. It was not just forgotten, or set aside because of World War II (Pearl Harbor was still three years into the future), but deliberately abandoned. Given the fact that this car was used as the basis for the Holden, its prior abandonment is of considerable interest. The GMH side of the program is well documented with copies of correspondence from Hartnett and his fellow executives to the engineers engaged on 195Y25. But Hartnett constantly complained about 'being kept in the dark'. There are comparatively few internal US records, that is, documents that were not sent to GMH. Nevertheless, there is valuable material, which has enabled me to construct a clearer picture. I also have some photocopies of 1930s Opel brochures and of German newspaper articles. So while it remains impossible to do much more than offer a carefully argued circumstantial account of how 195-Y-15 emerged from the new work done at Opel in the 1930s, I believe that a close 'reading' of the two vehicles themselves (engine capacity and number of cylinders, physical dimensions including length, width, interior space, and weight, etc.) supports my hypothesis.

Jack Rawnsley, one of the young Australian engineers sent to Detroit in 1945 to work on the first Holden, believes that the two '195' cars were built in Germany, even though the design was done in Detroit by Lou Thoms of GM's Central Engineering Office. Thoms would have determined the package size, mechanical specifications and body styling. The prototypes, Rawnsley says, were then shipped to Detroit for testing. Furthermore, he believes that Begg was in charge of the program. His view is supported by evidence that both Begg and Kuiper went to the United States in 1939 on two occasions, the second being when they were recalled because of the outbreak of war in September. Begg was on a ship out of Cherbourg on 10 February 1939 and docked in the United States on 17 February; it seems probable that Begg accompanied the experimental cars on their voyage to the United States on that occasion. This brings further implications for the correlation between the experimental cars and the Holden, which will be explored later.

Like the 1939 Chevrolet it somewhat resembles, 195-Y-15 has a six-cylinder engine. Unlike the Chevrolet its body and chassis are integral, making it a monocoque. Its outwardly identical twin, 195-Y-13, has a four-cylinder engine rather than a six. The essence of the experiment which explains their existence was: does a four-cylinder or a six-cylinder engine work better in a car of this size built to the latest lightweight monocoque design? It is likely that the question came from the Chevrolet division, which was considering the possibility of making a smaller vehicle for the North American market. And to answer the question we need to go back to Germany, to Opel, and take another brief look at the cars beyond the Olympia—the Super Six and the Kapitän—and their influence on the development of what would be known as the Experimental Light Car Project. There would also be strong export potential for a car of this size, American models being deemed too large and expensive by many prospective overseas purchasers. It may well be that the thinking was that the same car could be sold domestically as an entry-level Chevrolet, and in Britain, Australia, New Zealand and other important overseas markets as the first six-cylinder monocoque Vauxhall.

The 195-Y cars have a hint of contemporaneous Chevrolets but look even more like the Opel Olympia, especially from the front where an Opel-style grille makes a bold statement. In fact, inspiration for the entire exercise almost certainly came from the Olympia—developed in 1934–35 as General Motors' first all-new overseas product, and a great success. It was the first monocoque car both for the German automotive industry and for General Motors. Without the weight of a separate chassis, the Olympia was lighter than any direct rival, as well as being stiffer due to integral construction. Weight is the enemy of both performance and fuel economy; less weight allowed the Olympia to use its small four-cylinder engine to better effect.

At the time the 195-Y experiment began, design of the six-cylinder Opel Kapitän was in its final stages. This was a special car, designed specifically as a product of and for the Third Reich. The Kapitän would showcase Opel as a world-class manufacturer of high-quality cars and help to secure continuing viability for the US-owned company in Nazi Germany. First shown at the Berlin Motor Show late in 1938 as a 1939 model, design of the Kapitän probably began in 1935 before the Olympia went on sale. Here was the successor for the Super Six, which we have already seen was described as a blend of American and European themes. The Kapitän was, perhaps, more thoroughly a dialectical consequence of these different motoring expectations. By melding monocoque construction, a six-cylinder engine and a high level of standard specification, it offered the best of both worlds. But it was certainly not conceived with the same aims as 195-Y-15. Light weight and low fuel consumption do not rank high among the priorities of what is intended as a plush, upmarket kind of car, a *limousine* as the Germans would call it. Even Opel's own publicity for the Kapitän makes no

At the time the 195-Y experiment began, design of the six-cylinder Opel Kapitän was in its final stages. This was a special car, designed specifically as a product of and for the Third Reich. The Kapitän would showcase Opel as a world-class manufacturer of high-quality cars and help to secure continuing viability for the US-owned company in Nazi Germany.

special claims in terms of thrifty running costs. In praising the 'integral body and chassis construction method' as the best available, the brochure continues: '. . . the new Kapitän is more than twice as strong in regard to torsional rigidity than the conventional body and chassis type construction . . . all material is better utilized because the entire structure carries the load . . .'

In the Olympia's case the new design is credited with allowing better performance and fuel economy through reduced weight. Advertising for the Kapitän departs from this theme. Rather: 'Even with this all metal type of body construction an excellent power to weight ratio has been maintained.' That 'even' is partly a problem of translation, essentially meaning: the Kapitän is light and fast considering its physical size.

This was a substantial car, which weighed 2676 pounds (1216 kg), compared with the Olympia's 2032 (924 kg) and about 2646 (1203 kg) for the Super Six. But where the overall length of the Super Six was 172 inches (4370 mm), the Kapitän measured 182 inches (4620 mm). So the power to weight advantage conferred by unitary construction was used to provide additional vehicle size and more equipment rather than to reduce weight and improve fuel economy.

The Kapitän, then, was conceived as a more luxurious, spacious and attractive medium–large car with good performance and reasonable economy. It was Opel's statement of upper middle-class status in the motoring-obsessed Reich, where the issue of top speed on the *autobahnen* was already important to many buyers, and 78 miles per hour (125 km/h) constituted a good turn of speed. It was a car intended to show indigenous Daimler-Benz a thing or several. There was never any question of using a four-cylinder engine, as the Kapitän was to supersede the Super Six. In fact the same engine was retained. This was a 2.5-litre unit which developed 60 horsepower (an output identical to the Holden's a decade on—surely no coincidence, and we'll read later about the Kapitän's cameo appearance in the Holden design program). Fuel consumption was quoted as 12 to 15 litres per 100 kilometres, the same as that claimed for the Super Six. Opel's new medium-sized car was promoted as 'the most perfect and desirable car of its class' for 1939, joining the plush and elegant Admiral model in a show of Opel's capacity to build not just excellent smaller models but also to create benchmark larger cars.

Between the Olympia and the Kapitän

The defining question seems to have been: what if you want to make a somewhat larger car than the Olympia—do you stick with a 'four' or go to a 'six'? Or, to put the same proposition into an Opel context: if we built a Super Six-sized car as a monocoque, thereby saving considerably more than 100 kilograms, would it work better as a 'four' or 'six'? The Super Six, tellingly, is almost exactly the same size as the experimental models—172 inches (4369 mm) in length compared with 170 (4318 mm). This tells us that the Super Six almost certainly provided the 'package' size for the 195-Y cars. Here, I believe, is the true genesis of the Holden. Take the Opel Super Six, redesign it as the most efficient monocoque possible, then see whether it works better with a six-cylinder or four-cylinder engine. Because the Olympia was the first GM monocoque, the engineers erred on the side of caution in terms of making components heavier than perhaps they needed to be. (This experience would be repeated by almost every other automotive company in making its pioneering monocoque, examples including Jaguar with its 2.4 Litre sedan in 1955 and Rover with its 3 Litre in 1958.) Doubtless, the experimental engineers were confident they could now build a much lighter monocoque without sacrificing strength and, as the name implies, this was a major theme in the Experimental Light Car Program. The six-cylinder 195-Y-15 weighed just 2077 pounds (942.1 kg), only 45 pounds (20.4 kg)

> Here, I believe, is the true genesis of the Holden. Take the Opel Super Six, redesign it as the most efficient monocoque possible, then see whether it works better with a six-cylinder or four-cylinder engine.

more than the significantly smaller Olympia, showing the experimental engineers had already learnt more about how to make lighter unitary cars. Almost
certainly, these cars used the latest Ambi-Budd integral construction technology, as had the Olympia and Kapitän in the recent past.

We should hurry out of the studio now because those engineers could
be on their way to take 195-Y-15 as the starting point for the postwar
Australian car. Before we leave, though, should we lean a hastily hand-
written sign up against the dusty black 195-Y-15 prototype: 'Australian Car,
1938 version'?

More (cylinders) is better

The engineers of the Experimental Light Car Program evidently decided that
the six-cylinder engine worked better for the 195-Y vehicle size. Yes, the
extra cylinders added to the cost but using a four-cylinder unit required a
more robust gearbox, among other things. In the end, the sums were similar
but 195-Y-15 had far better performance while using comparatively little
extra fuel. Obviously the six-cylinder car could also command a price
premium in the market which would more than offset any slight additional
manufacturing cost.

Once 195-Y-15 had been tested at GM's Milford proving ground and
shown to senior management, it began gathering dust. The four-cylinder car
received no testing, having evidently been discarded soon after its arrival in
Detroit. This lends further weight to Jack Rawnsley's account. It is probable
that the US executives would not have sanctioned the idea of reintroducing
a four-cylinder Chevrolet, having used 'sixes' exclusively since 1927; such a
reversal might have been seen as diluting the brand. The fact that *both*
prototypes were abandoned raises new questions, some of which are beyond
the scope of this book. One obvious possibility is the intervention of World
War II. All automotive engineering was paused during the war and by 1944
thought was already being given to developing a more modern and radical
six-cylinder car of this size. This project, officially announced in May 1945,

was the Chevrolet Cadet. It is clear, though, that the engineers had acquired new intellectual property from the 195-Y experiment. Had there been no Australian Car Program, this property would doubtless have been used by General Motors in the brave new postwar world, but certainly not by Chevrolet. (On 15 May 1947, the Cadet program was cancelled; any thought of producing an inexpensive car for the US market was abandoned in the rush to maximise profits. As it happens, GMH was the primary beneficiary of the 1937–39 195-Y experiment.)

The success of the Opel Olympia vindicated the engineers' choice of monocoque construction for the 195-Y program. This method demands longer production runs to amortise the higher cost of tooling and the General Motors Overseas Operation (GMOO) product planners must have been confident that the German market would justify this additional investment. The Olympia marked a turning point for Opel, achieving immediate success not just in Germany but wherever it was sold in Europe. Larry Hartnett had even wanted to part-manufacture it in Australia. With the exception of the 1938 Admiral, an expensive luxury model, all subsequent Opel car designs would employ the monocoque method. GM's English subsidiary, Vauxhall, was also ready for new models, all of which would be monocoques, by 1940.

Back in 1937, as the world economy gathered strength after the Great Depression, GM's multinational plans were coming to fruition and there was always the prospect that the corporation would begin to manufacture cars in other markets. Australia, where GMH not only dominated the market but had developed some innovative body designs, was the most conspicuous candidate. If the body and chassis could be combined in one unit, then the road towards full manufacture of cars in Australia must have begun to look shorter. Certainly the technology to make engines was lacking before World War II, but surely imported engines could be installed in the locally produced monocoque? Hartnett's plan for the Olympia had been to build most of the car in-house, sourcing ancillary components from outside suppliers and the engine, gearbox, differential and steering system from Germany.

As a consequence of the 195-Y experiment, senior engineers within General Motors came to favour the use of six-cylinder engines in mid-size cars, while recognising the potential for less expensive four-cylinder models sharing the same bodywork. (In the early 1950s Vauxhall would have its six-cylinder Velox and Wyvern four, while Ford played a similar marketing game with its Zephyr and Consul models.) By the late 1930s General Motors' US-manufactured cars used six-cylinder engines in the main (a precedent derived from the 1928 Chevrolet 490, which was smoother and faster than the newly introduced four-cylinder Model A Ford) and Opel was a six-cylinder specialist. So, even if the contest between 195-Y-15 and 195-Y-13 had been close, the 'six' would be likely to have gained the final nod of approval. Among mass manufacturers, only General Motors took this approach across a range of car sizes by 1939. Even more significantly, only GM combined six-cylinder engines with unitary bodies in what Australians would call medium-sized vehicles.

Hartnett's vision

Let's step into our time machine again and alight on 20 December 1943, at Fishermans Bend, Victoria. Larry Hartnett is chairing a meeting. Dark-haired, balding and in his prime at 45, he is at the zenith of his career (although he does not yet know that). Larry is of medium height, and with his neat moustache may be a candidate for the adjective 'dapper'. Energetic, self-assured and a keen communicator, he commands unwavering attention from the small group of fellow GMH executives around the table.

Metaphorically speaking, Larry Hartnett still wears two hats, and is happy for his colleagues to understand that, as the Australian government's director of ordnance, he continues to play a senior role in Australia's defence during World War II. He is not just the senior local representative of a foreign-owned company but a man right at the centre of Australia's affairs— a player on the international stage. It is where he had always wanted to be: in a position of significant power and respected by men at the highest levels. Hartnett had told Australians war was coming long before the politicians had worked it out. He likes to mention his colleague Essington Lewis, who appointed him to the ordnance role in 1940. Lewis himself exercises more political power than any other industrialist in Australia, as director of munitions. In defence matters, Hartnett reports to Lewis. At General Motors-Holden's Hartnett reports to Edward C. Riley, general manager of GMOO, albeit now through Harry B. Phillips, a New York-based American who had replaced Hartnett himself as GMOO regional director. Hartnett and Phillips enjoy a harmonious relationship. He gets on well with Ed Riley, too, having recently been a guest at Riley's ranch. Just three days before this meeting, Larry had written to Ed thanking him for his 'friendship'.

Hartnett the Englishman, so much at home in Australia from the outset, appears confident that what he decides for GMH will usually be endorsed by Riley, despite some misgivings in the United States about his dual corporate citizenship as managing director of GMH and director of ordnance, (which explains why Phillips had replaced him as regional director). Both Essington Lewis and Larry Hartnett deal on a regular basis with senior government ministers while running enterprises of great importance to Australia. But Lewis is the managing director of locally owned BHP, and does not have to balance the difficulties of working for both the Australian government and an overseas-owned corporation. Hartnett himself rightly believes that concerns at head office about his own role in Australian policy extend to the very top of the organisation and the formidable personage of Alfred P. Sloan Jr.

Larry has called this meeting, at a time when many people are getting ready to relax for Christmas, to discuss the prospect of moving into the manufacture of complete cars; the timing implies a measure of urgency as far as Hartnett is concerned. This is driven in part by the difficulty of finding work for all his employees as the war effort winds down. The wartime contracts are

Larry Hartnett has some very strong ideas about what kind of car he wants to build, and it will differ in significant ways from the mainstream North American GM products.

drying up and already GMH factory workers are making pedal cars, filing cabinets, carpet sweepers and stainless-steel sinks while waiting for the supply of imported chassis to resume. Since 1931 GMH has manufactured car bodies to be fitted to these chassis, a process which began in 1917 when Holden's Motor Body Builders was formed.

Larry Hartnett has some very strong ideas about what kind of car he wants to build, and it will differ in significant ways from the mainstream North American GM products. By the 1930s there was a clash between the needs of North American markets and the still embryonic Australian market, of which Hartnett was keenly conscious. Before 1930, North American and Australian road conditions had diverged considerably. Those high-crowned unmade US roads of the first twenty years of the twentieth century that demanded a tough, high-riding vehicle such as the Model T had mostly vanished. Bitumen roads predominated. This had profound implications for car design and permitted Harley Earl to indulge his desire to build lower riding, sleeker cars. The Model T Ford was seen as outmoded long before its demise. Buyers wanted stylish cars which could travel at higher cruising speeds on the smooth roads between major centres; styling had already begun to predominate over function before the Depression partly because the pure functionalism of the early cars was redundant for US driving conditions. When the engineers at Fisher Body, a wholly owned division of GM, developed sleek new garments to dress the latest chassis designs, they did not need to concern themselves with the primitive and rugged kind of road conditions that still applied in Australia. Visitors from overseas were sometimes shocked by what passed for roads.

GMH could do nothing about the fully

> **When the engineers at Fisher Body, a wholly owned division of GM, developed sleek new garments to dress the latest chassis designs, they did not need to concern themselves with the primitive and rugged kind of road conditions that still applied in Australia.**

imported chassis, but its engineers created impressively robust bodies to clothe the mechanicals. The Australian subsidiary prided itself on this special local expertise. A 1936 GMH advertising brochure, *The Changing Trend*, which sounds as if it were written by Hartnett himself, says:

> Without questioning the knowledge and cleverness of other countries, the fact remains that Australia's roads and geographical conditions, and the special tastes, needs, habits and preferences of Australia's public provide unique problems. Australia's motoring public is large—the problems demand and deserve solution—yet no country but Australia is interested or concerned to solve them . . .
>
> . . . Nowhere else in the world are so many problems presented to the car body designer and builder. Bodies built overseas for use here will stand up to Australian conditions for a certain period but are never completely up to the Australian standard of requirement—because they were produced in countries where the product does not have to meet such arduous conditions as those existing in Australia.

The observation that 'no country but Australia is interested or concerned' to solve Australia's motoring problems implies latent tension between GMH and its parent. It also suggests that Larry Hartnett would have plenty to say about these special 'needs, habits and preferences' when it came to the design of an Australian car.

'Somewhere between the two types'

The meeting in Hartnett's office was about what kind of car would be suitable for Australia. Present were Norman A. Pointer, George A. Quarry, R.L. ('Bill') Abbott, D. Dunstan and Jack H. Horn, who, as assistant to the managing director, was taking minutes:

> Mr Hartnett was of the opinion that the present day US automobile was a bit too grandiose for Australia's actual needs, and, on the other hand, European cars were a little bit too much the other way. Perhaps a solution to the problem would be a car somewhere between the two types. He considered that the design should

reflect post war Australia, but admitted it was difficult to forecast what this would involve . . .

Desirable features in an Australian made car included 30 miles per gallon performance, light weight and comfort for long distance driving . . . weight [should be given] a good deal of consideration . . . [because light weight] not only improves performance but decreases the cost of production.

Jack Horn did not circulate his minutes of the pre-Christmas meeting until 4 January 1944. Nothing that Hartnett said at the time—and he presumably did most of the talking—surprised anyone present because his views had been expressed at even greater length in a document called 'Motor Car Manufacture in Australia: General review and market study', which had been published in May 1940.

In the 1940 report there is extensive analysis of Australian motoring preferences as evident in buying trends in the second half of the 1930s:

The Australian buyer fundamentally prefers the American type of passenger car because of its roominess, good ride and smooth high performance. However, his major considerations of:

> *List price*
> *Out of pocket operating expense*
> *Registration and insurance charges*
> *Resale value*
> *Size of car*

all combine him, against his natural preferences, in the purchase of the Low Priced small English car or the Vauxhall '14'—Willys type.

Comparison is made of the factors against the Ford/Chevrolet (large American car) type and the factors against the Vauxhall '14'/Willys (medium priced, medium size) type. The former suffered from excessive fuel consumption and depreciation, were more heavily taxed and insurance cost more. Tyre replacement costs were greater. They were more difficult to park and required more garage space. They tended to grow larger with model changes. And, significantly, they were a 'reminder of relative extravagance'.

> *Negatives for the Vauxhall 14 and Willys style of vehicle include a lack of stamina and ruggedness, restricted room, fussy engine and gearchanges, troublesome 'gadgetry' (eg, a telescopic steering column), inadequate ground clearance and poor brakes.*
>
> *It seems that the car which would best suit [the Australian buyer is one that is] more economical than the Chevrolet/Ford, has more roominess than the Vauxhall/Willys but is smaller than the Chevrolet/Ford.*
>
> *It would also have room for five passengers, offer better performance than the Vauxhall/Willys but use less fuel than the Chevrolet/Ford. The same formula, passenger space excepted, would also apply to the utility.*

More than three and a half years later, little change seems to have occurred in Hartnett's thinking; the meeting of 20 December 1943 elaborated exactly the same themes. Christmas was coming. More importantly, so was the end of the war. The timing was dictated by the sense that peace was nigh.

The concept of a car combining the economy of a smaller English car with the spaciousness, power and ruggedness of the larger American models was a radical one, which provides evidence of Hartnett's capacity to see the big picture. Why was this idea so radical? Simply because before World War II, despite the fact that to varying degrees General Motors, Ford and Chrysler could all be described as multinational corporations, most cars were designed specifically to suit the needs of their local markets. The concept of 'the world car' would not arrive until the 1970s, at least in any realistic sense.

> **The concept of a car combining the economy of a smaller English car with the spaciousness, power and ruggedness of the larger American models was a radical one, which provides evidence of Hartnett's capacity to see the big picture.**

In general, European buyers preferred small cars which were economical to operate, while North American buyers, for whom petrol was very much cheaper and incomes generally higher, were strongly inclined to larger cars and were less worried about operating costs. Roads were better in the United States and Canada (Hitler's *autobahnen* and the Italian *autostrada* excepted), distances between centres greater, and there was less emphasis on agile handling and good braking than, for example, in mountainous Italy. These national motoring preferences were consolidated by the 1920s and there was surprisingly little crossover. Some wealthy European buyers drove American cars, but comparatively few European vehicles were sold in North America. So there had never been a perceived demand for Larry Hartnett's type of car, even if a small number of English, European and US designs could have been said to combine some of the elements, and especially the six-cylinder Vauxhall 14/6 and the Opel Kapitan.

General Motors introduced its T-Series and V-Series cars in the 1970s. Both 'world cars' were sold under different names in many parts of the world. The T-Series was an Isuzu, Vauxhall, Opel and Holden (Gemini), while the V-Series was an Opel, Vauxhall, and—after a major mechanical redesign—the Holden Commodore. Some much earlier cars and especially the Volkswagen had been successful in widely diverse markets but were conceived with a more local agenda.

It was not until 1959 that General Motors, Ford and Chrysler launched their own vehicles of this type on the domestic US market. There had been aborted projects in the 1940s and early 1950s, the most notable of which was the Chevrolet Cadet. Apart from the extra profitability of larger cars, there was little evidence until well into the 1950s, when the Volkswagen drove its way up the US sales charts, that North American customers wanted to buy such cars. In the booming postwar market American consumers would buy whatever was on offer, and so the automotive manufacturers went for maximum profits until the Volkswagen (the car reviled by Henry Ford II as 'that little shitbox') challenge demanded a reluctant response.

Neither the 1940 report nor the December 1943 meeting got as far as adumbrating how the Australians' desired 'in-between' car might be developed. By what means could the proposed vehicle offer the performance of an American car with the economy of an English one, for example? The number of cylinders the car would use is not discussed (neither is its mode of construction; perhaps Hartnett saw unitary construction as a given), and a 'four' was assumed. The exclusion of the Kapitän not only confirms that a six-cylinder engine was off the agenda but also that Hartnett envisaged a more basic vehicle. He seems not to have known about the Experimental Light Car Program in 1940. Why then would he have considered anything other than a four-cylinder engine, given the emphasis on keeping operating costs down? Unaware of 195-Y-15, Larry would not have imagined using a six-cylinder engine in a car half a size smaller than the Kapitän.

In the booming postwar market American consumers would buy whatever was on offer, and so the automotive manufacturers went for maximum profits until the Volkswagen (the car reviled by Henry Ford II as 'that little shitbox') challenge demanded a reluctant response.

An (Australian) Englishman in New York

In *Big Wheels and Little Wheels*, Hartnett dates his introduction to the 195-Y cars to November 1944. He sets the scene graphically. Our hero has just returned victorious from a meeting with the GM Executive Committee, where he has convinced Sloan and his fellow committee members to endorse the idea of GMH's manufacturing a car in Australia, and is recounting the event. The speaker is Walter Appel, chief engineer at GMOO:

I've read your specifications for the job you want to make, and, Larry, this prototype six-cylinder car out there is very, very close to your requirements.

I'll tell you about them [195-Y-13 and 195-Y-15]. Bill Knudsen, president of Chevrolet, used to have a hell of a row in his committees. He reckoned a six-cylinder automobile could be made as cheaply as a four-cylinder job. This became literally a million-dollar argument.

So they drew up a specification of a car for the lower price-bracket and made one with four cylinders and one with six. Identical basic performance to give the same torque and horsepower. I think the six won the argument, because with a four you've got to put more 'beef' in the gearbox and back axle and clutch. But both cars are out there now, gathering cobwebs.

Hartnett's story is certainly located in the wrong time frame and may even be apocryphal, a trick that memory played twenty years later when he re-counted his memories to John Veitch for the book. Certainly Walter Appel may have had a chat with Larry about 195-Y-15, but it was already an impor-tant vehicle to the Australian Car Program, as can be found in the US document 'Australian Post War Car Manufacturing Program, October 25, 1944':

EXPERIMENTAL MODEL 195-Y-15

As the major specifications of the proposed car became more clearly defined, they were found to fall very close to those of a pre-war experimental model developed by the Corporation's Central Engineering Staff. This model, designated as Model 195-Y-15 was of integral body construction, approximately of the desired package size and weight, and its mechanical features, with a few exceptions, coincided with the concept of the projected Australian car. It was therefore used as the nearest criterion of size, weight, design and construction.

This report succeeded Hartnett's background briefing of 20 September, in which he claims to have given 'the finest presentation of Australia ever prepared for the enlightenment of Americans'. The September briefing was an exhaustive overview of Australia as seen by Hartnett and his team, with a view to persuading the executive committee that here was an appropriate country in which to manufacture cars. It even included a section on Aboriginals (in the general racist style of the era). This report provides a fascinating time capsule of early 1940s corporate/cultural thinking.

By contrast, the October publication is an extensive nuts-and-bolts technical analysis, prepared in New York by W.B. ('Bill') Wachtler, manager of planning and development, GMOO, which compares 195-Y-15 with a range of existing production cars including the Chevrolet, the Vauxhall '10' and '14' models, all of which were sold in Australia, and the Opel Olympia and Kapitän, which were not. This was a far more comprehensive analysis than that undertaken by the GMH committee in 1940, but appears to have used the Australian data as a starting point.

A memorandum dated 11 September 1944 (two months *before* Hartnett's alleged dialogue with Walter Appel) provides a way into a more accurate chronological reading of events. R.C. Rainsford, GMH's technical liaison representative working at GMOO, wrote to Hartnett:

> *As I mentioned to you over the phone last Thursday, we have been fortunate in locating a car which could be a good starting point for our Australian unit. This particular car is known as 'Light Car Project 195-Y-15' and was developed by the New Products group in 1938, at which time it was thought that the Corporation might market an American car smaller than Chevrolet . . .*

Rainsford's summation is enticingly short on detail, although that term 'American car' might provide a clue. Bill Abbott, one of the Holden engineers seconded to Detroit in 1945 for the Australian Car Program, referred to 195-Y-15 as a lightweight car designed by Lou Thoms 'very likely for Vauxhall'. Perhaps the idea was that the same basic car could be sold in North America as a Chevrolet and in Britain as a Vauxhall. It is probable that neither Rainsford nor Abbott were privy to these answers—but Walter Appel was. He refers to the intention to create a car 'only slightly smaller than a Chevrolet with American performance at a price sufficiently lower than the Chevrolet to be attractive'. This is the strongest clue we have that the 195-Y cars were conceived as prospective inexpensive Chevrolets. Any export prospects would be a bonus.

From Walter Appel's point of view, the superiority of the performance/economy equation achieved by 195-Y-15 made its selection as the starting point for the Australian car a foregone conclusion, even though Hartnett had planned for a four-cylinder engine. As we shall see in subsequent chapters, there were also implications here for the wider automotive industry.

It seems likely that Rainsford's letter was written shortly after the inclusion of 195-Y-15 in the planning process and that Wachtler's report would have taken most of the ensuing five weeks to prepare. Is it possible that Hartnett confused not only the timing of his introduction to 195-Y-15 but also the agent?

No need for a clean sheet of paper; we'll write on the back of this one!

The observations Hartnett attributed to Appel go to the heart of the Australian car program. The existence of the prototype made the task of creating the Holden a much shorter process than had it begun with the proverbial blank sheet of paper. The original plan was to put the car into production during 1947 for proposed release that year, which would have broken most world records before or since for designing a car and bringing it to a manufactured reality—a process which even in the 1950s generally took at least four years and more often six. Even in the 21st century, with all the advances of computer technology, four years is a remarkably short gestation period. But the preliminary work had already been done eight years earlier, another serendipitous factor in the Holden story. If the Australian government had put GMH on pole position in the Australian car race, the prior existence of 195-Y-15 effectively gave the company several extra years' start over its rivals.

It also seems that neither Hartnett himself nor any of his GMH engineers were consulted by the GMOO planning and development people, the Wachtler report being produced in-house in New York. Was Hartnett unaware of it? The lack of any comment in his letters on such a report and his erroneous account in *Big Wheels and Little Wheels* of how the prototypes became involved in the Australian car project reveal a significant subtext: General Motors Overseas Operations was already making its plans for Australia without seeing any need to involve Hartnett in the details. Why, for example, was he not invited to New York to join Wachtler's committee? Subsequent events lend further evidence that his desire for close involvement in the details of the project was not reciprocated within GMOO. So as far as the Export Company's senior personnel were concerned, the Australian car's genesis was to be the business of the Americans alone with Hartnett and his men involved only when, and to whatever extent, they deemed appropriate.

It was indeed a serendipitous coincidence that the 195-Y-15 car accorded so closely with Hartnett's concept. Hartnett himself leant more to the European than the American concept in searching for a car between the two, the Kapitän presumably erring too close to the latter for his liking. The question answered by General Motors by means of 195-Y-13 and 195-Y-15 was an uncommon one in 1937 because for most other manufacturers the boundary between four- and six-cylinder engines remained reasonably clear, as was the distinction between the kinds of vehicles each type powered.

Germany into USA equals Australia

With its use of a six-cylinder engine in a somewhat larger vehicle than the Opel Olympia and employing that car's still radical monocoque construction, 195-Y-15 was indeed 'somewhere between the two types'. The reality of the 195-Y-15 prototype was that it was almost perfectly poised between the United States and Europe, as if some curious dialectic were invisibly at work. This dialectic was itself a consequence of the uniqueness of Australia in the automotive world. Because the country had never manufactured cars in significant

> **... there was certainly more room for experimentation when it came to developing a car specifically for Australia, where the challenges of geography, topography, infrastructure and climate had found most imported cars wanting in some respects.**

numbers, no great inertia had developed. Buyer preferences shifted around considerably, although there had long been a leaning towards American models because of their power, size and greater ruggedness than most English models. But there was certainly more room for experimentation when it came to developing a car specifically for Australia, where the challenges of geography, topography, infrastructure and climate had found most imported cars wanting in some respects. Australia seemed to demand a different approach to the motor car. It is reasonable to say that the island continent's unique motoring conditions invited this type of lateral thinking about a car. But, critically, the dialectic was also an inevitable consequence of GM's work at Opel with a whole new range of cars developed to suit Europe not the United States.

Hartnett would certainly have conveyed his views to Ed Riley about what kind of car should be designed for Australia. So, to this extent, his claim to being the father of the Holden is valid. There does not seem to have been any serious challenge to the broad concept of a car something like midway between the mainstream Chevrolet and the Opel/Vauxhall four-cylinder vehicles. But equally, it seems that from the beginning, once they had accepted Hartnett's broad concept, GMOO management assumed full responsibility for the design process. The project car's size and weight was, as we have seen, also consistent with Hartnett's expressed ideal of a vehicle somewhere between US and English designs, a principle which became embedded in the project as run by Russ Begg. But the key point is that the decision to use 195-Y-15 as the springboard for what was to become the Holden was not taken by Larry Hartnett but by GMOO chief engineer Walter Appel, who wrote the blueprint. Besides, the 1948 Vauxhall Velox, work on which had begun before the Australian car decision was taken, was a monocoque of similar size to 195-Y-15 *and used a six-cylinder engine.*

Sloan approves the Australian Car Program

Let's jump into the time-travel machine again and speed straight back to 25 October 1944. We are in New York at General Motors Overseas Operations where a meeting critical to Australian industrial, cultural and social history is taking place. In the chair is Alfred P. Sloan Jr, still straight-backed in his seventieth year and absolutely in command, although always willing to delegate. Today he and

Hartnett would certainly have conveyed his views to Ed Riley about what kind of car should be designed for Australia. So, to this extent, his claim to being the father of the Holden is valid.

his fellow board members will hear Larry Hartnett put forward his case for an Australian-manufactured car. Each board member has a copy of a 96-page report on the subject.

The title of the report makes for dull reading but it is likely that the product planning team responsible for 'Market, Product and Cost Data Related to Projected Motor Car Manufacture in Australia' was enthusiastic about its task. This was radical new territory demanding lateral thinking. They 'decided that the approach should start with an examination of the entire problem on the basis of 1939 conditions'. No need seems to have been felt to look beyond General Motors vehicles to assemble relevant comparative data, at least as far as dimensions were concerned, although a broader study was made on the running costs of cars available in Australia in 1939. The team examined two Chevrolets, two Vauxhalls and two Opels, all of them 1939 models. There was a seventh car, 'the experimental model 195-Y-15, developed by the Corporation before the war'. The projected Australian car, the report stated, should combine:

package size 4–5 passengers, interior dimensions approximately the same as the Vauxhall 14/16 or Opel Kapitän, similar in construction and design to 195-Y-15, curb weight about 2100 pounds [952 kg], and embodying modern American appearance to a degree consistent with cost limitations and Australian market requirements and preferences.

The reference source for Australian tastes and probably the starting point for the entire exercise was the May 1940 GMH report, 'Motor Car Manufacture in Australia: General review and market study'. Just as the Australians had done, the US engineers compared 'small British' with 'typical American' models, listing the advantages and disadvantages of both. The advantages of the former were listed as 'low first cost' and 'low operating costs' but the list of debits was longer: small package size, poor performance, outmoded appearance, small boot and long stroke/high speed engines.

By contrast, the American cars had only two negatives (which happened to be the obverse of the British cars' strengths), and four positives—large package size, good performance, modern appearance and large, lower speed engines. Would it be possible to combine all the advantages with none of the disadvantages? This was a question American engineers had perhaps never asked, even if they had come close to it in devising the 1939 Opel Kapitän, the design of which was being finalised at about the time the 195-Y cars were built (1937–38). (Perhaps the two experimental models immediately succeeded the Kapitän on Russ Begg's schedule?) Operating economy had not been a primary objective of the Kapitän program. It is probable that the US team noted not only that the top eight preferences of Australian buyers defined in the 1940 report did not include styling but also that 'Australians have become conscious of what they consider the extravagant size and overall appearance of the American passenger car'. In order, these eight preferences were list price, operating costs (petrol, oil, repairs), registration and maintenance charges, resale value, roominess/ride comfort, size (garaging/parking), reputation of maker and replacements. There were several reasons, then, for giving the projected car a more modest style than its US counterpart, including the fact that the typical Australian garage was only 15 feet (4.6 m) long.

So fuel economy and weight were major considerations from the start of the program, influencing even the appearance of the car: 'Exaggerated styling, involving increased weight . . . is not in keeping with the fundamental requirements of the proposed GM Australian car.' The planners set objectives which included fuel economy of 30 miles per gallon, a top speed of 74 miles per hour (119 km/h, identical to that of the 195-Y-15), and ground clearance of 8 inches (203 mm). The report compared no fewer than fifteen cars on the first criterion, ranging from the Buick 40 which gave 15.5 miles per gallon, the mainstream American Chevrolet Master and Ford De Luxe 8, both of which came in at 18 miles per gallon, through to the Vauxhall 10, which was the most frugal on 34.9 miles per gallon but could only manage a top speed of 60 miles per hour (97 km/h). Project 195-Y-15 weighed 2076.98 pounds (942.1 kg), compared with the projected 2100 pounds (952.5 kg) for the Australian car. The difference was described as an 'allowance of 23 pounds [10.4 kg] for modernized styling (13 lb [5.9 kg] body, 10 lb [4.5 kg] chassis sheetmetal)'.

Although Walter Appel had written the blueprint he had severe misgivings about the project, a vital point in the early development of 195Y25 that has never previously been examined. On 28 March 1945 Appel began a long letter to GMOO Regional Director H.B. ('Bud') Phillips. It was sent two days later with copies to Begg, R.W. Seeley, V.W. Stacey, Ed Riley and Wachtler. This letter, more than any other document in the Holden's gestation, implies the enormity of the task of turning a discarded prototype into a production-ready car for tortuous Australian conditions. It provides the explanation for changes in 195Y25's specification during 1945–46:

Although Walter Appell had written the blueprint he had severe misgivings about the project, a vital point in the early development of 195Y25 that has never previously been examined.

I feel that you should know that I have some misgivings about the Australian car program. I am somewhat skeptical about the possibility of being able to develop a car of the package size, performance, and weight, as it is contemplated for Australia and at the same time incorporate the durability which it must have to establish a reputation as a satisfactory product.

There is also a question in my mind as to whether the car we are proposing for Australia represents the best car for the market.

Appel unfolds a long discussion about the relationship between weight, durability, performance and economy. In essence, he offers the opinion that 195-Y-15 represents a poor starting point, having been developed for a different purpose, namely to 'evaluate the commercial possibilities' of an inexpensive Chevrolet-type vehicle. The weight was fixed at 2000 pounds (907.2 kg), most 'refinements' were eliminated. 'In this instance, therefore', he continues, 'the package size and weight were fixed, leaving the durability as the unknown to be proven'. He clearly thought the experimental light car had been a marginal exercise:

The 195-Y-15 was given a 5000 mile [8047 km] test on the Belgian block road at the Proving Ground after which it was decided that it was of no further use to the corporation. The 5000 mile test was insufficient to be conclusive and later investigation has shown that many short cuts were taken to reduce weight which would not prove commercially practical at the present time.

The durability testing that had been done involved a car weighing 2000 pounds. But, wrote Appel, the curb weight of the Australian car 'will be around 2200 pounds [998 kg] . . . almost 10% more than the chassis units were originally designed to carry and hence invite the possibility of fatigue failure'. He referred to Australian road conditions as being severe. It looked to him as if the engineering team had bitten off more than it would be able to chew:

. . . I feel that the gap between what has been accomplished commercially to date and what we are trying to accomplish weight-wise is considerably wider than it appears we can possibly accomplish in the program we have set up.

We are hoping to achieve satisfactory durability in this size, weight and performance. If we are successful, we shall have an outstandingly light car for its size . . . What are the chances of our success?

Our present problem is to take 2100 pounds of finished material and use it so as to produce the most acceptable car commercially, having the following characteristics in their order of importance:

(1) Durability

(2) Economy of operation and maintenance

(3) Performance

(4) Package size

Our present approach to this problem, in which the package size and performance are pegged, is in directly the reverse order leaving the first and most important factor as the questionable one.

The car which we intend to build in Australia will be a General Motors car. It must represent all that General Motors tries to build into their products: 'Customer Satisfaction and Dollar-Value'. That means that the car must be durable, pleasant and easy to operate, low in first cost and maintenance and free from annoying troubles. This sounds like an 'Ideal' specification. It is and we will probably never reach it 100%, but our aim must be in that direction.

General Motors' experimental engineers were probably the first in the world to consider using a six-cylinder engine where a 'four' would do. This became a hot topic in the 1950s.

- At the 1950 London Motor Show, Ford of England announced its all-new mid-size cars in two versions, the four-cylinder Consul and the six-cylinder Zephyr. The Zephyr had a longer wheelbase and was 1 inch (25.4 mm) shorter than the Holden in overall length. But in Australia the Consul cost only £34 pounds less than the Holden in April 1953—£1076 compared to £1110. But the Zephyr at £1168 cost £58 more than the Holden. These English Fords grew out of the stillborn Chevrolet Cadet program of 1945–47. Inadvertently, GM had given Ford the car with which to challenge Holden and Vauxhall.

- It took the British Motor Corporation forever to understand the Australian demand for roomy six-cylinder cars and by then it had been swallowed by Leyland. BMC began full local manufacture in Australia in 1959 using the Wolseley 1500 as the starting point. The Wolseley name made way for the choice of Austin or Morris. A restyle unique to Australia brought a bigger boot with horizontally themed grilles. The Austin Lancer, billed as 'the Family Car Answer', showed that BMC had misunderstood the Australian question, while the Morris Major served to make its Minor sibling seem diminutive. In 1962 buyers were invited to 'Make Way for the Freeway' but few did. This was the Austin Freeway with the 'Blue Streak' six-cylinder engine, a truly belated challenger to the Holden. The Wolseley name was dusted off and applied to a mechanically identical car known as the 24/80, complete with leather and timber. The 24/80 might have been a challenger to the forthcoming Premier but just looked too old fashioned. And too English.

- In 1955 Armstrong Siddeley Motors bewildered the motoring world with two new cars known as the Sapphire 234 and the Sapphire 236. Outwardly identical, the main differentiator between the two was the engine. The slightly more expensive 236 used a 2.3-litre six-cylinder engine, developed from a pre-war design, while the 234 used a 2.3-litre four-cylinder engine, which was basically a cut-down version of the 1953 Sapphire 'six'. Try explaining to the public that the 'four' was the high performer while the 'six' was aimed at more conservative motorists. Yes, that's right, the cars failed spectacularly, playing a major role in the end of the Armstrong Siddeley marque within five years. Another victim of Jaguar.

Chapter 5

'Chief engineers are not very good correspondents'

The buck for the Australian car program stopped with C.L. McCuen, General Motors' vice-president of engineering. Late in 1944 and within weeks of the crucial board meeting which endorsed the project, McCuen chose Russell Begg to be chief engineer. The program now had a name, 195Y25 without hyphens, reflecting its gestation from 195-Y-15. From 1936 to 1939 Begg had held the enormously important role of assistant chief engineer at Opel, which meant he had been involved in the Kapitän program. The evidence suggests that he also developed the 195-Y cars in Germany, probably after the Kapitän engineering program was completed. The imminent threat of war in Europe led GM to recall its personnel from Opel, and so Begg found himself back in the United States, having boarded the *Manhattan* along with most of his colleagues on 24 September 1939 from a remote port on the French Atlantic coast.

From 1934 to 1936, Begg had been chief engineer of special engineering assignments for Lou Thoms, who is reputed to have designed the 195-Y cars and reported directly to McCuen. It is probable that Begg spent much of this time in Germany developing the Olympia, before being appointed to the role of assistant chief engineer. The evidence for this is circumstantial: so important and radically new was the Olympia, it is difficult to imagine who else but Begg could have done it. History throws up no other names. Significantly, too, his contacts with the Ambi-Budd company were strong and he had previously worked for Budd in the United States in the late 1920s when that company was at its creative peak. Ambi-Budd appears to have provided the technology and helped produce the Olympia's all-steel body and mode of construction.

Begg's immense experience

Begg's pivotal role in the Holden is a kind of historical given, but the nature of his prior experience has never been outlined at length. Some elements of his curriculum vitae, especially his work first at Budd and then at Opel, provided him with unique insights directly relevant to the development of the Holden. These skills were unique in the industry. Elements of Begg's approach were questioned by Walter Appel, senior engineer at General Motors Overseas Operations, but in the end Begg always prevailed; indeed, there is no evidence of a significant debate and Begg just got on with his job, doing things his way.

By 1944 Begg had notched up about 35 years in the industry, having graduated from the University of Michigan with a Bachelor of Science in 1909. He worked at many of the leading US automotive companies through the industry's formative years, spending time at Packard and at Hudson before being appointed assistant chief engineer at the Thomas B. Jeffrey Company in Kenosha, Wisconsin. Jeffrey (the second largest maker of bicycles in the United States), made an eponymous brand plus Rambler. That was in 1912, just four years after the debut of Henry Ford's Model T. In 1916, Begg joined Eddie S. Jordan and two others from Jeffrey to form the Jordan Motor Company, established in Cleveland, Ohio. Their strategy was to build an upmarket niche model somewhere between Buick and Cadillac. Begg served as a director and chief engineer until 1928, meaning he was there when Jordan, an advertising genius, dreamed up the 'Somewhere west of Laramie' advertisement. Their designs were overtly sporty and intended to appeal especially to women. Jordan focused on quality by using the best available suppliers and latest engineering developments. From the start Jordan used aluminum body panels and introduced all-steel bodies in 1925.

Following the collapse of Jordan, Begg went to Budd, the industry pioneer in all-steel bodies, before proceeding to the highly prestigious Stutz Motor Company as chief engineer. He then joined GM, probably in 1934, immediately after the collapse of Stutz.

Few engineers could have been as sympathetic to the needs of a pioneering automotive culture as Russ Begg. He was old enough and, more to the point, experienced enough to understand what the road conditions of the early twentieth century demanded in terms of vehicle ruggedness. (Begg could be said to belong to the second generation of automotive pioneers, the first including Henry Ford and Billy Durant, founder of General Motors.) If the Australian car had to be engineered for conditions not all that much better than those in the United States 40 years earlier, then so be it. Begg was aware that he had been handed a challenge few other engineers had ever been given: to design an all-new car for a specific market. But he was almost certainly the best man in the world for the job. The young Australians who worked with him quickly came to respect him, although he could be quite authoritarian. Bill Abbott was one who commented on this. He described Begg as 'a fanatic for weight saving, hence detailed weight estimates all along the line'. Jack Rawnsley, who worked very closely with the

> **Few engineers could have been as sympathetic to the needs of a pioneering automotive culture as Russ Begg. He was old enough and, more to the point, experienced enough to understand what the road conditions of the early twentieth century demanded in terms of vehicle ruggedness.**

Begg had also surrounded himself with excellent senior engineers, some of whom had almost as much depth and length of industry experience as he.

chief engineer, enjoyed much favour. 'I was the apple of his eye', the indefatigable 96-year-old commented in 2007.

Begg had also surrounded himself with excellent senior engineers, some of whom had almost as much depth and length of industry experience as he. His careful selection of a top-class team reinforces the brilliance of the GM decision-making process that put Begg behind the wheel. Oscar C. Kreis, for one, started his working life as a toolmaker with the Leland Faulkner Company, which later became the Cadillac Motor Company. From 1905 to 1908 he was a designer for Packard and worked for other automotive companies before taking the position of engine engineer at Adam Opel AG in 1937, reporting to Begg. Chester S. Carlton's career included stints at Jordan, Peerless, White, Continental Motors, Ford and General Motors Research. He, too, went to Opel, according to Jack Rawnsley.

Milton A. Trisler had a distinguished engineering career before he went to Opel as an engineer in 1936. (There is a pattern developing here: first Jordan for some, then Opel and almost certainly the 195-Y cars, then GMH.) Trisler had worked with GM from 1923 to 1926, mainly in experimental engineering, and returned to GM in 1927 when he joined the Cadillac division for a short time before accepting a position with the Holley Carburetor Company. Trisler resumed his career at GM in 1936. When World War II broke out, he was recalled to Detroit where he worked in the Vauxhall development section with engineers seconded from England. So he was deeply involved with what would become the postwar Vauxhalls before joining Begg's team during 1945 as carburetor and electrical engineer on the Australian car development staff. Milton Trisler's postings illustrate again the experience brought to bear on the first Holden: Cadillac, Holley, Opel, Vauxhall.

For his chief experimental engineer, Begg chose his old friend G.C.R. ('Kipe') Kuiper with whom he had worked at the Jordan Car Company from 1916 soon after Kuiper's arrival in the United States. Evidently the German-born and educated young engineer impressed Begg because Kipe followed Begg first to Budd and then to Stutz. In 1937, one year after Begg's appointment to his Opel job, there was Kipe again, in the same role of chief experimental engineer: he must have been a lay-down *misere* for the 195Y25 project.

The best of all automotive worlds

It is curious how history works, but all the evidence shows that the conflict with Germany actually helped rather than hindered the Australian Car Program. As war drew nigh, some very experienced people left Germany and returned to the United States where important work was found for them. During the war they helped with the General Motors munitions effort, but as it became clear that the Allies would win, the impetus shifted back to the needs of the postwar international automotive culture. Few, if any, engineers in the world could have brought such a blend of US and European experience to bear on a new car as Begg, Kipe, Kreis, Carlton and Trisler did. This was precisely what was needed for the challenge of the Australian Car Program.

Arguably, no other car in history has been so carefully conceived for a unique set of circumstances as the Holden was. First, it had to suit the

Arguably, no other car in history has been so carefully conceived for a unique set of circumstances as the Holden was. First, it had to suit the very demanding conditions imposed by Australia. Second, it had to showcase General Motors' international knowhow to the watching postwar world.

very demanding conditions imposed by Australia. Second, it had to showcase General Motors' international knowhow to the watching postwar world. Because, by 1944, for the senior operators at General Motors the world was indeed their oyster. They wanted to succeed everywhere that General Motors made or sold cars.

No one had ever developed a mass-production car to suit Australia. Sloan himself, reflecting on the likelihood of full local manufacture in Australia after the war, had made it clear in January 1940 that he 'would not prejudice to any extent whatever, the proposed design by establishing a relationship to any other car produced anywhere else'. So, if the '195' cars had not existed Begg would have been empowered by the chairman of General Motors to begin with a clean sheet of paper. As it was, Walter Appel was able to draw up a 'plan of operation' which put 195-Y-15 at the heart of the new program:

> *Two steps are involved; first, the redesign of the 195-Y-15 model to incorporate the latest American styling and Engineering knowhow and develop tested and proven models, second, the translation of this model into Australian materials, accessories and manufacturing processes.*

The plan was to create a 'modern concept of a motor car based on the 195-Y-15 and having a curb weight of 2100 pounds'. By contrast, the Opel Kapitän weighed 2676 pounds (1214 kg). Walter Appel knew that this formula would yield a remarkably high size to weight ratio. His insistence that this weight target be met would be reflected in Begg's subsequent directives. 'It is important', the plan continued, 'that major emphasis be placed on the weight since it is only by not exceeding the weight for which the 195-Y-15 was designed that we can be reasonably sure of freedom from trouble in service'. Unlike its four-cylinder sibling, 195-Y-15 had been submitted to durability testing.

So 195-Y-15 gave Begg's team an elaborated frame of reference rather than a precise blueprint. If the same people who went to work on 195Y25 had also engineered the experimental cars this surely made their task slightly less challenging, albeit still complex; regardless, they were in new territory, adapting a largely untested prototype into a vehicle ready for the rough and tumble of the sunburnt country and suitable for manufacture in Holden's facilities with high Australian content. The chassis engineering, which included suspension design, steering, brakes, wheels and tyres, would be done specifically for 195Y25, so that in the end there was little evident similarity between the prototype of 1937–38 and the production car of a decade later. The Holden would get a fashionable column-mounted gearchange to liberate its six-seater potential, and a more advanced front suspension system. A glance at the comparative specifications shows the technical superiority of the Holden (superior economy, higher performance, wheelbase an inch longer, weight up by just 5 per cent to 2240 pounds—1000 kg) even before considering the specific Australian engineering input and the modern styling.

Frank Hershey, 'international designer for Opel in Germany, Vauxhall in England, and Holden in Australia', was in charge of the aesthetics, although heavily overseen by Earl. His task was to develop 'the latest American styling'. Does this mean that his efforts at Opel and Vauxhall were also deemed 'American'? It is more likely that a styling dialectic was already at work with American themes being applied to much smaller cars. The Holden surely came closer to the worlds of Opel and Vauxhall than it did to Chevrolet. Regardless, with hindsight it seems clear that Hershey faced an easier task than Begg, who was the key target of Hartnett's barrage of suggestions.

The challenges of the 195Y25 project

Because of his depth of previous experience, Begg probably knew that he would face many challenges as chief engineer of the 195Y25 project. Not only did he have to design the first Australian mass-produced car but he was in a sense caught between Appel's scepticism at higher executive level and the pressures from within his own team to incorporate this or that weight-adding feature. But there was a wild card in the Australian car game. Russ

Begg had not yet met Larry Hartnett, although he would have gathered that Hartnett enjoyed a slightly mixed reputation among the senior GMOO executives in New York. Bit of a troublemaker, some said. Pretty darned sure of himself. Not really a team player. But Begg had his instructions from Appel and it was entirely clear that he, Begg, was to run the program; he expected a free hand and was certainly not ready for interference from across the Pacific, expecting rather that specifically Australian concerns would be raised by the engineers seconded to the program. Soon, however, he would find himself having to deal with an increasingly aggrieved and intrusive Hartnett, who was, of course, not even an engineer by training.

Bill Abbott, one of the young Australian engineers seconded to the program, described Begg as 'an absolute stickler' on the weight question. It is easy to see why this was so. Recollecting the early engineering history, Abbott wrote: 'Objective was to keep car weight as low as possible, therefore we made comparitive [sic] operating stress estimates and for 195Y25 used the highest of any used by a then current GM car giving satisfactory service.' Abbott noted that GMOO chief engineer Walter Appel 'had considerable doubts about Begg's high stress-low weight approach'. The first prototype weighed 2200 pounds (998 kg), and after durability testing an extra 40 pounds (18 kg) of weight was added to strengthen it. Begg had proved his point.

A close reading of documents housed in the Holden archive shows a difference of philosophy between Appel and Begg. While they were unanimous on the need for durability and economy, Begg believed there was no need to sacrifice either of the other two major parameters—performance and package size. Appel's recommendation was apparently to use a less powerful engine, which would provide a top speed of just 65 miles per hour (105 km/h) rather than the 74 miles per hour (119 km/h) achieved by 195-Y-15. It seems that, at least initially, Abbott held similar reservations: 'When we first saw the original 195Y15 [sic] specification and weights in Australia, we thought that the job was rather cut down for our conditions but with the proposed revisions to weight, and possible reduction in performance, it looks a bit better.'

Appel had described the durability testing of 195-Y-15 as 'inconclusive', but perhaps he was unwilling to put anything more negative down on paper. George Quarry, GMH's technical liaison representative in Detroit, was more forthright. He wrote to Hartnett on 7 October 1945: 'The 195Y15 [sic] is an experimental vehicle of "X" package size and 2078 lbs. [945 kg] curb weight, designed and tested to determine durability, and found so deficient in this respect as to result in its shelving by the Corporation as of no commercial interest.'

Six months earlier Bill Abbott had reported:

I have been going through the experimental log books on the 195Y15 [sic] job extracting items which require investigation and correction before the 19525 [sic] is finalized. The number of items is about 400, and it illustrates very well the point that even with experienced designers a lot of troubles always crop up with a new job.

. . . most of these are of a relatively minor nature, but they do show that the 195Y15 [sic] was not at the stage where it could be released for production when the development work was discontinued.

Taking all these documents together it does seem probable that Quarry's claims were accurate and that Begg embarked on a project even more difficult than historians have previously acknowledged because it was based on an inadequately durable design. But Begg himself was well aware that the experimental model would require a great deal of engineering finessing. Also, by this time, he had developed his own philosophy about the inter-relationship between performance, economy, durability and weight. His thinking is made clear in a fascinating letter from Quarry to Hartnett:

It does seem probable that Begg embarked on a project even more difficult than historians have previously acknowledged because it was based on an inadequately durable design.

Russ, Kuip and I were out in the 2-litre Kapitän sedan which, while weighing 2676 lbs. [1214 kg] curb, with a 150.9 cubic motor on a 106.1" [2695 mm] wheelbase, has very similar internal space and performance factor as our job (actually 90.3 compared with our 90.1). I told Russ that I felt that Australia would have accepted a somewhat reduced performance factor, especially if it had a beneficial effect on weight and cost; his reply was that such a move is quite in the other direction, as any substantially lower performance factor means a different and heavier transmission to handle the greatly increased second gear work.

I appreciate that such things are simple and fairly elementary, however, my belief is that we still need to pick up an awful lot of such experienced knowledge before we can depend on sound judgement for changes, etc.

It is easy to see the respect Begg commanded from Quarry. It is also easy to see how it was better that Begg's judgement rather than Appel's misgivings prevailed when it came to the design of the Holden. His 'quite in the other direction' thinking flew in the face of mid 1940s conventional engineering as expounded at length by his superior, Walter Appel. This was the brilliance of Begg, and this short quote demonstrates his power over what we might call the ideology of 195Y25. By October 1946 any thoughts of a less powerful engine had vanished. The top speed of the prototype now was identical to that of the Kapitän at 80 miles per hour (128 km/h).

A 'cute little car'

Why no Holden historian has identified the car's designer is mysterious, because it has never been a secret. The Holden's styling was the work of Frank Hershey, one of Harley Earl's most trusted lieutenants. Hershey was chief designer at Pontiac from 1931 to 1935 before going to Buick. He was then given the job of redesigning the whole line of Opels. Hershey went to war and had a gap of several years between conceiving the Admiral and Kapitän models for Opel and his next car: 'When I returned to GM after leaving the Navy in 1944, the first project was to design a new small

Australian car called the Holden. This I did with no help except for a layout man and modelers. It turned out to be a cute little car about the size of a Toyota Corolla.' But the substantial shadow of Harley Earl always hovered over Hershey, and in the end the car came out rather differently. (See Chapter 9, 'Diamonds Are a Grille's Best Friend'.)

While styling the Holden was an important job it was far from being a highlight of Hershey's distinguished career. His next appointment was to put his name in the history books forever. Bill Mitchell, chief stylist at Cadillac, was still in the navy so Hershey was asked to take over his role for the duration, brief though it turned out to be. This gave him a window of opportunity: '. . . I did the '48 Cadillac', he says. Cadillac was GM's most prestigious marque, bearing the slogan 'The Standard of the World' (which had actually been conferred in perpetuity in 1912 by the Royal Automobile Club). The 1948 model, an all-new car, was judged by posterity as one of the critical pieces of early postwar American car design. Here, for the first time, the world could see General Motors' idea of how a postwar car of the grandest type should look. Cadillac represented the cutting edge, where Harley Earl could dazzle Detroit, and thus the world.

As well as having charge of Cadillac, as if that were not enough, Hershey and his assistant Ned Nickles were also entrusted with looking into the future. They prepared two or three models of incredibly futuristic design. A photograph of a running prototype appears in Edson C. Armi's important book, *The Art of American Car Design*.

It is no wonder Hershey has little to say about the Holden because the following year he conceived cars that would, in most respects, still have looked radical twenty years later, but were rejected as too much of a step into the future. He himself describes them as 'far too advanced. As far as I know, we finally destroyed them'. Interestingly then, the production 1948 Cadillac, which ushered in the postwar era for General Motors and was the first car with tailfins, was far more restrained than Hershey's work immediately after the Holden. Ever since Alfred P. Sloan Jr had formulated General Motors' product policy in the 1920s, radical new styling themes had been put into production first on the expensive Cadillac and then progressively in the less expensive cars, eventually finding their way into Chevrolets.

So Hershey's 1948 Cadillac can be said to be the first of the new wave of postwar GM designs, expressing themes that had not been developed when Hershey took on the Australian car. Don Loffler has observed that many people are reminded of the 1948 Buicks when they look at the Holden's grille. That should be no surprise, given Hershey's experience at Buick before he went to General Motors Overseas Operations, specifically Opel. Michael Sedgwick, whose landmark twin studies of the cars of the 1930s and 1940s, and those of the 1950s and 1960s remain the most comprehensive ever written, describes the Holden's 'sedan configuration' as 'obviously inspired by the 1938 Cadillac Sixty Special', which places it a decade behind Hershey's re-interpretation of the marque.

It is perhaps best to say that the Holden was styled by the most talented GM designer available late in World War II, that it was sandwiched in Hershey's CV between the Opel Kapitän and the 1948 Cadillac, and obviously drew on the very latest thinking within GM at the time but came slightly too early to benefit from the new themes Hershey himself would develop in 1946. By that time it was clear that, even if his experiments were too bold for the company to allow into production, postwar automotive architecture would favour the longer-lower-wider look, with mudguards faired into the bodywork. There was indeed another car being developed elsewhere within General Motors by 1945 that was similar in size to the Holden but which incorporated this type of styling, which will be looked at later.

So the Holden was composed right on the cusp of postwar modernity and represents a halfway house between pre-war themes and those originally expressed in the 1948 Cadillac (finished during 1946), a design language partly inspired by fighter jets and redolent of triumphant victory in World War II. Harley Earl was keen to incorporate these themes into a new General Motors design idiom, always with Cadillac leading the way. The other divisions would not get their fresh, entirely postwar styling until the following model year.

Compared with what was to follow in the early 1950s, Hershey's only Cadillac was a masterpiece of elegant restraint. The Holden stirred more controversy in its early stages. On Friday 31 August 1945, after some significant revisions, the Holden was ready to be signed off by Earl himself:

The clay model is now in its final stages and was reviewed by Mr. H. Earle [sic] late Friday afternoon. We have got what we consider as an acceptable side body and fender design but have had considerable trouble in achieving a nicely balanced distinctive front end design but we believe we now have the proper motif for this and it is being developed on the clay model this week. Mr. Earle [sic] told the writer that in his opinion we had achieved a well-balanced, harmonious, attractive design. Something which is not a scaled-down version of modern American cars but is considerably more advanced in styling than English cars and is a design which he believed would set a different styling trend but which is at the same time not easily dated and will have enduring value.

Despite being styled before General Motors, Ford or Chrysler had really conceived their postwar architecture, the Holden was unquestionably more modern in appearance than most of the European cars planned for early postwar release. Most of these drew on late 1930s, early 1940s American themes but none was conceived under Harley Earl's *aegis*. The Standard Vanguard, for example, was inspired by the 1942 Plymouth, while the Austin A40 Devon was a smaller clone of the 1940 Chevrolet. Both were restyled in the early 1950s and their successors looked barely newer than the 1948 Holden. Hershey's retrospective descriptor 'little' and the fact that the Holden effectively came at the end of a line of Opels, all of which were designed for European markets, puts it outside the Detroit mainstream.

The Holden design also preceded two other 1946 cars that would have enormous influence on the direction of automotive styling into the 1950s and beyond. These were the 'coming or going' Studebaker Champion and the Pininfarina-designed Cisitalia (see Chapter 9). The Studebaker gave Ford its packaging blueprint for the postwar Custom, and Rover the basic look for its 1950 P4 models, which would stay on the market until the mid 1960s and be referred to affectionately as the 'Aunty Rovers'.

One designer . . . Holden, Cadillac, Thunderbird . . .

In the Detroit styling studios of General Motors, the Holden enjoyed at best a footnote of fashion, sandwiched between the carryover pre-war designs which were reintroduced as 1947 models and the rush of the new; 'a cute little car'. Contrast Hershey's Holden comments with his praise of the 1955 Ford Thunderbird, which has been widely, although somewhat controversially, attributed to the same designer: 'You can come up with a philosophy to explain anything! What could be more lean or clean than the first Thunderbird?'

The Holden's styling, helped no doubt by the heavily chromed grille which came late in the process, earned Harley Earl's approval and perhaps Hartnett agreed that it was not 'another gaudy American job'. But for the artists in Detroit a new small car for Australia was never going to allow the full exercise of their talents. Utility and light weight were higher priorities. The available evidence also suggests that Earl had not clarified his own thinking about future directions when Hershey styled the Australian car. By approaching it as a basic vehicle, then embellishing it with a bold Buick-style grille and handsome hub caps, Hershey did not have to risk striking out in the wrong direction. 'In the fall of 1946', said Hershey, 'jet-powered fighters were making their first public appearance, and they displaced the propeller-driven P–38 in the imaginations of designers'. Thus the pre-war Cadillac Sixty Special with its formal proportions gave way to the sleek, curvaceous 1948 Cadillac.

The most striking aspect of the Holden 48–215's styling was the radiator grille, a lavish chrome affair with more than a passing resemblance to that of the expensive Buicks of the immediate postwar era. This 'face' of the Holden was surely consistent with the nationalistic pride many would feel in the car; it was smiling, optimistic, well fed. Interestingly, the radiator grille was far more heavily chromed and bolder than the design for the 1949 Chevrolet, which had to take its lowly place in GM's North American domestic car line-up beneath Pontiac, Oldsmobile, Buick and Cadillac.

So the Holden would look far more modern than the 1948 Chevrolet, which was essentially a 1942 model dressed up with a new, horizontally themed radiator grille. Arguably, in this respect (although probably in no other), the timing of its debut was premature. Had the car been styled in 1947–48 rather than mid 1945, it would probably have still looked contemporary by 1955. The most informative comparison here comes from within General Motors. The E-Series Vauxhalls, of similar configuration to the Holden but somewhat less roomy inside, made their debut at London's Earls Court Motor Show in August 1951. Their shape would remain in production until 1957.

'The E-Type was engineered and styled at Luton', writes historian David Burgess-Wise in his history of Vauxhall, 'and although it bore a certain family likeness to the Australian Holden, that was only to be expected, since the Holden had, in part, been based on design studies for a new six-cylinder Vauxhall that had been sent to Detroit at the beginning of the war'. Maurice Platt, chief engineer of Vauxhall during this period, noted that Vauxhall had sent drawings to Detroit in 1939. But I have found no evidence that these had any influence on the final design or appearance of the Holden. Burgess-Wise also claims that 'a large proportion of British-made parts shipped from Luton' were 'incorporated' in the Holden. It is hard to agree with 'a large proportion', given the Holden's 92 per cent local content from the start of production.

Although Vauxhall's history of styling its own cars was a reasonably distinguished one, the final decision would still have been Harley Earl's, and the same principles informing the appearance of the Holden, although updated by about three years, would doubtless have applied to the Wyvern and Velox models. Interesting, too, is the fact that these two General Motors models echoed 195-Y-13 and 195-Y-15 by using four- and six-cylinder engines in the same body. Their immediate predecessors, launched in August 1948, also shared the same essentially pre-war body.

When the E-Class models went on sale in Australia in 1952, they were assembled from imported packs because production space was needed for Holdens. Despite being comparably priced to the Zephyr, the Velox sold quite strongly in Australia, helping Vauxhall to secure the position of fifth top-selling brand for 1952 and doubtless bringing some consolation to those not prepared to wait for 'Australia's Own Car'. The majority of the work on the E-Type Vauxhall's design would have been done in 1947–48, with the stylists already familiar with the forthcoming General Motors American models and also the Holden 48–215.

Among the major surprises hidden by the Australian car's neat but conservative styling was an astonishingly roomy interior. This was also a feature of the 195-Y cars. If Larry Hartnett had hoped to have much of the interior size of a Chevrolet in his car 'between the two types' then surely the outcome would have delighted him. On the key measurements of front and rear leg room, head room (at a time when hats were a factor) and seat width, the Holden not only outclassed the Opel Kapitän but equalled and in several cases beat the physically very much larger Chevrolet. In the GM context, its space efficiency was unsurpassed.

Take a break, Larry

Larry Hartnett is unable to hide his surprise one day in December 1946 when Harold Bettle, a higher ranked GM executive, arrives to see him. But he stands from his chair, plasters a smile on his face and stretches out his hand to shake Bettle's. 'What on earth are you doing in this neck of the woods, Harold?' he asks, but has already guessed the answer. How difficult to believe how wrong things have gone in these last six years.

When Hartnett instigated the 1940 report which defined in broad terms the concept for an Australian car, he was at the height of his powers within General Motors. And in November 1944 he won approval from General Motors for the Australian car largely on his own terms. The concept outlined in 1940 had provided the starting point for the design of the car and this had served to further his sense of ownership of the program.

But trouble was already brewing and Hartnett himself was aware of it. The bigger picture is that the Australian car was a General Motors program, not a Larry Hartnett one. In *Big Wheels and Little Wheels*, Hartnett points out that Sloan seemed to regard both him and Australia with some suspicion. An interjection he attributed to Sloan during the September 1944 presentation has the ring of authenticity:

> **The bigger picture is that the Australian car was a General Motors program, not a Larry Hartnett one.**

Halfway through my address, the chairman of GM, Alfred P. Sloan, a crusty old Tory, who, I always thought, considered me too venturesome, interrupted me with the remark, 'I don't like this country Australia. It's a socialist sort of place: the government owns the railroads, doesn't it?'

As we have seen, Sloan insisted that Jim Mooney 'lay down the law' to the Australian Englishman before he returned to Fishermans Bend. But Hartnett wanted to play a definitive role in the car program. He bombarded Begg with detailed design suggestions. As early as February 1945, the GMH liaison officer in the United States, George Quarry, felt obliged to write to Hartnett:

> *Russ Begg, having full responsibility for designing a vehicle . . . cannot set up to review all details of another vehicle being developed in Australia . . . he has been very short of manpower.*

But 'another vehicle being developed in Australia' is not accurate. Partly because he wanted to have maximum input into the appearance of the new car and also because he was desperate to keep his people employed with war orders in decline, Hartnett had ordered a number of styling exercises for the future car as an early stage of Project 320, comprising a series of nine scale models with numbers from 2000 to 2008. It seems that the nature of this work was misconstrued in the United States, leading to the conclusion that Hartnett was trying to hijack the program. When the models arrived there, tensions escalated.

Regardless of the details, which remain obscure, by early 1945 it was already clear that the process of designing the Holden was viewed differently on the two sides of the Pacific Ocean. Hartnett wrote to Harry Phillips, the GMOO regional director, that 'we feel rather in the dark as to what progress has been made by the team in Detroit'. Appel had formulated the plan late in 1944 but there was evidently some misunderstanding—doubtless fostered by Larry himself—about the extent of the responsibility GMH would have for the development of the car. A 'directive from the office of the managing director' under the heading 'Basis of Understanding with General Motors Corporation' and dated 15 January 1945 included this clause:

> That GMH will be held responsible for the performance of this project under all headings—that is, design, manufacture, applicability of the product to the market, effective performance, materials, timing, and that the general nature of the product will enhance the name and reputation of General Motors.

The following month Larry was disabused of this notion. Harry Phillips delivered a flow and procedure chart which defined 'design responsibility as resting with the Vice-President in charge of Engineering. In turn, the Vice-President delegates this authority to a Central Engineering Product Study Group, of which the Australian team are members'.

Hartnett did have some good ideas and fortunately Begg was prepared to listen when a logical argument was put to him. R.C. Rainsford, the liaison officer between Begg's group and GMH, wrote to Hartnett on 14 May 1945: 'Here again, the tendency seems to be to sacrifice ground clearance for appearance.' The GMH boss handwrote on this letter: 'We are very zealous to preserve ground clearance because of our operating conditions.' This appears to have been a victory for Hartnett, and one that had a positive influence on the Holden's design. The Australian engineers working on the project would certainly have backed him up and Begg evidently paid heed. The ground clearance was raised by half an inch (12.7 mm) from the prescribed 8.0 inches (203 mm).

Hartnett was relentless in his attempts to become more involved with the design process. This time he was concerned about the configuration of the interior, writing to Ed Riley on 26 June 1945:

> The admirable work they have coming out of Detroit is very interesting, and we are now comparing their findings with our own, but I do hope that our work will be well tabled [i.e. considered]
>
> . . . [The] trend of the smaller car class is towards three passengers in the front and two in the rear. We have enough information from England to indicate that they are thinking that way in their treatment of relatively small cars.

Note, first, the patronising tone of the opening clause, and the idea of 'comparing their findings with our own' is also surely too much of a challenge to be ignored.

Hartnett perhaps had some success in influencing the exterior styling of the Holden, but not as much as he would have liked. The scale model of GMH's Project 2008 styling exercise arrived in the United States sometime after 1 June 1945 to a very cool reception. George Quarry, GMH liaison officer and ostensibly Hartnett's representative in the United States (and a big fan of Russ Begg), was, according to Hartnett biographer Joe Rich:

> reluctant even to table the design in Detroit, declaring it could 'only further belittle our technical reputation.' When it was tabled a 'Superficial investigation,' he reported, 'revealed serious defects' and 'raised doubts as to the maturity of our thinking' . . .

Among the features of this car was a seating configuration which placed three people in front and two behind. Even without its defects, the scale model would have been unwelcome, viewed by Begg and his team as interference. His US bosses, probably not especially mindful of Hartnett's ulterior motive of finding work to keep his engineers and designers busy, saw him misusing his authority, and not for the first time. Friction, already considerable, intensified when this scale model arrived. Ed Riley, mincing no words, penned a letter ordering Hartnett to butt out:

> . . . We cannot afford, however to risk going into production on our first model in Australia on the basis of a design which is the product of an untried and untested engineering department. I'll be glad at any time to review models which you could develop in Australia and consider them for production in Australia for future programs. I am not willing, however, to plunk down our blue chips on the production of this, our first car, on the basis of such design . . . I just cannot put our money on your crowd for this first job.

It seems probable that Ed Riley was the corporate meat in this sandwich, that he had Russ Begg's engineering team on one side and Larry Hartnett on the other. Regardless, his patience had run out, and perhaps from this point on Hartnett's future was pretty much sealed. But Harnett's frustration continued to build towards an inevitable showdown. It seems that the trans-Pacific correspondence was mostly one way. Finally, on 28 August, Begg responded in an apologetic tone. 'Chief engineers are not very good correspondents', he begins.

> . . . we are all hopeful that the new style will give Australia something which is unique and which combines the best features of Continental and American styling without in any way being a copy of either.
>
> Your Australian boys have fitted into our program very well and I think that they are gaining much from their experience with us and have been able to contribute to us an Australian outlook and Australian viewpoint.

Please be humble

What correspondence was exchanged between Begg and his immediate bosses at GMOO? It is likely that he implored them to get Larry Hartnett off his back. On 26 April 1946 E.S. Hoglund, the operations manager for GMOO in its New York head office, wrote to his regional manager, Harold Bettle:

> Maybe this sounds cockeyed to you, Harold, but if in your own words you can get Larry Hartnett to leave this idea with the boys coming over, I am sure that it would do the boys here an awful lot of good and would greatly facilitate both their work and the work of our engineers here.

This evidence of Bettle's early involvement in the Australian car development process—rather, the politics of it—is especially interesting, given that Bettle would be the man chosen to replace Hartnett as the managing director of GMH. On 6 February 1946, Bettle had written to Hartnett ordering him to discontinue any work being done in Australia 'in connection with the Australian Car Project', and five days later he rebuked Hartnett for acting unilaterally. On 20 June the outspoken Quarry sent a letter to Hartnett with a copy to Bettle, effectively rebuking his boss:

> *Regarding our moot point of sound engineering, I think we must leave this one for a while, as it is almost impossible to thrash out by letter—all I can say is this:- The majority of schemes sent from Australia to improve the thinking and design of this vehicle have definitely transgressed sound engineering principles, and of this there is no contradiction.*

Begg remained diplomatic in his dealings with Hartnett, aware that he would probably be reporting to him when the project moved across the Pacific. On 27 June 1946 he wrote:

> *Dear Larry*
> *Your letter of May 24th was very timely and much appreciated because at the moment I was feeling pretty low.*
> *I agree that most of the anxieties on both sides arose from the distance which separates us . . .*
> *Although we have been through many programs of this nature, we still think that the developing and building of a new automobile is a very tough job and therefore believe that both the Americans and Australians should be very humble in their approach. We have been led to believe, through cables, letters and personal contacts, that the Australian group does not appreciate the magnitude of the job to be done, and this has occasioned considerable concern.*

'The Australian group does not appreciate the magnitude of my job'—little reading between the lines is required here to make out 'and especially you, Larry' in invisible ink. Russ Begg and his people just got on with the job, despite constant attempts to interfere by those Australians not seconded to the United States for the program. It seems that thinly veiled hostility prevailed across the great divide of the Pacific Ocean, and that Hartnett finally offered an olive branch which Begg accepted.

This, however, did not end the tension. On 24 October 1946 Hartnett wrote to his immediate boss, Harry Phillips, one step below Edward Riley on the GM corporate ladder, expressing his astonishment at not being able to 'see the car we are planning to manufacture'. But by late 1946 and two years out from the Holden's actual launch Hartnett's star had paled almost to invisibility. Edward Riley dispatched Harry Bettle to Australia to take over as managing director of GMH—the successor uncomfortably doubling as messenger. Bettle's task was to hand-deliver to Larry the letter which told him he was being recalled to America for re-indoctrination in the General Motors culture. Hartnett's own summation of the reasons is surely close to the truth. 'I was too Australian', he says. Hartnett had started out as a General Motors executive in the 1920s but his senior Australian posting brought out the entrepreneur in him. His role as director of ordnance during World War II intensified his contacts within government circles and probably his sense of destiny. It was harder for his bosses to make him stick to the General Motors rule book.

Sometimes when we think of rule books, we think only of bureaucratic red tape or rules for the sake of rules. But, as history has shown, when it came to developing the appropriate car to launch in Australia in the late 1940s, the GM rule book, with the hand of Alfred P. Sloan constantly upon it, was a wonderful thing.

- **1908** Henry Ford's Model T marks the start of mass motoring and gives Alfred P. Sloan Jr his point of departure for the early 1920s (when the Ford remained current). The T's utility inspires GM *style*. Its simplicity provokes GM *complexity*. Sloan turns the Model T into a competitor for a *used* Chevrolet.

- **1928** The Chevrolet gets a six-cylinder engine instead of the old four. This is the serious beginning of the history of sixpacks.

- **1935** The Opel Olympia brings monocoque construction to GM and to Europe's biggest market, Germany.

- **1937** The Opel Super Six provides the real starting point for the Holden. The Experimental Light Car Project of 1937–38 amounts to seeing how a car of these dimensions will work as a monocoque. Should it then be powered by a 'four' or 'six'? These questions and answers shape the Holden and Australian motoring history.

- **1938** The Opel Kapitän also feeds the Holden program. Its monocoque construction allows it to be bigger and plusher than its Super Six predecessor, but barely heavier. GM engineers are learning bucketloads about the potential of the monocoque. Extra size or less weight? That might depend on whether you wish to impress buyers in the Third Reich or a very different market in Australia.

Chapter 6

From Milford to Melbourne, 1945–48

No new car has ever before had such a background of scientific skill and achievement.

—*General Motors New Australian Car: HOLDEN*, Australia, 1948

Even if many of the cars that traversed Australia's imperfect roads in 1948 were battle-weary pre-war models, the cultural landscape had changed dramatically since 1939, shifting its focus from Britain to the United States in the aftermath of the Pacific War. The new American alliance greased the political wheels that would drive 'Australia's own car', which of course was really the American–Australian car, just as the monocoque Opels of the 1930s were American–German and their Vauxhall counterparts were American–English.

There had never been serious doubt that colonial Australia would follow Britain into World War II, but while the struggle for Europe finished in May 1945, Australian troops had three more months to fight alongside their American allies in the defence of Australia against the Japanese. Like any change at the top, this political realignment would have profound consequences on how ordinary citizens thought and felt about Australia's place in the world. Children in Australian primary schools still learnt about the Mother Country and coloured large sections of their Mercator's projection maps pink, but in 1948, when the Holden was launched, Australia was in some respects already more oriented towards the United States than to Britain. While in the 1930s Australians favoured American Chevrolets over British Vauxhalls and watched more films from Hollywood than from England, the country still thought of itself—and indeed generally described itself—as a British nation. As late as 1939, when the outbreak of World War II distracted even tycoons like Hartnett from the automotive business, the very notion that an Australian car might be sourced from General Motors rather than, say, Austin or Morris, was barely conceivable. As discussed in earlier chapters, Larry Hartnett's proposal to build the Opel Olympia in Australia was dismissed by the government as being prejudicial to the English industry's sales. There can be no doubt, then, that the shift in cultural focus towards the United States was one of many issues of timing which worked in favour of the Australian car program.

As the war in the Pacific was drawing towards its close, the finishing touches being put to the nuclear weapon and the *Enola Gay* being readied for its terrible duty, Russell Begg and his team were preparing to submit the first 195Y25 prototype to durability testing. Project 195Y25's ultimate proving ground would be Australia in geographical and cultural terms, but there was much preliminary work to be done before the three US-made prototype cars would turn their wheels on the other side of the Pacific.

Begg, pursuing Walter Appel's plan of operation, took no short cuts in readying the Australian car for production. Once the design was complete, it had to be proved in actual road testing. This was to be no haphazard process, for General Motors had an outstanding facility at Milford, 65 kilometres from Detroit, Michigan, where the prototypes could be tested on different surfaces, driven up steep gradients and generally given a thorough workout in complete secrecy and without the exigencies of public traffic.

A documentary film of the Milford testing of the 195Y25 can be viewed in the Holden Collection at the Mortlock Library in the State Library of South Australia. Although rival manufacturers tested their vehicles, certainly the American and English Fords sold in Australia in the early postwar era did not have to undergo such a rigorous process. Problems experienced by the Consuls, Zephyrs and Customs in Australian conditions are documented by Geoff Easdown in *A History of the Ford Motor Company in Australia*.

The final piece

In a sense, the Holden was the final large piece in GM's international jigsaw puzzle of the 1925 to 1945 era. It was never just 'the Australian car' but a car developed specifically for Australia, using General Motors' unique expertise at developing vehicles to suit overseas markets. The fact that the demands of Australia were even more exacting than those of Germany or Britain meant that General Motors' achievement in creating the Holden was arguably its most significant since the 1920s when Alfred P. Sloan Jr developed the corporation's product policy and set Chevrolet against Ford.

So why was the Holden superior to all rivals in terms of uniquely Australian motoring requirements between 1948 and 1953? In this chapter and the next, I want to show how the Holden's success in the market and its superior design reflected Sloan's corporate vision, that the Holden was absolutely the right car at the right time for Australia, and that it ushered the nation into the era of mass motorisation. The car also influenced a number of designs both within and outside General Motors. Although it was not the first six-cylinder monocoque sedan of this size, it was the first with postwar styling and the first to draw international attention from the specialist motoring press. And in doing all this the Holden set a pattern for

Although it was not the first six-cylinder monocoque sedan of this size, it was the first with postwar styling and the first to draw international attention from the specialist motoring press.

the local car market which would not be seriously challenged for more than half a century.

GMH itself published a booklet after the announcement of the Australian car but before the public release of the Holden. This carefully worded advertisement puts the Holden into the broader context of General Motors, depicts the testing process and observes that the car constituted 'the first opportunity to cater for the particular requirements of Australians'. An even more extravagant claim follows: 'No new car has ever before had such a background of scientific skill and achievement.' That is because General Motors had the 'biggest overseas organisation in the automobile industry, being represented in more than 100 countries', and was the repository of the largest design team and the most extensive research. Just like GM's domestic American cars, the Holden was tested at the General Motors proving ground at Milford, but where American cars were tested for the equivalent of 25,000 miles (40,230 km) of normal motoring, the Holden was given double that trial and performed excellently.

Holden prototypes go to Milford

Opened in 1924, Milford was the world's first purpose-built proving ground and another Sloan innovation. Although Sloan's stated intention was to increase shareholder value, he was also resolute that this should be achieved by building the best engineered and most sharply styled cars in the market. As for the idea of *proving* cars before their public release, the evidence backs the claim made in the booklet that General Motors did this more thoroughly than all its rivals at the time, not just at Milford but also in those overseas markets where it manufactured cars, notably Germany and Britain.

Sloan recalls in *Adventures of a White-collar Man* overseeing the ineffectual attempts of the GM team to test the recently developed four-wheel brakes:

> *We went to a place back of Pontiac, Michigan, which was convenient to all, intending to run some tests. We had seven or eight cars, and quite a large party of executives and engineers. It was a public road, and as our tests had to be conducted at speed we would no sooner get started than it was necessary for us to stop because someone would come driving along the road. The futility of a great organization doing its engineering work under such conditions became overwhelmingly apparent to me as I waited time after time to get the tests started and then restarted.*

It was then that Sloan came up with the idea of a 'great outdoor laboratory, with all types of roads that existed anywhere, so that the test cars could be subjected to all conditions'.

Fiat had a banked track on the roof of its Lingotto (Turin) factory in the 1920s and various other makers had their own small facilities, but the Milford proving ground was still unique in the industry by the time Russ Begg took his precious prototype Australian cars there, the first of them late in August 1946:

> *It covers an area of 1268 acres [513 ha] at Milford, Michigan, near Detroit, and represents the world's largest outdoor laboratory . . . a fact finding institution which has developed its own special techniques for testing cars far beyond the point of endurance reached in normal driving.*

It was a public road, and as our tests had to be conducted at speed we would no sooner get started than it was necessary for us to stop because someone would come driving along the road. The futility of a great organization doing its engineering work under such conditions became overwhelmingly apparent to me as I waited time after time to get the tests started and then restarted.

In the span of just over 24 years, since the first car drove its first measured mile at the G.M. Proving Ground, brakes have gone from two wheels to four wheels; cylinders have multiplied from four to sixteen; helical gears have supplanted spur gears in the transmission; the bumps in the road have been levelled out by independent front wheel suspension, and coil springing on all four wheels: synchromesh transmission, gear shift on the steering column, and now, automatic transmission have been developed . . .

The 195Y25 car did not have a sixteen-cylinder engine or automatic transmission, nor did it have coil springs in the rear suspension, but a comparatively basic specification did not preclude the Holden from a full Milford initiation, which included emergency braking tests, hill climbing and water sealing.

The first 195Y25 at Milford would be joined by a second car a month later. On 14 October the third US-built 195Y25 prototype was completed, but according to official documentation testing finished the following day, probably to allow sufficient time to prepare for the coming boat trip to Australia where further testing was scheduled. More time at Milford, however, certainly would have helped and it is difficult to see how just three months or so for the first prototype could be deemed exhaustive, even though the prototypes performed well. As it happened, some problems were discovered after the cars had made their transatlantic crossing.

Secrecy surrounds the Holden

On 4 December 1946, with its cargo of three cars and 86 passengers, not all of whom were associated with the Australian car project, the first-class Tasman liner *Wanganella* left the port of Vancouver on its 25-day voyage to Sydney. From Sydney the three top-secret prototypes were driven overnight to Fishermans Bend. During the *Wanganella*'s time at sea, Harold Bettle had time to install himself as Hartnett's successor, meaning American management was firmly in control of the program, officially renamed Project 320, by the time it had crossed the Atlantic. Such precise timing was surely not coincidental: presumably the decision to relieve Hartnett of his post was hastened by the Americans' desire to retain full control of the Australian car program. There appears to have been a further lull in testing until 12 February 1947.

On 12 February 1947 all three prototypes were registered in Victoria as 1946 Chevrolets. The cars had to be registered under a brand name and Chevrolet must have seemed as good as any, especially since it was GM's top-selling car in Australia. This intriguing detail might even have resulted from a spur-of-the-moment decision made at the motor registry. For the casual observer or interpreter, the fact that they were registered as Chevrolets could have constituted proof that they were actually Chevrolets. Was it an official attempt to suppress interest? If so, it was partially counterproductive, undoubtedly contributing to rumours that the Holden was nothing more than a discarded smaller Chevrolet, originally designed for the North American market.

These three US-built prototypes were joined by two Australian-built cars later in the year. All five were submitted to a rigorous testing process on sealed and unsealed roads around Melbourne. But it was the outback trials that were most revealing, and fatigue cracking of the body in the firewall area vindicated such thoroughness. The Project 320 cars were not only the first in the world to be tested by a manufacturer under the harshest Australian conditions, they inaugurated a culture at GMH which persists into the 21st century. Even the Milford proving ground could not (and had never tried to) replicate Australian country roads with their corrugations and bulldust, and high temperatures in summer. This was a lesson about the 'sunburnt country' which should have been absorbed into national folklore but Ford Australia's almost disastrous experiment with the Falcon in 1960, which will be covered later, suggests it was not.

There was a paradox embedded in the culture of secrecy around the car. For GMH, there was a risk of being placed in the boy-who-cried-wolf category. Leading up to World War II, and gathering momentum from about 1935, numerous rumours about forthcoming Australian cars had circulated through the embryonic motor industry. In the immediate aftermath, as Project 320 neared production-readiness, there was a level of scepticism among GMH's own employees and the outside companies who would be required to supply componentry for the car. But it was necessary to retain employees and to ensure that prospective suppliers knew the Australian car was about to be invented or, more accurately, realised. As Don Loffler observes, the culture of secrecy 'contributed to this notion' that production was improbable. Harold Bettle countered the scepticism by giving secret previews of the car, which sometimes involved 'large groups of people who needed to be convinced'.

On 25 August 1947, the car was shown to all the employees at the Woodville plant where the bodies were to be manufactured. Bettle noted in a report to E.S. ('Pete') Hoglund, assistant general manager of GMOO:

> To show the car to our employees and to a select list of suppliers this far in advance of production is, of course, an unusual procedure, and if we were already manufacturing complete cars in this country, this would never have been considered.
>
> However, I cannot overemphasise the amount of scepticism that still exists on the part of some suppliers on whom we shall be dependent, and on the part of our Woodville employees.

Doubt and mistrust were problems but incapacity was a bigger one. It looks likely that Larry Hartnett had been overconfident about the incipient local supplier industry's capacity to meet the huge challenge of complete automotive manufacture. Pragmatic Bettle had to sort out any inherited problems. In a letter written to Pete Hoglund three days after the Project 320 car had been paraded before the Woodville employees, Bettle said:

> Over past years the Australian public have been told in the press of local car manufacturing ventures, all of which have fallen by the wayside . . . [but] there is

Australia-wide acceptance of the fact that the project is well under way. This has been achieved without divulging any important technical details or information regarding the car's performance. No photographs have been released so actually those who have viewed the car have only a mental picture of it.

So much for the scepticism. But Bettle was still very concerned about the Australian resources at his disposal, fourteen months to the day before the official launch of the car, and the letter continues:

Our experience is demonstrating more clearly every day that there does not exist in this country the independent background and knowhow that had been counted upon. It is really very thin and just about one layer deep . . . with practically everything there is only one source, or at best, two, and the difference between first and second is so great that we are really confined to one source for material, parts or components or technical services.

There was so much pressure to get as many production-ready components as possible that Bettle's boss, Ed Riley, vetoed a request from Vauxhall for a full set of 320 parts, whether gift-wrapped or not. The British subsidiary of GM was at the start of its planning process for the E-Series Vauxhalls to be launched at the end of 1951 and the engineers probably believed they could incorporate many elements of the Holden's design; in fact the Vauxhalls were quite similar in most respects, albeit built on a shorter wheelbase. And the six-cylinder Velox was slightly heavier than the Australian car. A Vauxhall delegation including managing director Sir Charles Bartlett and designer David Jones had viewed the Holden styling model in July 1945 with Harley Earl himself. The Holden's styling was not to chief engineer Maurice Platt's taste and he described it in his memoirs, *An Addiction to Automobiles*, as having a 'work-horse look which was sadly unattractive'. This was before the Holden put on its jewellery—that magnificent grille. As it happened, Bartlett and Jones helped Ed Riley make the case to Harley Earl for significant revisions which were signed off on 31 August. (See Chapter 9, 'Diamonds Are a Grille's Best Friend'.) When the E-Series

. . . the unique place of the Holden in the General Motors world: a product of Detroit but tailored to specific Australian needs and minus some of the customary 'cellophane'.

Vauxhall finally arrived, it had more of the look of a scaled-down Chevrolet. (David Jones may not have liked the early Holden clay model, but in general he was an ardent admirer of Harley Earl, says Maurice Platt.) Once again, we see the unique place of the Holden in the General Motors world: a product of Detroit but tailored to specific Australian needs and minus some of the customary 'cellophane'.

The name game

Given that Bettle and his team were worried suppliers were sceptical about whether the projected Australian car would eventuate, one would have thought a photograph on the front page of the Melbourne *Herald* would have been viewed positively as free advertising and proof of its existence. On 8 October 1947, prototype number four was shown in right front three-quarter forward view, having been caught by a *Herald* photographer on its standard test route, news having no doubt reached the newspaper about strange new cars without identifying badges being seen regularly on the same roads. Had the scoop occurred three months earlier, before the viewings by supplier groups and employees, Bettle's response may have been different, but initially he was angry.

When the Australian car was shown to the *Herald*'s readers it was not yet named. Harold Bettle had sent a list of suggested names to GMOO on 1 April 1947. Despite it being April Fool's Day, Bettle's attached letter was entirely serious:

The name should be short, catchy, easily pronounced, preferably identifiable with Australia, but one that would be acceptable on any overseas market that might be

developed later on. The consensus of opinion is that the name should be 'Canbra'.
This is the phonetic spelling of the word 'Canberra'.

Indeed, but were Bettle and his advisors unaware of the abbreviation of the word 'brassiere' and how 'Canbra' could have been the butt of so many jokes as to harm the car's sales potential? It could have been the first time in history where an advertisement for a car could have been mistaken as one for a sports brassiere or its 1940s counterpart. Possibly this objection may never have been raised. Runners up on Bettle's list, in order, were 'GMH', 'GeM', 'Lion' and 'Holden'. The managing director himself favoured 'GMH'.

Ed Riley was almost certainly behind the decision to name the car after the Holden family. Hindsight says we should be in his debt: the name linked the American-designed car with a highly respected Australian company to reinforce the sense that it was truly a GMH product. Bettle's letter of 1 December 1947 suggests he responded to pressure from above because the Holden name was down in fifth place on the Australian list. The 'selection' was plainly made in New York:

Acting on the authority which you have given me in our last telephone conversation,
we have decided upon the name 'Holden' for the Australian car. We have no serious
objections to the name selected, although some of us feel that the initials 'GMH'
would be more appropriate. In any event, we have now officially released the name
to Engineering and Manufacturing for design and tooling purposes.

The key word here is 'objections', which strongly implies that some kind of moderate pressure had been brought to bear on Bettle to choose the Holden nameplate. Riley's history with the family dated back to 1923 and the agreement that Holden Motor Body Builders' new Woodville facility would be used exclusively to produce bodies for General Motors products. If Hartnett could claim to be the non-custodial father of the Holden, then Riley was its godfather.

So the '320 car', as it was commonly referred to by insiders, did not have an official name until a year before its launch. Having satisfied employees and suppliers that the project was genuine, Bettle and his fellow executives were nevertheless determined to keep the 'Holden' name a close secret, but by mid 1948 rumours mentioned 'Holden' more frequently. Bettle decided to announce the name at a special press function to be run over two days, 31 August and 1 September 1948. Seventeen journalists were invited and at the end of proceedings they would see the car itself.

Once the name was in the public domain, there was still a question mark over when the car itself would be launched. Announcements over when the Holden would be released into dealer showrooms were timed to maximum advantage by GMH's marketing team under Harry Cavanaugh. The Melbourne announcement capitalised on the excitement surrounding the Melbourne Cup, with the GMH gold cup (a replica of the Melbourne Cup) presented to the winning jockey. Thirty-seven radio stations around Australia broadcast this program at 9.30 p.m. on the day of the race.

Standard testing procedure at Milford involved:

- a hill start on a 27 per cent grade
- a 'Belgian Block' road to test suspension and body rigidity
- a 400-metre water splash

and much more. The first Holden prototype completed 10,000 miles (16,100 km) of hard driving at Milford on 14 October 1946, and then the three prototypes came to Australia. An 86-mile (138 km) road loop around Melbourne was used to complete urban durability testing, although there was a lot of dirt in those 140 or so kilometres! Then the cars went to the outback.

But the first owners did the final testing. Few faults emerged.

The official launch on 29 November 1948 built expectations still further. Yes, here was the car and people could read its specifications and compare it with other vehicles on the market, and they could even go to a local showroom to inspect it, even though this might have been a case of standing four or five rows back and peering between the heads and shoulders of those in front. At this stage, though, the Holden still represents a promise of the future because retail sales will not begin until February 1949.

Chapter 7

Smile, the war is over
. . . or is it?

One particular sequence of photographs among the many taken at Fishermans Bend on 29 November 1948 lives on in Australia's cultural memory. In terms of placing a bookmark into the industrial-socio-cultural history of Australia, this image stands with those of the Sydney Harbour Bridge nearing completion or Dupain's photographs of the Opera House in construction. Here is Prime Minister Ben Chifley smiling beside the newly launched Australian car, the Holden 48–215 (later, popularly, known as the 'FX'). The image is celebrated not just because it shows the first Holden but because the car and the prime minister are shown together in what amounted both to a statement of intent and a promise for the imminent future into which we could drive in our Holdens. (Or, rather, we would be able to when the car was actually released for sale, if we were high enough up the waiting list, and provided we could obtain sufficient rationed low-grade petrol to drive where our fancy might take us.)

For a country to manufacture its own car represents a kind of coming of age, and in this process Australia was half a century behind other western industrial nations including the United States, Great Britain, Germany,

France and Italy; even Japan had been making cars for many years before the outbreak of World War II. Among these countries, only the United States could claim mass motorisation as a consequence of its industry, but long before 1948 all of them not only made cars but had developed what might be termed a distinctive national automotive culture.

The process of developing a strong, self-sufficient car-manufacturing industry was not just about building a stronger economy. World War I had shown the extent to which even quite rudimentary motor vehicles could serve the purpose of national defence. The United States, Britain, Germany, France, Italy and Russia to varying extents depended on their automotive manufacturers to furnish the weapons of war. And the intellectual armoury and technical ability of industry was enhanced by the experience of war. But the most conspicuous illustration of how effectively the automotive industry could be used as an instrument of national power had been provided throughout the twelve years of the 'Thousand Year Reich'.

While Hitler's policies brought cheaper cars and gave enormous momentum to the automotive industry, his aim was always world domination. When in 1935 the Nazis asked Opel to build a new factory with a view to manufacturing the mooted *volkswagen* the stipulation was that it should be located inland, out of reach of enemy bombers. The *volkswagen* contract did not of course eventuate and the new factory at Brandenburg, 60 kilometres west of Berlin, was used to build Opel Blitz trucks for the Wehrmacht. Without mass production of cars and trucks, and later armaments and aircraft, the Third Reich could not have got itself onto a strong enough footing to launch World War II. Germany's enormous strides towards mass motorisation between 1933 and 1938 were, for Hitler and his cronies, a pleasing spin-off. The major player was, paradoxically, General Motors'

Without mass production of cars and trucks, and later armaments and aircraft, the Third Reich could not have got itself onto a strong enough footing to launch World War II.

wholly owned subsidiary, Opel, which during this period joined the world industry leaders in car design on the strength of American know-how. The mooted Volkswagen also came into being but would not be available as a car the *volk* could buy until after World War II. Even the great increase in new vehicle registrations between 1933 and 1938 did not give Germany anything like the level of motorisation that had been enjoyed in the United States before the Great Depression, but the advent of mass production served Hitler's terrible vision.

By contrast, successive Australian governments had done little to encourage private purchase of cars, beyond protecting the local motor body building industry and privileging chassis imported from Britain via a lower tariff regime. Australian suppliers of componentry such as tyres, batteries, upholstery, fastenings and springs were protected, in some cases before World War II. But it would not be until 1936 that the government would invite the Tariff Board to consider the 'question of the best means of giving effect to the Government's policy of establishing in Australia the manufacturing of engines and chassis of motor vehicles with consideration to the general national and economic aspect'. Roads were almost uniformly poor even into the 1960s and beyond. Public transport was, as Sloan noted disapprovingly, publically owned and funded, and thus in competition with the automotive industry.

By 1944 John Curtin's Labor government had come to see the need for a locally manufactured car, but Curtin's emphasis was typically on the need for high levels of postwar employment and the development of secondary industry rather than on the virtues of personal mobility. In this second-last year of the war, no new cars were available to private buyers, petrol was rationed and cities were still blacked out at night. But Curtin was looking to the future, at what Chifley would later call 'the light on the hill'—it might have been a metaphor for secondary industry.

The image of Ben Chifley with the Holden is worth ten thousand words. When Curtin died in office in July 1945 he was succeeded by Chifley, who was also a keen advocate of the Australian car. But even by the time

GMH was ready to launch its Holden, rationing continued and, in the context of the fast-changing mood of Australians who were eager to move forwards and put the past behind them, this had become a divisive political issue. It must have seemed to some observers a surprising disconnect:

The image of Chifley with the Holden is worth ten thousand words.

the government gave support for the Holden while continuing to impose restrictions on private mobility even though by this time World War II was more than three years into the pages of history. But this disconnect tells the story of the Holden's significance for the government. When Chifley looked at the Holden he saw the surge of secondary industry in dangerous times, but most Australians saw the prospect of a shiny new sedan to drive into the fifties.

If anything, this paradox made the public launch of Australia's first mass-produced car an even more significant event in Australia's cultural history than it might otherwise have been. For here was the prime minister of an avowedly social democratic government taking centre stage with the product of the world's most successful and influential multinational corporation. With hindsight it seems that Chifley and his variety of Australian Labor Party government was already anachronistic in 1948; there was indeed little public support for the continuation of wartime austerity measures, the nationalisation of banks, nor for the overtly socialist 'planks' of the ALP platform. By contrast, the Holden car staring boldly into the camera on that overcast Melbourne day at the end of spring is almost as much metaphor for the future as product of the present.

Although the Holden was manufactured in Australia with 92 per cent local content, it was nevertheless the product of General Motors. The car was designed and engineered in Detroit, Michigan, and not at Holden's Woodville plant in South Australia, where GMH's own engineering team was located.

Chifley's smile is proud, almost possessive, and—especially when invested with nearly 60 years of hindsight—hints at a deeper complicity than mere readiness to pose for the obligatory photograph. Why does the social-istically inclined prime minister of Australia look so happy to be launching a product developed in the United States by a US multinational? Beyond this crisply composed black-and-white photograph lies a complex jigsaw puzzle. We have assembled several pieces already but more are needed to complete the bigger picture surrounding Chifley and the first Holden. As for this evocative image, it is like many other photographs in that a great deal can be learnt by examining not just what the lens captures but also what it excludes.

It is notable that the subject matter of the photograph may be summed up as Prime Minister Chifley plus Holden 'Number One' (although the subject car was not literally the first down the production line). Chifley is not shaking anyone's hand, although he reportedly shook a great many on the day. Nor is he behind the wheel or in the passenger seat as the car is driven off the line. (That task had been reserved for Harold Bettle and Russell Begg for an earlier occasion, almost a month before the official launch.) There is no-one else with whom the prime minister shares smiles and congratulations. Could this have been an oversight? Might it have been seen as *in*appropriate, given the extraordinary circumstances that occurred in the four-year period between the initial proposal for the car and its arrival as a gleaming, photogenic *product*, that the photograph puts just one indi-vidual in the frame with the car? Or was Chifley's role principally symbolic? Was this perhaps the way General Motors' publicity machine wished to present the new car: as a gift to Australia and thus a kind of public relations tour de force? Perhaps it was the coded message the Australian government itself wished to disseminate? (And whose interests did the image principally serve—Australia's or General Motors'? Or was this such a very special symbiosis that there was no difference, as in the famous case of Charles ['Engine Charlie'] Wilson, who had been invited in 1952 by his friend, Presi-dent-elect Dwight D. Eisenhower, to surrender his presidency of GM and become the US Secretary of Defence. During a senate committee hearing Wilson said: 'For years I thought what was good for our country was good for General Motors—and vice versa. The difference did not exist.')

Most likely of all is the simpler explanation that the photograph was a spontaneous event which went on to inspire the Australian cultural imagination and linger in many people's memories. Chifley was an iconic and appropriately self-made 'man of the people' style of prime minister at an especially patriotic time in Australia's national history, and it is difficult to think of any other figure (except perhaps Larry Hartnett) whose presence beside the Holden would have signified much at all to most viewers in 1948. Chifley's famous 'light on the hill' metaphor and his habitual pipe are indelibly attached to his memory, as are his origins as the son of a Bathurst train driver; his being perceived as archetypally Australian had to do with the accurate perception that he was egalitarian. I hope it is not irreverent to suggest that had Ben Chifley been a car, he would have been the 1948 Holden. Of the numerous images captured on 29 November of that year, it is this sequence which continues to define the Holden's role in the history of postwar national pride and industrialisation.

Chifley's influence on the Australian Car Program

Spontaneous or not, it is no confected smile-for-the-camera image. Without the direct involvement of Chifley in 1945 it is probable that the Australian Car Program would not have proceeded, at least not at that time. In a sense then, the Holden was itself a kind of war baby, conceived in hope and desperation, with peace seemingly a brief moratorium amid intensifying international conflicts. On 29 November 1948, at the launch of a motor car, Chifley spoke about the risk of a third world war, which sets the glamour of the occasion against a darker background and suggests much about the government's enthusiasm for the project. The prime minister's speech reveals a shift in political rhetoric and perhaps also in political will between 1944–45 and 1948, following the US bombing of Hiroshima and Nagasaki. Even before the end of the war in the Pacific, the Cold War had begun and fears of an imminent conflict with Russia strengthened in the period between mid 1945 and late 1948. The prospect

The prospect of a third world war, Chifley told the 1100 guests, was a terrifying one. The thing that mattered most in the world today was peace.

of a third world war, Chifley told the 1100 guests, was a terrifying one. The thing that mattered most in the world today was peace.

It was at Chifley's insistence and in response to a request from the then managing director of GMH, Larry Hartnett, that the federal government underwrote Project 320. General Motors itself provided most of the sense but none of the dollars, although it agreed to guarantee the loan and, through GMH, paid the interest. For Chifley, the Holden was not just a symbol of Australia's new industrial capacity but of its newly independent nationhood, a nationhood imperiled by the threat of World War III and dependent on secondary industry to provide the means of defence. General Motors would make the profits but the Australian government had underwritten the program—given Alfred Sloan's intense dislike of government intervention in private enterprise, here was an intriguing paradox.

The only person immediately identifiable in these images apart from Chifley is standing out of the limelight, probably somewhere around the rear right mudguard of the Holden. This is Harold Bettle, managing director of General Motors-Holden's since December 1946 when he replaced Hartnett. In the open space to the right of the vehicle there is a considerable crowd of people, mostly looking at the Holden although one or two focus on the camera, aware perhaps of the historical significance of the occasion. After all, GMH had invited 1100 people to a handsome function. Dressed to the nines, these guests were served champagne, beer and soft drinks by thirteen hostesses wearing dresses of an identical red to the leather upholstery of the cream Holden on display. An eight-piece orchestra played light classical music, and speakers included Ben Chifley, the premier of Victoria, Thomas Hollway, and Harold Bettle.

BHP steels Holden's future

One of the guests at the launch was Essington Lewis, managing director of BHP and director of munitions during World War II. Lewis had worked closely with Larry Hartnett; as director of ordnance, Hartnett reported directly to Lewis. The two men were friends and Lewis had assured Hartnett that BHP would be able to supply the necessary quantity of steel to ensure local manufacture of the car could proceed. Essington Lewis towered over Australian secondary industry in the era of the Holden. You might have expected that Hartnett and Lewis would both have taken their places at the small VIP luncheon hosted by Harold Bettle before the launch ceremony commenced. But only Lewis was there, initially having declined the invitation because of a prior commitment, but later deciding to attend just the lunch. Most of the other luncheon guests were politicians—Chifley and at least two state premiers (Hollway of Victoria, Playford of South Australia)—and senior executives of General Motors. But Hartnett certainly did not dine with Bettle, Chifley and the others. Not only did he receive no luncheon invitation but he was not even on the list for the larger function.

So the most important exclusion from this or any other photograph taken at Fishermans Bend during the official launch of the Holden was certainly Larry Hartnett, the man generally credited as being the 'father of the Holden'. Hartnett had left General Motors' employ in May 1947. Even so, he clearly expected an invitation to the launch. The fact that none was forthcoming appears to be a measure of the distance senior General Motors executives from the overseas office wished to place between the company and Hartnett and, besides, his presence might well have proved embarrassing; he had not been taken as any kind of prisoner of General Motors' machinations but was essentially a victim to be forgotten at the earliest opportunity. At least one senior government official took offence at the exclusion of Hartnett from the festivities. John Jensen, chairman of secondary industries, refused the invitation because his friend Hartnett had not received one. 'I feel sorry for the man pushed outside', he noted in a letter to Lewis. Essington Lewis's almost inestimable contribution to Australian manufacturing capacity during his time as director of munitions played a major part in creating the context in which full car manufacture became viable. Lewis had also asked to be allowed to purchase the first car off the line and refused to accept his Holden (which was not among the first ten built—those being retained by GMH) as a gift.

There is no record of what was said over lunch, but friendly exchanges between Ben Chifley and Essington Lewis may be taken for granted: we could probably call them mates. Chifley had actually worked under Lewis during World War II when the BHP boss was made director of munitions. It was Lewis who recruited Chifley to the position of director of labour. Laurence Hartnett (director of ordnance) and John Jensen (assistant secretary of the Department of Supply) were two other senior Lewis appointments. The evidence suggests that all four were on friendly terms, and there can be no doubt that Larry's friends in high places are an important piece in the Holden jigsaw puzzle.

It would be impossible to complete this puzzle without looking at Hartnett's role in the creation of the Australian car and at the circumstances surrounding his departure from General Motors, where he had served as a senior executive for almost twenty years, first for the corporation's British subsidiary Vauxhall where he was export manager and then as managing director of General Motors-Holden's (from 1934). During the years in which the Holden car was being developed, Hartnett's relationship with his employer grew strained and in 1947 it broke completely. It was not until 1976 that a reconciliation between Hartnett and GMH was effected by the then managing director, Charles S. ('Chuck') Chapman, and from this time until his death in 1986 much fuss was made of him.

A Storey of talent

John (later Sir John) Storey would not have been a candidate for a photo-graph with Chifley and the Holden but he played a big role during the lead-up years, influencing both Australian government policy and the expansion of GMH. Storey, like his close wartime associate Essington Lewis, did much to create a manufacturing context where the challenge of an Australian car seemed far more achievable. It was Storey who wrote the automotive section of the Scullin government's revised tariffs schedule of 1930, which he himself described as a significant step towards the eventual manufacture of cars in Australia. In 1934 he became director of manufacturing for GMH and was appointed to the board. He then chose the sites for new GMH factories at Fishermans Bend, Melbourne (completed in 1936), and Pagewood, Sydney (completed in 1940), and supervised the refurbishment of the Brisbane and Perth plants. In 1936 he was appointed alternate director to Larry Hartnett on the board of the Commonwealth Aircraft Corporation, when GMH joined Essington Lewis' syndicate to prepare Australia for war. Then in March 1940 he was put in charge of the program to produce (with much assistance from Britain) the Bristol Beaufort fighter for the RAF and RAAF. But Storey fell out with Hartnett in 1940 when Larry refused to release him to accept a senior position on the Aircraft Production Commission for the duration of the war, and Storey resigned from GMH to serve the government.

After the fall of France in June 1940, Britain placed an embargo on the export of war materials, among which were the engines for the Australian-built Beauforts. Storey 'decided to follow a good old Australian policy and give it a go', confounding sceptics who did not believe Australia had the capability to manufacture aircraft engines and thus entire Beauforts. In the process he sub-contracted production of components to more than 600 companies, ensuring a strengthening of the supplier base which would later be critical to the successful manufacture of the Holden.

Sir John's story is one of many which just happens to indicate the depth of talent in GMH management during the 1930s. There were other board members whose influence extended far beyond the automotive industry. John Butters was one. Butters was chairman of the Federal Capital Commission from 1924 to 1929 and insisted Canberra would have 'none of the terrible eyesores which mar so many of our cities'. He was knighted for his efforts. In 1931 he was invited to be a member of the foundation board of GMH. He played a significant role in revisions to the Sydney CBD during the mid 1930s, especially Macquarie Street and Circular Quay. He was chairman of Associated Newspapers, Radio 2UE Sydney, The North Shore Gas Company, Hadfields Steel Works and Hetton Bellbird Collieries. Sir John Butters was president of the Royal Automobile Club of Australia from 1937 to 1949 and then vice-patron until 1969.

Harold Bettle: quiet achiever, team player

It is no surprise that Harold Bettle appears pleased with proceedings on the day of the Holden's launch. But he had faced a tricky start to his Australian job. As Hartnett's successor it had been his uncomfortable task to hand-deliver a letter from the United States, effectively dismissing that maverick tycoon from the top job at Fishermans Bend. Bettle arrived in Australia too late to have much influence on the car itself, a job already done. It seems beyond dispute that Bettle was selected as Hartnett's successor because he was seen as a corporate team player in a way that Hartnett was not.

Bettle, by contrast, does not seem to have displayed any of Hartnett's egotism or solipsism. His speech at the launch of the car barely uses the first person. He defines the significance of the Holden not just in Australian terms but in the context of the General Motors Corporation:

This is an historic and significant occasion—significant insofar as General Motors-Holden's Limited is concerned—because it marks the birth of a new product that will take its place proudly alongside such famous cars as Cadillac, Buick, Oldsmobile, Pontiac, Chevrolet and Vauxhall . . . We undertook this new project fully realizing our responsibilities in establishing an industry that will have a new and lasting influence on the national economy.

That 'we' seems to mean 'we at General Motors Corporation', not just 'we at General Motors-Holden's; there is no hidden 'us' and 'them', which characterised Hartnett's position between 1944 and the end of his career with GM. It was as if Hartnett's primary loyalty was to GMH rather than the broad corporation. But Bettle, like most of his senior colleagues, was a company man first and his involvement with the political process seems to have only been to further the corporation's interests. The Holden is depicted in his speech not so much as the Australian car, but a member of the broader family of General Motors cars; it is, like he, a team player.

Another key figure missing from the photograph is Russ Begg, chief engineer of the Holden. But unlike Hartnett, Begg does appear in other important early images. Begg sat next to Bettle when the GMH chief executive drove the 'first' Holden off the line on 1 October 1948 at a special pre-release function organised for the media and made into a clip for *Movietone News*. Begg, more than any other individual, nurtured the Holden from design to production.

The imprimatur of Sloan, thousands of miles across the ocean

When the Holden was launched, Alfred P. Sloan Jr, who still effectively ran General Motors as chairman, (he had relinquished the presidency in 1937), was not among the guests. Imagine the arch-conservative and patrician Sloan shaking hands with former locomotive-driving, working-class hero, socialist Prime Minister Benjamin Chifley in front of the smiling chromium

And if Sloan's motives for proceeding with Australian car manufacture were entirely different from Chifley's, they nonetheless dovetailed perfectly in a win–win outcome.

face of the 48–215 Holden: what could they have said? Would they have had trouble understanding each other, Sloan with his educated but still Brooklyn-tinged accent, Chifley with his broad Australian accent and insistent local vernacular, as heard in 'She's a beauty'? Would they have discussed the pros and cons of nationalisation? In any case, Sloan would not have been expected to venture down-under for the launch of the Holden. But this is not to detract from the car's importance to General Motors; Sloan had always been a brilliant delegator. Had he even seen the prototypes on trial at Milford? We will never know, and it does not matter. The Holden carried Sloan's imprimatur firmly upon it, as did every product emerging from the GM world between about 1924 and 1956—perhaps not in detail but always in principle. And if Sloan's motives for proceeding with Australian car manufacture were entirely different from Chifley's, they nonetheless dovetailed perfectly in a win–win outcome.

The Australian car was developed in conformity with key parameters established by Sloan, working through his committee system introduced in the 1920s. Its styling was signed off by Harley Earl, who oversaw all General Motors design from 1927 to 1958. Hartnett finally had little say beyond setting the general concept of the car—its size, passenger accommodation, ability to tackle rough roads, and its thrift.

Importantly, it is impossible to imagine Sloan relishing the enforced *cosiness* of the relationship between his Australian subsidiary company and the government that had provided the funding to put the Holden into production. Indeed it was Sloan's misgivings about the Australian political system that forced Hartnett in early 1945 to go outside the corporation and turn to Prime Minister Chifley for help in raising the necessary finance for the Australian Car Program. Chifley's involvement dated back to at least mid 1944, although the unspoken assumption was always that General Motors would finance any program by GMH to manufacture a car in Australia. On 12 July 1944, Chifley wrote to Hartnett: 'I am interested to hear that during your visit to U.S.A. you propose to discuss the possibility of producing complete motor cars in Australia.'

In 1944, when he was minister for postwar reconstruction and not yet prime minister, Chifley's portfolio responsibility loomed large. Many of the skills honed by wartime industrial requirements were in precision engineering and the metal trades. Rapid expansion of labour in these specialist areas during the war would have created the likelihood of high unemployment afterwards. This was probably Chifley's secondary concern in a July 1944 missive to Hartnett.

> *The Government is anxious that Australian needs of such vehicles should be made to the greatest extent possible by Australian production, particularly if this can be associated with a reduction in selling prices to the public. The technical development of Australian industry during the war provides, I believe, an opportunity for a rapid development of the motor industry in Australia . . . and its development can contribute significantly to the employment of Australian workmen who, during the war, have acquired skill and experience in this class of production.*

Note, first, that there is a more relaxed tone here than in the 29 November 1948 speech. The Cold War does not lurk between these lines. Rather, Chifley as federal minister is doing his job of careful planning for the postwar period; reconstruction rather than national survival is the theme. There is no reason to doubt that Hartnett had kept Chifley informed of his plan to convince the General Motors board to approve the manufacture of entire cars in Australia. Hartnett's forthcoming visit to the United States was for this purpose. Just five days before Chifley composed his letter to Hartnett, another key government player had made what might be regarded as the first formal step towards striking a deal between the

Australian government and General Motors-Holden's. On 7 July, John K. Jensen, chairman of the Secondary Industries Commission, wrote to his colleague and friend, Larry Hartnett. In the hectic job of running the ordnance division, Hartnett had been in regular contact with Jensen and the two men had established a strong rapport. This letter may be seen as an invitation to GMH to occupy pole position in the race towards local automotive manufacture.

> *I turn first to you for an answer because it seems to me reasonable that your company, with its heavy investments in Australia, with full knowledge of the motor car trade and with its own technique, would wish to capitalize upon this desire and enter the field of motor car production . . . frankly, the Secondary Industries Commission would appreciate from you a positive statement as to whether or not your Company is interested in the manufacture of the complete car in Australia as an early post-war venture . . .*

Driving through the tyranny of distance: defending Australia

But there was, by 1948, that even more emotional imperative behind the Australian government's rekindled anxiety to grow the automotive industry: defence. As Geoffrey Blainey and other historians have observed, there was a common view that World War III may well have followed shortly after the end of World War II. Where the Great War of 1914–18 had been billed as the 'war to end all wars', its unpredicted successor was viewed more as a major and tragic skirmish leading to a probably brief cessation of hostilities. The outbreak of the Cold War even before the conclusion of hostilities in the Pacific reinforced this belief. The success of the local industry in general, and that of GMH in particular, in making equipment for war use encouraged Curtin and Chifley to push for local car manufacture. After all, in 1939 GMH workers had made Whitney and Pratt aero engines, and they had manufactured 2-pounder, 6-pounder and 25-pounder guns as well as Gray diesel marine engines and a variety of boats. So why not a car? John Storey's work with the Bristol Beaufort fighter provided a brilliant precedent for Australia's ability to free itself from dependence on imports. But it was more the overarching need for advanced secondary industry capability rather than cars in their own right that underwrote this urgency. In government circles there was a conviction that GMH was the best company for the job, its manufacturing effort throughout World War II at the heart of this belief. Hartnett's personal connections could only have helped in the process.

Larry had responded with alacrity to the government's encouragement in 1944. By 1940 he had already formed the view that GMH should proceed as quickly as feasible towards the manufacture of entire cars. On 1 July of that year he wrote to his regional manager Harry Phillips at General Motors Overseas Operations saying that 'GMH want to manufacture a complete car in Australia directly the war tempo enables the project to be satisfactorily handled'.

Just three years earlier he had told a Tariff Board enquiry that 'definitely we do not favour the manufacture of cars in Australia; we prefer the nice conditions that now exist'. Between 1937 and the outbreak of World War II, the debate had already begun to move forward; war accelerated this process for two deeply interconnected reasons. First, war increased the sense of isolation and the need for self-sufficiency and, second, this need fathered a dramatic increase in industrial capacity. In April 1935 Hartnett had said that the time was near when 'the design of motor cars will not allow the independent manufacture of a body to be fitted to a chassis', an observation reflecting concern about the longer term future of his motor body building business. His unspoken concern was that GMH could only survive in its current guise by making entire cars.

Shortly afterwards, Hartnett put forward a proposal to the Australian government and to GM via Jim Mooney that GMH should 'part manufacture' the Olympia in Australia in exchange for exports of wool to Germany. Interestingly, the Australian government's rejection of Hartnett's proposal included reference to the Olympia's small size.

By August 1937 Hartnett was already considering the possibility of managing an independent Australian car manufacturing company. Perhaps his uncomfortable chat in mid 1936 with Sloan about the Australian aviation industry, mentioned earlier, and his sense of being out of favour with the General Motors president, encouraged Hartnett to consider an alternative career.

Chifley's letter of 12 July 1944 uses Hartnett's imminent visit to the United States as a 'handle' on which to hang his implicit invitation to GMH to advance a proposal for the manufacture of a car in Australia. Hartnett was already marshalling his arguments to put to Sloan and the General Motors board as to why GMH should take on this project. Two days after Chifley wrote to Hartnett, the former Labor prime minister, J.H. Scullin, a long-time advocate of an Australian car, put pen to paper under the letter-head of the Federal Parliamentary Members' Rooms in Melbourne:

> *As you are probably aware, it is the policy of the Commonwealth Government of the day, to foster secondary industry in Australia, whenever practical and economical, and the automotive industry is certainly one which should be developed to its maximum in this country. The fact that we are already manufacturing most of the car in Australia suggests that we should have no difficulty in producing a motor vehicle in its entirety.*

Hartnett hatches plan B

The letters from Jensen, Chifley and Scullin gave Hartnett another strand to ply if necessary, namely that the Australian government was hell-bent on getting its car regardless of whether or not General Motors came to the party. There was also surely an implicit threat: if the GM board did not back Hartnett, then he was ideally placed to negotiate his own separate deal with the government. There seems to be abundant evidence that he would have done so, had he been denied by the board. He also knew there would be an opening for him because his mate, John Jensen, had written to him on 7 July 1944:

How is this car to be obtained? . . .

. . . I turn first to you for [sic] answer . . . It is for you to decide, but surely manufacturers in other spheres will seize the opportunity if the present established industry does not. If industry does not respond then I suggest the Government may find it necessary to take some other action to consummate this Australian desire.

While making no mention of Hartnett in *My Years with General Motors*, Sloan seems to have been alert at least to the possibility that if General Motors didn't manufacture cars in Australia, some other company would. 'The alternative to manufacturing would doubtless be a declining share in a protected market', which was indeed the fate that greeted Ford! Frederic A. Donner, chief executive officer of General Motors during the 1950s, made the same point in his 'The World-wide Industrial Enterprise' lecture: '. . . the chances were that if we did not accept the challenge, some other manufacturer would.'

Had General Motors not agreed to the Australian car and the government then jumped into partnership with an ex-GM Hartnett (with all his accumulated intellectual property and hands-on experience), this would have posed an immediate and serious threat to General Motors' continuing dominance of the Australian market. The tone of Hartnett's discussion of his mission to 'persuade' his bosses suggests he relished the challenge. But, equally, he expressed some doubt about his chance of success. It is extremely difficult to believe that Hartnett was aware that Sloan, that 'crusty old Tory', had already, if reluctantly, approved the idea in principle. Nowhere in his memoirs does he leave such a possibility open and he even begins his small section on the Holden with the observation that, in view of how much money General Motors had made out of the Holden, it was ironic that the corporation had been strongly against the proposal in the

Had General Motors not agreed to the Australian car and the government then jumped into partnership with an ex-GM Hartnett (with all his accumulated intellectual property and hands-on experience), this would have threatened General Motors' continuing dominance of the Australian market.

first place. There is a certain political—or, more specifically, corporate—naivety evident in Hartnett's memoirs. He does not attempt to locate Australia within General Motors' rapidly expanding international operations. He appears to be oblivious to Sloan's master-minding of GM's international operations from the early 1920s through to the post-World War II era. Nor does he pay attention to the outstanding credentials of Russell Begg and the other members of the engineering team. Narcissism is always a risk in auto-biography; Hartnett gazes more deeply into the pool than most, and on Rich's evidence had always done so. (If he imagined Sloan looking over his shoulder, it was little more than a niggling distraction; for Hartnett, the Australian car was *his* baby, to be born if necessary out of corporate wedlock.)

A meeting of General Motors' Overseas Policy Group in Sloan's New York office on 15 June 1939 noted that:

[the] Corporation's substantial investment in Australia . . . and dominating market position and good-will, make it most desirable to discover some common ground on which the objectives of the Australian Government can be attained . . . and the Corporation's interest be preserved.

Eight days later Sloan acknowledged that General Motors should 'adjust our course accordingly' in response to the Australian government's determination to achieve 'self-containment [in] motor car production'. By June 1943 this position had been formalised.

General Motors does not believe that the basic conditions required to support complete manufacture of cars and trucks exist, or will be found to exist for some time, in any countries abroad which did not already have such manufacture before the war. An exception to the above is Australia, where a strongly supported program of automotive manufacture had made considerable progress prior to 1940.

Sloan lays down the rules to 'Mr Hartnett'

Sloan's innate political conservatism and his bold multinational philosophy may seem to have been at odds but actually they were not. It is easy to see how someone schooled in the private enterprise, free market system and so focused on maximising profits and expanding the General Motors empire would object to the idea of a 'socialist sort of place', as Hartnett quotes him as describing Australia. But it is equally easy to see why Sloan's longer term plans for General Motors would constitute his primary motive for endorsing the Hartnett program. It would probably have suited the GM board better had a Labor government not been in power in Australia, but Sloan clearly believed that, if the right controls could be instituted, the fact that the Australian government of the day might not have been to General Motors' corporate liking need not hinder the process, provided Hartnett could be kept under control. He wrote to Jim Mooney along these lines even before Hartnett and his team had begun their return journey after the November 1944 board meeting where they had given the final presentation of the Australian case:

. . . this approval on the part of the Corporation [of the Australian car manufacturing program] is predicated upon the general presentation of the problem which Mr. Hartnett and your organization have made. Frankly, I am always suspicious and skeptical when I see any Government approaching the area normally occupied by private industry. It is clear to me that there are possibilities, perhaps even probabilities, of something of this kind in Australia. While Mr. Hartnett has given us the impression that free enterprise will prevail, I am not so certain that this is necessarily

so. Australia has already seen more experiments with the economy from this standpoint, than many other countries.

What I am saying, perhaps not very clearly, or definitely, is, that this proposal is being approved on the basis of our being able to operate within the scope of the free enterprise system and in order to be sure that this is thoroughly understood, I think it would be as well to lay down the rules very definitely to Mr. Hartnett before he leaves.

Hartnett, however, tells a ripping yarn without being too distracted by the facts. To read *Big Wheels and Little Wheels* and any number of histories of the Holden or the Australian automotive industry that have been written subsequently, you would be led to believe that all the credit for the GM board's decision should go to Hartnett. And so Larry leaves Detroit with official blessing to proceed with the Australian car project, but without seeming to have understood that Australia was just another country within General Motors' multinational plan. By 1943 when the Overseas Policy Group singled out Australia as a potential venue for car manufacture, Hartnett's personal star was already waning in the GM firmament. Sloan probably enjoyed the opportunity to make Hartnett work hard to present his case. It is likely that he had decided not to make anything easy for him.

The GMH proposal

The Curtin Labor government—via the Customs Department—had by this stage already issued its invitation to the major automotive companies in Australia and many other industrial concerns to submit a proposal to manufacture a car. About 80 letters were dispatched on 5 October. It seems probable that only Larry Hartnett had been approached directly before the issue of this invitation. Regardless of that, it is certain that GMH was the first company to respond with a formal proposal, which was submitted on 5 January 1945 and said, among other things:

We would undertake to manufacture in Australia a five-seater sedan car and related utility which would be specifically designed for the economic and operating conditions of Australia.

Such design is not predicated on any type previously in production in any country but will be of a specification to expressly cater for the Australian requirements.

The objective of General Motors-Holden's Limited is to manufacture Australian motor vehicles in the low price group to sell competitively with imported vehicles without subsidy and without increase in the customs tariff rate prevailing in 1939.

Whereas there have been available to Australian buyers in the past only chasses [sic] designed to meet the economic and operating conditions applying to such countries as Canada, England and the United States, by specially designing a car for Australia as we propose to do, the product will better fill the needs of the country.

For something as significant as an automotive manufacturing industry to be introduced to a country, there needs to be a certain concord between private enterprise and political willingness. The political willingness was there in spades and, even though Prime Minister Curtin promised that it was 'the Government's intention to treat uniformly all firms submitting plans for the manufacture of motor cars', the GMH proposal was accepted before some of the others had been submitted. In *War Economy 1942–1945*, co-authors Butlin and Schedvin note that 'important decisions were taken without due process'.

Was the government's acceptance of GMH's proposal premature? Perhaps. Were all proposals treated uniformly? Almost certainly not. But GMH was the right choice because of its demonstrated technical capacity, its dominant pre-war market share, its financial strength and access to 'advanced technical knowledge', as well as Hartnett's own obvious capacity for innovation, his significant contribution to the munitions industry, and the fact that senior government figures had already worked closely with him during the war.

Just how urgent this whole issue was for the Australian government is made clear in two letters. The first was from Chifley as minister for post-war reconstruction on 22 January 1945, in which he wrote: 'I had hoped it would be possible for the Government to let you have a full reply at an early date, but there are still one or two matters on which I desire clarification.' The second was from Prime Minister John Curtin to Larry Hartnett on 3 February, with less than a month having passed since the proposal had been submitted:

Your letter of 5th January, 1945, relative to the establishment and development of the motor car manufacturing industry in Australia, addressed to the Chairman of the Secondary Industries Commission [J.J. Dedman], has been placed before me by the Minister for Post-War Reconstruction. It is a communication of very great importance in the development of secondary industry in Australia, and it is with due appreciation that I have read it. It is to be regarded too as a valuable contributor to the future defence of Australia. Likewise it is a practical token, after no doubt an exhaustive survey by disinterested authorities, of confidence in the future and stability of Australia.

A vehicle with war on its agenda

As late as mid 1945, there was still confusion as to what *type* of car GMH would deliver. On 19 June, the Melbourne *Herald* published a letter from John Dedman, who had taken over Chifley's portfolio of post-war reconstruction, saying that the government's 'approach to the Australian car had been from the viewpoint of having in Australia a type of production suitable for defence needs should Australia again be involved in war'.

With its bold, chromium-plated grille and shiny metallic paintwork, the production Holden hardly looked like a vehicle developed with military operations in mind; indeed, it is incongruous to imagine the Chifley/48–215 photograph with the caption: 'A type of production car suitable for wartime use.' So it was perhaps just as well that no such image was around in June 1945. By this time Hartnett was deeply enmeshed in arguments with some of his American colleagues about the styling of the forthcoming car. He was insisting that it should not be 'gaudy or flashy'.

When he read the *Herald* story, an alarm bell sounded; Hartnett wanted a car of restrained style, but he was not focused on military requirements. He wrote to Dedman the next day:

> . . . *I particularly note your 'approach to the Australian car had been from the viewpoint of having in Australia a type of production suitable for defence needs should Australia again be involved in war'. I should be pleased if you would amplify this point for the guidance of my Company . . . [we] have, in the main been directed to applying ourselves to producing a low-priced passenger car so that the largest section of the buying public could afford to purchase.*
>
> *Contained within our specification and engineering design, there are already many features and assemblies which we know from experience are particularly applicable to needs of war; however, we could give fuller cognizance to these things if the requirements of the Services were made known to us at this stage.*
>
> *May I strongly commend to you that the actual product being produced in times of peace invariably has relatively little value compared with having resources, skill and qualified men in the country, who, at short notice, can design and engineer for the specific needs when war is imminent or declared. Furthermore, the skill and facilities to design and produce tools within the country at short notice, together with the manufacturing equipment makes the total facility of the greatest value for many needs of war.*

To the GMH boss it must have seemed that Dedman was striding down the garden path hand in hand with the military pixies. Hartnett was focused primarily on matching supply and demand in a civilian, consumer market, with any military applications a welcome side benefit. Furthermore, he probably believed he had already explained himself clearly in the formal proposal.

But this difference further illuminates the strong sense within government ranks during the 1944–45 period that a locally manufactured car was necessary not just to Australia's economic prosperity but to national defence. Behind Dedman's concern was the terrifying tyranny of distance that had forced the country to develop greater self-sufficiency during both World Wars. During the First, the motor body building industry burgeoned. During the Second, factories in which cars had been assembled were given over to the production of armaments, marine and aero engines, airframe assemblies, small marine craft and, as we have seen, even advanced fighter planes.

Cars and trucks were in great demand by 1945, partly because the worldwide industry had essentially been diverted from six years of production. General Motors' research showed that in 1944 the average age of cars in Australia was 14.2 years. General Motors-Holden's was not the only automotive company to throw its industrial weight into the war effort, but its effort was almost certainly larger than any other company's, including that of Geelong-based Ford. Additionally, GMH's principal, Hartnett, with bright feathers in his government hat, had been instrumental in promoting new technical expertise in Australian industry. By July 1944, this confident and self-assured technocrat was in a bullish mood about what he could do with his company for the good of Australian industry and his adopted country.

The resentment of rationing

The federal government would continue to follow a policy of vigilant austerity into peacetime. Even moving beyond John Dedman's June 1945 concerns, there remained an implicit contradiction between the heavily chromed grille of the 1948 Holden car and the prevailing economic and social mood of that year. After eight years of petrol rationing, Australian voters were poised to make this a major issue in the imminent federal election.

Paradoxically, the Labor government, which did much to facilitate the process that led to the reality of the Holden car, was intractably on the other side of this political argument. A famous *Bulletin* cartoon, published on 30 November 1949 (one year and one day after the Holden launch), showed Prime Minister Chifley at the wheel of a '1921 Socialisation Mark II' model car, while Bob Menzies steps out of a brand new Holden to seduce a female voter to move from Chifley's car into his, which she does with a tellingly backward glance. Many observers attributed Labor's 1949 election loss largely to this single issue, while few appear to have observed the rich irony involved. Chifley paved the road for the Holden; Menzies merely drove it.

To juxtapose this cartoon with the Chifley/ Holden photograph is to begin to unpack some of the strange history which surrounds the first Holden. Significantly, one of the Menzies government's first acts was to end petrol rationing.

Bob Menzies steps out of a brand new Holden to seduce a female voter to move from Chifley's car into his, which she does with a tellingly backward glance.

Only GMH had the right idea

As for the unsuccessful proposals from Ford, Chrysler, Nuffield (makers of Morris cars) and others, they provide implicit support for the government's choice. I have suggested a disjunction between the Holden's bold chromium-plated 'face' and the Labor government's continuing preoccupation with austerity in the early postwar years. Both Ford and Chrysler proposed to build large cars and Ford's would have been powered by a V8 engine—in a time of petrol rationing. Road tests of Ford V8 models of the era show they used almost twice as much precious petrol as did the Holden. Had the Australian car been a big Ford powered by a V8 engine, the government's petrol rationing policy would have seemed even more out of keeping with the times as well as making government support of a private enterprise proposal to manufacture such a car appear incongruous at the least.

In the case of Nuffield, the declining sales of English cars throughout the 1950s and into the 1960s suggests that whatever type of Morris Lord Nuffield had proposed to sell here would hardly have generated the ferocious enthusiasm that met the Holden. Nuffield himself had shown a disinclination for Australian manufacture. His company merged with Austin in 1952 to create the British Motor Corporation, but the combined model line-up of Austin, Morris, Wolseley, MG and Riley barely dented demand for the Holden; as will be seen later, these cars were simply unsuitable for Australia's motoring conditions—or, rather, were a great deal less suitable than was the Holden.

Difficult to quantify, but evident nonetheless, was a shift in cultural allegiance that followed the political reorientation towards the United States announced by Curtin in 1942. The fact that GMH was US owned was largely perceived as a good thing in 1948, with the war in the Pacific such a recent memory. At the launch of the Holden, Prime Minister Chifley spoke of the war and of Australia's need to be self-sufficient in the context of the new alliance with the United States:

> *The project which you have here today is only, as Mr Hollway and Mr Bettle have said, another link in that relationship. But it has become necessary because, after all, although one must fight for peace, one must always keep one's gun powder dry. Therefore, it becomes an essential thing, as it was proved to us with double emphasis in the last war, that when we were here on this perimeter of the Pacific, needing things badly, in fact in hundreds of cases, and thousands of cases, we had to improvise for the things that are necessary for our own protection, and to render that help which our allies sought, including the United States, who joined with us in this Pacific fight.*

Here are echoes of the theme espoused by Curtin in his letter to Hartnett more than three and a half years earlier and before the conclusion of hostilities in the Pacific, but by this time the tone is more intense, reflecting the escalation of the Cold War. The impact of World War II was universal and the fear of an even more devastating conflict informed major political decisions. Historians of the Australian car have been insufficiently conscious of the Chifley government's motivation in bonding with GMH to bring the Australian car manufacturing program into being. This decision was more about military preparedness and industrial capacity than it was about either employment or individual mobility. Perhaps the excellence of the product itself and Australian national pride has obscured the darker issue. Consciously or unconsciously, Chifley and his colleagues must have learnt from the Third Reich: without Hitler's massive rearmament program, Germany simply could not have initiated World War II in 1939. And, finally, it was the world's first superpower, the United States of America, which brought the Pacific War to its terrible close. It looked like the briefest of breaks in conflict, that it was to be a case of Germany and Japan first, then Russia in World War III. The Cold War was reaching its zenith by the time Chifley unveiled the Holden car with a speech where World War III loomed darkly over the car he called 'a beauty'.

'A beauty', as Chifley quipped, she may have been, but the Holden's glamour was secondary in Chifley's thinking to her utility. So the government persisted with its spirit of austerity despite Australians' desire to put wartime memories behind them and build a comfortable future with a house in the suburbs, a car (preferably a Holden) in the driveway, and at least two healthy children. But despite a continuing dread of war, the prime minister was able to smile for the camera on 29 November 1948.

Chapter 8

'An absolute confounding of the croakers'

You and your organisation should be feeling very proud of your great achievement. I was thinking on Monday of the initial stages, the almost impossible task you had set yourselves, the air, nevertheless, of quiet confidence amidst a good deal of pessimism (I saw more probably of the latter than you did) and although it seems no time since the commencement of operations,

to-day [sic] the Holden car is on the road, acclaimed on all sides as a first class job; a surprise to a great many people and an absolute confounding of the croakers.

—J.K. Jensen, Chairman, Secondary Industries Commission, to
H.E. Bettle, Managing Director, GMH, 2 December 1948

The immediate success of the Holden is an historical given, with demand exceeding supply for more than two years, but exactly why this US-designed General Motors product was so enthusiastically received invites a closer look. Specialist early-model Holden historian Don Loffler has done a first-class job of detailing public response then and now. In *She's A Beauty!* he shows that, on a range of criteria, the 48–215 and FJ Holdens were superior to other mainstream cars available in Australia at the time. How well though did the utilitarian car developed for Australia compare with the finest immediate postwar designs from Europe and the United States? And why, indeed, would anyone choose to pay double the Holden's price for an English Jaguar or an American Buick? From that dusty black 1938 prototype, General Motors gave Australia its family car answer years before others had even framed the question. But not only did the Holden satisfy as much as half of the total postwar Australian market, it also set a new international benchmark for mainstream family sedans. In this chapter we will see how enthusiastically the leading English motoring magazines received the Holden, and how superior its overall specification was to most contemporaneous vehicles, even some that were twice the price. At the end of the 1940s and well into the fifties, regardless of price, the Holden was unquestionably the best all-rounder on local soil; the Holden was to Australian motoring what Keith Miller was to Australian cricket.

The Holden was to Australian motoring what Keith Miller was to Australian cricket.

Before World War II the best-selling car in Australia had been the Chevrolet, with Ford in second position. From October 1929 until July 1933 a publication called *The Motor Trade Journal* listed new car registration figures. The November 1929 issues reported Chevrolet monthly sales (probably for September 1929) of 858 with Ford on 580 and the Overland Whippet on 375. The top-selling British car, well down the rankings, was Austin with 251 units. The Depression brought a collapse of the market, but by the time *The Motor Trade Journal* produced its last issue the recovery was in process. Chevrolet and Ford continued to be the top-selling cars, usually in that order, until the outbreak of World War II. During the war vehicles were produced only for defence purposes and it took at least two years from the cessation of fighting for vehicles to begin emerging in any significant numbers from the world's automotive factories. Whatever cars remained in service from the pre-war era came into the 'old bomb' category by 1948. New American models became prohibitively expensive due to US currency limitations in Australia, and the Chevrolet ascended from mainstream to luxury status. The same thing happened to the Ford V8, but at least General Motors-Holden's knew it had precisely the machine to fill the gap left by postwar economic rearrangement. In this sense, the Holden may be regarded as a replacement for the Chevrolet.

The delay of retail sales of the Holden until February 1949 was an unintended marketing triumph. Anticipation built, and then came the waiting list! Many people were keen to be the first in their street with a Holden. Some cars had cloth upholstery and some had leather, and the distribution appeared random. But there were no model names in the first years, no Standard or Special, just the Holden. Years later, the public retrospectively dubbed this first model (coded 48–215) the 'FX'. Fittingly, BHP's managing director, Essington Lewis, was the first retail customer in Australia to receive one. It was delivered on 24 February 1949. Given Lewis's major role in bringing the Holden to market, his enthusiasm was both understandable and indicative. Thousands of others within the supplier industry and GMH itself felt a similar sense of identification with the new Australian car, and this in itself was another factor driving the huge demand. To use much newer vernacular, to own a Holden represented the height of cool. Colonel Harley Tarrant, who had produced Australia's first petrol-powered car in 1897, succumbed to the excitement and ordered one for himself: it had been a half-century's wait between Tarrant and Holden. In 1953 author Frank Clune bought a brand new Holden in which to drive around Australia. 'I had no hesitation', he said, 'in deciding to use a Holden car for this motor-marathon'. Later that year the Holden would be the choice of many entrants in a more competitive version of Frank Clune's adventure, the Redex Round Australia trial.

By the time the first Redex event was run, there was no questioning the Holden's dominance of the market, even if supply had long since met demand, which just about everyone had underestimated in 1948–49. In the March 1949 edition of GMH's in-house magazine, *Pointers*, general sales manager Harry Cavanaugh said that the company planned to produce 20,000 Holdens during that year—this compared with 8853 Chevrolets and 7272 Ford V8s in 1938. While it was part of Cavanaugh's job to make confident sales predictions, it is difficult to believe that neither he nor any of his fellow executives nursed private doubts. After all, the Holden was an unknown product and significantly smaller in size than the pre-war Chevs and Fords that Australian buyers had favoured. Some dealers were initially worried that the car was *too* small.

In fact the Holden was the right car at the perfect time, a new and happy 'medium'. Much smaller than the Chevrolet, it was similar in size to a number of postwar British vehicles including the larger models of Vauxhall, which was GMH's top-selling brand with 4340 cars sold in Australia in the second half of 1948 compared with 2308 (supply-constrained) Chevrolets. By the end of 1948 it could be said that the Holden had supplanted the Chevrolet as the 'aspirational' car for Australian buyers, and by 1950 the price of the larger American car further reduced its appeal.

The shift in buyer choice towards more economical vehicles was encouraged in part by government policy from 1930 which applied lower tariffs to imports from countries within the British Empire, with the lowest rate of all (40 per cent) applying to British cars; buying British was seen as patriotic. A GMH internal report of May 1940 noted the 'definite increase in the share taken by English cars, and a corresponding decrease in the share commanded by American cars'. In 1935 the English share was 21.8 per cent compared with 78.2 per cent for US/Canadian cars, but by 1939 English vehicles held 43.8 per cent and North American models accounted for 56.2 per cent. This was a massive swing which Hartnett was right to identify as a trend rather than an aberration. A lower purchase price and love of the Mother Country were well and good, but, as Hartnett was keenly aware, Australians preferred the American cars to their more modest British counterparts.

What a blessing, then, that the Holden's driving characteristics and general feel were American rather than British. Strong engine torque combined with tall gearing to provide the kind of long-legged effortlessness typical of American models, most of which used engines of around 4.0 litres. The much lighter Holden entailed no compromise in performance, while delivering vastly superior fuel economy and comparable space for occupants and their luggage. All three factors were largely consequences of its more modern design, particularly the unitary construction, which Holden advertising termed 'Aerobilt'—it was built rite, if not spelled right.

Furthermore, the Australian car was sold through the same dealer network, which meant that existing GMH customers could merely shift their choice from Chevrolet to Holden without having to sever a long-term business relationship, and this was especially important in rural areas. If you regularly sit near your Chevrolet dealer in church, for example, you don't want to have to go elsewhere to buy a car. So there can be no doubt that one contributing factor in the surging demand for the new car was its GMH provenance. Regarding size, there is little evidence the Holden was seen as 'small' by Australian buyers, despite being empirically small by American standards. I still find it strange to hear the Holden described as 'small' or 'little': here, in the late 1940s, a Morris Minor was 'small' and a Chevrolet was 'big'. In embodying the happy medium, the Holden made most other cars look either small or big. Its one-size-fits-all nature created a new and enduring Australian norm.

To describe Australia as car-starved when the Holden made its debut in November 1948 is to overdose on understatement. Vehicles of any kind were in short supply, which explains why so many uninspired ones, especially of English origin, fared well. In the year of the Holden's debut, British cars accounted for 72.7 per cent of the market, compared with just 14 per cent in 1928. It was much the same in the United States and worse in Britain, where postwar austerity dictated an 'export or perish' policy. The 1.2-litre Austin A40 Devon made its debut in 1947. Despite the 1942 looks and modest performance the Devon, barely available on its home market, sold well both in the United States and Australia, until the real thing, as it were, came along. For US buyers that was the 1949 Ford or Chevrolet with faired-in guards and generally low-slung lines. Here the real thing was, instantaneously and in a love-at-first-sight kind of way, the Holden. By 1951 the little Austin had suffered a permanent fall from buyers' grace, becoming Devon sausage meat to the Holden's hefty rump steak. Another stalwart of the immediate pre-Holden years and, to be fair, a strong seller for some years afterwards, was the bulbous and upright Standard Vanguard, a vehicle whose design was inspired by the 1942 Plymouth. The automotive historian Michael Sedgwick used the term 'Vanguarditis' to cover this type of British and European scaling down of early 1940s US styling. Other culprits included the Devon and the 1950 Fiat 1400. Alongside any of these, the Holden's styling was almost graceful.

By 1951 the little Austin had suffered a permanent fall from buyers' grace, becoming Devon sausage meat to the Holden's hefty rump steak.

In preparing their postwar models, British manufacturers faced a dilemma. Should they rework pre-war themes, dating back to 1939, while they worked on the next generation? Or should they look to the United States, where automotive design had continued until Pearl Harbor? Rover was one company that reworked its 1930s model as a stopgap and then used the 1947 Studebaker as inspiration for its all-new Rover 75. By contrast, Austin and Standard looked to the early 1940s American cars with the result that their offerings already looked old when they were new in 1947–48, by which time the 'coming or going' Studebaker was cruising the streets.

So Australian new car buyers accepted the English offerings because the wait for a Holden was prohibitively long. Most of these were under-powered four-cylinder models which had never been engineered with Australia's road conditions on their agenda—quite a paradox, given the British government's policy of meeting export demand first. There had been some negative consequences for participants in the late 1930s trend to smaller vehicles. Hartnett and his colleagues knew in 1940 that the English cars were less durable than American models. They may have served adequately in English lanes and even in the countryside where motorways were unknown, the topography was sometimes demanding, the roads clogged with heavy vehicles, and where typical cruising speeds were in the order of 40 to 45 miles per hour (64–72 km/h), but they were challenged in Australia. Even some very high quality cars coped poorly. Great distances between capital cities, higher temperatures and appallingly corrugated country roads applied an Australian blowtorch to the belly of British automotive engineering. A retired Holden executive, Marcus McInnes, who joined the company in the 1950s and drove Holdens success-fully in rallies, says:

> In those days there were no dual lane roads outside the cities and few within. The Hume had steep hills on which the lower-powered cars and trucks slowed to crawling pace. When I was in national service near Seymour in 1956/7/8 it took over two and a half hours in favourable conditions to drive from Melbourne to Seymour a distance of only 60 miles. In NSW conditions were worse, between Gundagai and Jugiong there were one-lane bridges, very winding roads, steep hills and pavement in many places was broken up and barely two lanes wide. Well into the '60s my interstate truck driver neighbour only drove half way to Sydney before stopping overnight to return next day in a different truck.

In these sort of conditions good acceleration for overtaking and rugged suspension were critical. No other family sedan matched the Holden on both these attributes.

With no new cars available for the better part of a decade, this poor durability was further underlined: many of the surviving 'old bombs' were British. Even Ford Australia, after a quarter of a century of assembling cars in Geelong, experienced reliability and longevity issues heading into the 1950s. The English Ford Pilot and Consul/Zephyr and the American Custom V8 all developed rapid wear problems when used on Australian country roads. Max Gransden, who was Ford Australia's director of sales and marketing through much of the 1970s and 1980s, explains how cars that worked well in other markets did not necessarily cope here in the early postwar years: 'If something was wrong we would have to go back to the source. But they would say, "Well, we haven't got that problem here", and they didn't because the cars they were building did not have to take the torture of our rough Australian roads.'

> Great distances between capital cities, higher temperatures and appallingly corrugated country roads applied an Australian blowtorch to the belly of British engineering.

While neither the English nor American cars were engineered specifically for this country, the latter were regarded as more suitable, which in large part explains the continuing (if reduced) dominance of Chevrolet and Ford in the pre-war era. As Hartnett understood, the trend towards the smaller British models from the mid 1930s was driven by thrift rather than desire. In 1948 the Holden blended Austin thrift (when driven at comparable speeds rather than to its far higher limits) with the allure of postwar high performance and style, plus the singular credential of having been specifically engineered to suit Australian conditions.

Worth the wait!

When retail sales of the Holden began, the waiting list was quoted at two years and by the end of 1949 at least one rural dealer was threatening an unfeasible seven. The factory was simply not geared up for the rush. An exacerbating, if short-lived, factor was the national coal strike that ran from 27 June to 15 August, seriously disrupting Holden's production tallies just as capacity was beginning to improve significantly. The monthly numbers clearly show the impact of this strike. In January GMH made 387 Holdens but had ramped this up to 840 in June. Just 452 emerged in strike-bound August, but September brought a leap in production to 1100, although this rate was still well short of Cavanaugh's forecast. For August 1950 the tally was 2204 and by the end of that year sales of 19,196 brought the Holden into third place behind Austin (24,528) and Ford (23,883). Some eager buyers were prepared to pay a premium of 50 per cent just to cut the waiting time. This is despite the fact that Harold Bettle himself said that he thought 'the price had been set at about the upper limit'. It looked as if many people were not in the market for a *car* but only for a *Holden*. Bettle was probably being conservative. As one newspaper pointed out in its road test, an English car of comparable power would probably have cost £1000, and certainly many with similar performance to the Holden cost more than twice its £734. As for the drab and dated Devon, its price was £705.

It looked as if many people were not in the market for a *car* but only for a *Holden*.

Many dealers were literally cashing in on buyers' enthusiasm, a phenomenon perfected in the United States and doubtless well practised in Britain. Stories abound. As noted by Ed Cray in *Chrome Colossus*: 'A gray and black market flourished. . . . Dealers resorted to a variety of cunning ploys to circumvent the rules . . . one veteran paid the ceiling price for his new car, as well as $300 for the cat asleep on the front seat.' Alfred Sloan, who kept his hands firmly on the steering wheel of General Motors until December 1946 (wisely reluctant, it seems, to trust any successor to keep the corporate car on the right road), had correctly predicted the enormity of postwar demand, but even he may have been surprised to learn that 'as late as May 1948, dealers were scoring $700 above list price for a

Chevrolet, $500 for Pontiacs and Dodges'. Sloan had understood that cars would be snapped up wherever in the western world they could be supplied. This was one reason why approval of the Australian car program came so easily.

But not even the prescient Sloan in the United States nor Harold Bettle on location in Australia had completely understood the extent of pent-up postwar demand. In some respects this hunger was for any new car, but there were significant differences between the US and Australian situations. Timing for the Holden launch was to a tee: all new cars were in short supply, memories of World War II and its associated privations were fresh, and patriotism was probably at some kind of zenith, although this is difficult to quantify. 'Australia's Own Car' drew ravenous consumers as if all Christmas dinners had come at once. Petrol was rationed until February 1950; cars may as well have been too!

The black market for the Holden began even before retail deliveries. People would sell their place in the queue at a profit. This passion was evidently about much more than the car itself. If in the United States owner-ship of the latest car, in compliance with the Sloan-initiated annual model change, was a sign of having achieved a certain status, the Holden phenom-enon in Australia was surely about participation in a national coming of industrial age. The Holden was symbolic of the increasing independence of a country finally emerging from the shadow of British colonialism. Having ridden on the sheep's back, Australia could now promenade in its own car towards a proud new postwar identity. Besides, from January 1951 the sheep could be carried in the 50–2106 utility version of the Holden, a vehicle that became even more dominant in its market sector than the sedan.

The short supply of the larger American cars further fanned desire for the Holden. Call it the Six-Cylinder Factor, if you like. Doubtless some buyers would have preferred a Chevrolet but chose to wait less time for a Holden, which drew from the same gene pool; General Motors had the biggest and most widespread dealership base of any manufacturer and there was considerable long-term brand loyalty on which to draw, the Chevrolet having been Australia's favourite car since the late 1920s. Don Loffler's uncle Ron Schulz was one of those willing to settle for a Holden in lieu of a Chev. In 1947 his local dealer had been allocated just one sedan for the entire year and Ron missed out on it. At least he got the solitary Chevrolet truck. Loffler writes:

> *When the Holden came onto the market and was an instant success in 1949, Ron decided to order one on the understanding that he would take whichever came first, the Chevrolet or the Holden. No delivery date was promised and the months went by without any news. While he was at the Royal Adelaide Show in September 1951, where he showed his cattle, he met the General Motors-Holden's regional sales manager, Alwin Schulz, who told him he would be pleased to know his Chevrolet had just been sent up to Kapunda.*

So the wait for the Chevrolet faced by a regular customer was some four years, but after two years on the Holden waiting list there was still no indication that delivery was imminent. As it happened, Ron Schulz's dealer actually sold the Chevrolet to someone else, so he approached the local Chrysler/Standard dealer. At this time there were three closely related American models sold by Chrysler dealers—Plymouth, Dodge and De Soto—and Standard dealers were selling plenty of Vanguards in the late 1940s, though not to Loffler's uncle:

> *Ardie [Fahlbusch] was delighted to have an order from Ron, but it had to be on the understanding that he would take a Plymouth, Dodge or De Soto, whichever came first, and then only if the car came before a Chevrolet or a Holden. He would not take an English Vanguard, however, under any circumstances.*

In the wash-up, patient Uncle Ron eventually got a 1952 Chevrolet, but his preferences were interesting—big General Motors car first, smaller General Motors car second, other large American third, Standard Vanguard never. GMH used full-page advertisements to tell prospective customers that

'Holden Is Worth Waiting for'. The major thrust was the car's exceptional fuel economy as testified by owners.

The 'Australia's Own Car' rhetoric notwithstanding, buyers (and especially, one imagines, those whose hearts were set on a bigger American car) would not have queued for years had the Holden itself not been well received by commentators and had they themselves not been satisfied when they tested it. As noted by Frank Clune:

> Sentiment would not enter into the argument, if the quality of an Australian-made article were inferior. But when anything made in Australia is as good as, or better than, imported articles at competitive prices, no Australian buyer could hesitate to support an industry which creates employment and prosperity in Australia.

Even some of the road testers combined a practical assessment of the Holden's merits with a generous dose of patriotism, one tester stating that: 'If durability matches performance—and the past record and two years' road trials of the test cars suggest that it will—the car should prove a credit to Australia's industrial skill.' In a sense, what was being sold by GMH and promoted here by this unnamed writer was not just a worthy car but also participation in Australia's increasing industrial maturity. While eager American consumers sped into the 1950s aboard flashy looking new cars with 'straight-through' mudguards and generous helpings of chrome, Australians were just proud the Holden was locally made. Externally, only the elaborate and heavily-chromed grille, reminiscent of the GMH-built Buick of the time, was suggestive of postwar American styling trends and implied the presence of a powerful engine.

'Unbelievable' performance for the 1940s

The Holden's performance was widely regarded as astonishingly good, even 'unbelievable'. For 21st-century motorists this might require some explaining. Any late model car feels brisk enough in everyday use and will climb the majority of highway hills without the need to change down a gear, not that the majority of drivers need to think about gear-changing at all these days. (A late 1930s Hillman ad ran: 'How does Hillman go up a hill, man?' 'Over the top in top, Pop.' A friend of mine had a 1954 model when I owned an FJ Holden of the same age. My car would *accelerate* up a certain hill in top gear, while his struggled to hold a constant speed in the third of its four ratios.) A typical early postwar car—let's say the Austin A40 Devon, Australia's best-selling model in 1949—took about three seconds to struggle to 15 kilometres per hour in first gear and another three to get to 30 in second. Accelerating flat out from rest to 80 kilometres per hour was the noisy work of 22 seconds. What a contrast the Holden provided, zipping to 30 in first gear, then requiring just a single gearchange to reach 80 in just over half the time taken by the Austin. Or if you drove it hard for 22 seconds from rest as per the A40 your road speed would already be approaching 100 kilometres per hour. Try comparing a new Toyota Camry with a Porsche 911 and you'll have the idea.

To get such performance without paying the price in fuel was the truly astounding aspect of the Holden, especially given the generous space the vehicle provided. Sixty brake horsepower was a reasonable number in 1948, but the key element was not the output of the engine but the power to weight ratio. The Holden was almost certainly the lightest family sedan to boast 60 horsepower at the time of its launch. (See box on page 185.) Contemporary road tests of the Holden invariably commented on its unique performance to fuel economy ratio. In late 1948 it was almost certainly the only car in the world to combine these attributes: seating for six, fuel economy of 30 miles per gallon and top speed of 80 miles per hour (128 km/h). Few customers minded that it used a three-speed gearbox because the strength of the engine more than made up for the extra ratio provided by many English and European makers.

Some comparisons highlight the uniqueness of the Holden's blend of performance and economy at a time when both were important, albeit for different reasons. The A40 Devon had a 1.2-litre four-cylinder engine, which developed 40-brake horsepower and gave average fuel economy of 30 miles (48 km) per gallon. The top speed was less than 70 miles per hour (112 km/h), and there was seating for four. Launched at the 1949 Earls Court Show for model year 1950 were the new 2.3-litre Armstrong Siddeleys. Based on the 1946 2.0-litre models, which were the first all-new British postwar cars, they had 75-brake horsepower (compared with the Holden's 60) and a top speed of 80 miles per hour (128 km/h). The Armstrong Siddeleys, costing twice as much as the Holden in Australia, were not direct rivals in the market but competed instead with English Jaguars, Rileys and Rovers. They offered similar interior room, but weighed almost half as much again as the Holden, due in part to their use of a separate body and chassis. Fuel economy averaged a little more than 20 miles per gallon. Acceleration times from zero to 50 miles per hour (80.5 km/h) for the Austin, Armstrong Siddeley and Holden were respectively 26.9, 13.5 and 13.3 seconds.

The closest direct comparison possible in 1949 was between the Holden and the English Standard Vanguard, which was powered by a large 68-brake horsepower four-cylinder engine. The 'four' was nowhere near as smooth as the Holden's 'six'. More expensive than 'Australia's Own' by some 10 per cent, the Vanguard was correspondingly heavier and more fuel consumptive, as well as slightly slower in acceleration. Like the majority of late 1940s cars the Vanguard was of body-on-frame construction, and this difference accounted for many of its extra kilograms. Consider, too, the highly relevant case of the Chevrolet. *The Autocar* magazine's road tester observed:

> *The Holden thus offers a remarkable combination of body space, performance and fuel economy. It even turns out to have a slightly better acceleration and maximum speed than were obtained from the best seller of all the General Motors range, the Powerglide Chevrolet tested recently by* The Autocar, *and it does this with an engine of 2.2 litres against 3.9 litres.*

Note that this test was published almost three years after the Holden's debut and the Chevrolet in question is the model introduced at the Waldorf

Hotel in New York City in January 1949 as the division's first truly postwar offering. Although the Holden only beat its Chevrolet cousin to public introduction by two months, the Chevrolet development process was shorter.

Despite the Holden's evident superiority to all comers in its blend of performance and fuel economy, there were still some niggles about the price. The *Australian Monthly Motor Manual* said this was 'too high for average purses', but reported that 'a recent test of two Holdens, over a 600 mile [965 km] course of varying surfaces at an average speed of 35 m.p.h. [56 km/h] an economy of 37 m.p.g was recorded'. This was not their own independent test but one conducted by GMH and reported in identical fashion in an early advertisement. Road testing had a way to go in Australia! Petrol rationing was still in place and would be until February 1950, when the incoming Menzies Liberal and Country Party government fulfilled the key election promise to abolish it; the number of miles—always finite— your petrol coupons could be translated into was a paramount concern beyond the mere hip pocket nerve of consumption. Remember that Ford Australia's proposal for the Australian car specified a V8 engine—an egregious misreading of the government's invitation.

Remember that Ford Australia's proposal for the Australian car specified a V8 engine—an egregious misreading of the government's invitation.

Under the heading 'The Australian Holden', *Australian Motor Sports* (*AMS*) delivered a much more comprehensive report, also in its edition of 15 March 1949. Where Keith Winser's *Motor Manual* had a brief tabloid-style report focusing on price, *AMS* was one of the few Australian publications to provide a lengthy review in which the Holden was considered in the broader context of car design, as the opening paragraphs show:

It is an engineering maxim that it is usually more difficult to build well, but cheaply, than it is to make an inferior article at greater expense. General Motors-Holdens, makers of the Holden, have clearly kept this maxim in mind, and we have no hesitation in saying that their product is a leader in the medium price, medium size field.

Its performance is striking, due to its good power and well balanced suspension; its appearance is practical and devoid of frills; its shape is one which would probably be found to be quite from an aerodynamic viewpoint as there is little wind noise when it is travelling fast; and the short stroke gives its engine an effortless quality at high cruising speeds. Interior appointments are restrained but adequate.

Possibly its most surprising feature is the very good fuel consumption; during our road test the Holden was not spared, yet it returned a figure of just over 30 miles [48 km] per gallon to which, for a 21 h.p. car weighing well over the ton with the three passengers it carried, the term phenomenal could quite aptly be applied.

Wrapping up its comprehensive report, the magazine said: 'Altogether, we found the Holden a car to covet, and congratulate General Motors-Holdens on their achievement.' This conclusion was quite typical of reports on the original Holden.

One might expect a jingoistic element—muted in the *AMS* instance—to have flavoured Australian reviews of the country's first ever mass-production family car, but English testers would surely have been more inclined to stick to the technical facts and their overall impressions? *The Autocar* had published a report by its Australian correspondent in its 26 August 1949 edition but followed this up for the 5 October 1951 magazine with a full road test (number 1445) of the Holden on British roads:

The building of a car can be regarded as a symbolic act indicating that a country has come of age industrially, for the many skills required in the car factory itself must be backed by efficient forges, foundries, press shops and many ancillary industries to produce the parts and components. The Holden, Australia's first car, therefore, has a special significance in its own country, and although it appears at first sight to be an orthodox car of simple and straightforward design, closer acquaintance shows it to be one of unusual interest.

Implicit here is what attracted many buyers to the Holden; the car's 'special significance in its own country' could hardly be overlooked, especially in the immediate postwar context. It is interesting that *The Autocar* took more of a big-picture approach in its report than did most local accounts. Motoring journalism was long established in Britain and this particular journal was first published in 1895. *The Autocar*'s first report on the Holden appeared a week after the official unveiling and summed up its broader significance thus:

> *In some ways also the Holden represents General Motors' post-war idea of a medium-sized car approximating to those made in this country. The vast Detroit corporation has plenty of experience in building the smaller European type of car, through its connections—for instance—with Vauxhall, and with Opel . . .*

In its first report rival English magazine, *The Motor*, noted in passing that: 'The design is an interesting example of American design freed from any restriction of existing jigs and tools.' Those 'existing jigs and tools' played a big role in ensuring that monocoque design would not arrive in the Detroit mainstream for some years yet; the whole manufacturing process was predicated on mounting the body to a separate chassis. The fact that virtually all of GM's overseas cars were of unitary ('Aerobilt') construction suggests that this would have been the choice of the American engineers had the manufacturing and cost constraints been removed. Not until 1959 did Chevrolet finally launch a smaller car, the Corvair. Like its rivals from Ford and Chrysler, the Corvair was of monocoque design. (Unlike them, it was a sales disaster, skidding backwards—oversteering— down the road to nowhere, proof if any were needed that General Motors knew less about car design in 1959 than it had in 1949, or, rather, made worse decisions.)

The Autocar's road test was predominantly positive, especially as far as the Holden's engine performance, fuel economy, comfort and spaciousness were concerned. The brakes were quite big enough for the car's weight. The overall tone of the report suggested strong interest and the writer obviously came away from his experience with a positive opinion of Australia's first foray into the mass-produced motor car. Because the Holden was a new General Motors product, comparison with the larger Chevrolet must have seemed relevant to British readers, but it was probably even more so to those who lived in a market where the Holden was, at least theoretically, available. There is no doubt, however, that the Australian car attracted considerable interest in Britain and not just from motoring journalists. Don Loffler reports that the agent-general for Tasmania, Sir Eric von Bibra, frequently had to push his way through a crowd to get to his specially imported Holden in London.

If the introduction to *The Autocar*'s test is strong and places the Holden into a broader context of automobility, and the body of the article is garlanded with praise, the conclusion is right to the point:

> . . . the Holden showed a remarkable performance and demonstrated its ability to cover over 30 miles on a gallon of fuel at moderate speeds. It has a tireless ability to cover big distances almost regardless of road surfaces and is an outstanding example of the results which can be achieved by single-minded concentration on the production of a simple utility car without mechanical complications or eye-catching gadgets.

'A simple utility car'

While Russ Begg can take the credit for the 'single-minded concentration on the production of a simple utility car', the absence of 'gadgets' was only in part due to the design blueprint. The early Holdens were criticised at the time, but much more strongly in later years, for lacking some features found in many contemporary vehicles. There were no heating/demisting arrangements, the windscreen used flat glass in two panes vertically separated and the wipers which strove to keep this glass clean were of old-fashioned vacuum design rather than electrically operated. This was one of few areas where the production car departed from the plan laid out in 1944, where electric wipers were specified. As for the Holden's electrical system, it was of 6 volts. That was principally because, while 12-volt systems were common in Europe, 6 volts were still the norm in the US industry when the Holden was designed. In an interesting twist which highlights the great emphasis on keeping weight down, GMH advised owners not to upgrade their car's electrical system because various components were not designed to carry that extra weight. In 1948 very few cars made anywhere in the world had curved glass mainly because suppliers did not have the technology to manufacture it. Even the one-piece windscreen was not to be taken for granted—this was one change made by Jaguar for its 1957 Mark VIII. Curved glass would remain rare until the mid 1950s (although the 1951 Ford Zephyr had a curved one-piece windscreen), making its Holden debut on the FE of 1956. As for electric windscreen wipers, the Holden did not get these until the start of the following decade, and while it is credible that no Australian supplier had the capacity to produce motors in sufficient quantity in 1948 or even 1955, this was probably not the case in 1960 and Holden management may simply have been allowing complacency and cost cutting to dictate their product planning. Heating/demisting arrangements were also not to be taken for granted in 1948, but the Holden did not include a system as standard equipment until it was legislated for safety reasons some twenty years later, and given the huge profits being dispatched to shareholders in the United States, this looks like corporate stinginess.

The early Holdens had wipers which worked on engine vacuum and tended to slow down when they were most needed, for example, when accelerating hard to overtake a truck. Conversely, they sped up when the driver lifted his/her foot off the accelerator pedal. The valid excuse of 1948 looked dubious by 1960, when most cars sold anywhere in the world used an electric motor to ensure the wipers worked steadily all the time. Interestingly, GMH imported Bosch electric windscreen wiping systems from Germany during the 1930s.

The Holden becomes Australia's best-selling car

It was no surprise when the Holden became the bestseller for 1951 as production capacity increased almost to the point of meeting demand. Although the so-called 'humpy' shape was familiar and becoming dated, especially when compared with the latest American models arriving here in limited numbers, buyers seemed unperturbed. As for the use of a four-cylinder engine in the Consul and a 'six' in the Zephyr, was this perhaps a much later echo of 195-Y-13 and 195-Y-15, from which the Holden evolved? Local sales of these English Fords were never even close to those of the Holden, and while many buyers would willingly pay considerably more than the retail price to obtain their Holdens more quickly, comparatively few were prepared to pay an extra 5 per cent or so to obtain the striking new Zephyr, any more than they had been prepared to accept immediate delivery of a similarly priced Vanguard. The visually similar four-cylinder Consul was actually built on a shorter wheelbase and was priced very close to the Holden, and was thus uncompetitive on value. And the Zephyr's visible and sexily low-sprung presence on Australian roads did serve to make the Holden look quite dated by 1951. These English Fords boasted what was arguably the most avant garde mainstream design of the time.

In performance, economy and accommodation, the Zephyr was quite close to the Holden although certainly not superior overall, despite being newer. The straight-through style also provided superior interior width in relation to the exterior width because separate mudguards inevitably bulged outwards beyond the doors. Occupants in the Fords sat lower in the car. Nevertheless, Ford had not utilised the inherent lightness of the monocoque to such advantage and the similar sized Zephyr weighed considerably more than the Holden. Predictably, the low-riding Ford cornered better and had more sporting characteristics overall than the local champion, as *Australian Monthly Motor Manual* found in its January 1953 comparison test between the Holden, Zephyr and Austin A70. Motoring reports of the 1950s were rarely overtly critical and some reading between the lines was often required:

The cornering characteristics of the Holden are good for a car of this type, and providing one is not too enthusiastic in a tight turn, body roll is not too noticeable.

The one criticism to be offered in the handling characteristics of the Holden is that owing to its high powered engine and its light 20 cwt. body, the car on some surfaces is inclined to float when maximum speed is approached.

But there is little evidence that the Holden's handling inferiority to its Ford rival was judged to be worth a small hill of beans as far as most motorists—infatuated with the idea of owning not just any car but *Australia's Own Car*—were concerned. And the downside of the Zephyr's superior dynamics (to import the modern term that covers handling, roadholding, steering, ride and brakes) was all too apparent on Australian roads: it had 2 inches (51 mm) less than the Holden's 8½ inches (216 mm) of ground clearance and people said it was 'too low-slung'. Ford's own advertising proudly described the Zephyr and its four-cylinder Consul sibling as 'underslung', meaning you stepped down over the doorsills into the car and that the floor was closer to the road. And its heavier weight meant that the Zephyr could not quite match the Holden on fuel economy, still judged to be very important in 1953.

For Australians, the Zephyr was probably somewhat too modern and its perceived English-ness, despite the American styling, might also have counted against it. Despite its clean 'three-box' design and one-piece windscreen in curved glass, the Ford made no unique appeal to Australian aspirations. 'Ford of England', said the badges, but this emphatically lacked the charisma of the 'Australia's Own Car' Holden advertising theme which had struck such a chord. Before World War II the Chevrolet brand was more popular than Ford, and by 1953 Holden was far more popular than Chevrolet had ever been. As for 'Ford of England', it was associated with febrile little Anglias and Prefects as well as the poorly built Pilot with its ancient side-valve V8 engine that many Australians bought in lieu of anything much else in the very early postwar years. The Zephyr's 5 per cent price premium, reflecting the difference between manufacturing the entire car locally (Holden) and assembling it from a mixture of imported and locally made components, was presumably the crowning reason for its failure to mount a serious challenge to GMH's product. The Holden was, as it were, the only Australian trophy car. We can apply poet Robert Lowell's 'his Chevy . . . was garaged like a sacrificial steer' just by substituting 'Holden' for 'Chevy'.

By the end of 1951 more than 53,000 Holdens coloured Australian roads, and the 100,000 landmark was achieved on 19 May 1953 when a car registered GAW 190 drove off the assembly line to play its part in increasing Victorian motorisation. Holden had achieved market leadership in 1951, selling 21,184 units compared with rivals Austin (17,258), Ford (17,054), Morris (15,944) and Standard (10,280). The figures for 1952 were: Holden 23,721, Ford 20,956 (boosted by the Consul/Zephyr models), Morris 15,238, Austin 10,081 and Vauxhall 5081 (reflecting the arrival of the E-Series Vauxhalls).

Despite the Holden's dated appearance, demand continued to exceed supply until the original 48–215 model had been on sale for almost four years. The Loffler family bought its Holden in January 1953, just a month or so before Frank Clune took delivery of his round-Australia car. Theirs was one of the last 'old suspension' models. Don's parents rejected the dark green car available for immediate delivery and had to wait just ten days to get theirs in Gawler Cream. By 1953, with production matching demand, the Holden's dominance was fully evident. Sales reached 33,611. The combined total for second-placed Ford (24,035) and third-placed Austin (9635) of 33,670 beat the Holden by just 59 units.

By 1953, with production matching demand, the Holden's dominance was fully evident.

But how safe?

Regardless of its outstanding sales success, there were some issues with the Holden. Because unitary construction was still unfamiliar to motorists whose initiation into motoring had been in Chevrolets and Ford V8s, more than a few prospective and actual buyers worried that the car might be lacking in safety and would not stand up well in a crash. Some sense of 'tinniness' encouraged this impression. A second concern was that the car could behave in a wayward fashion on loose surfaces. And here emerges a delightful paradox: the fact that a number of Holdens crashed, and mostly stood up quite well even when they rolled over, served to assuage anxiety about the radical mode of construction.

> The opening scene of the 1975 movie *Sunday Too Far Away* depicts a 48–215 coming to grief on a dirt road, occupants unhurt. This could be a metaphor for the ubiquity of the Holden and its role in Australian rural life.

The instability was partly due to the suspension design and from February 1953 Holden began to equip its cars with telescopic shock absorbers rather than the old-fashioned lever type, and heavier duty rear springs. To have promoted the 'new suspension' at the time would have amounted to acknowledging a previous deficiency, so little was said. The timing was interesting, too, and suggests a measure of urgency with the new model due in October. As Loffler observes, those accustomed to pre-1953 models would have noticed the superior ride and handling of the FJ. In this way, GMH was able to mask one of the few shortcomings of its first Holden.

It seems that GMH's publicity people accepted a subtler means of promoting the Holden's 'roadability' and ruggedness. When best-selling author Frank Clune decided that his convalescence after surgery would take the form of a drive around Australia, his timing was excellent because GMH had just begun to produce its 'new suspension' model. He would almost certainly have been happy with the earlier car and makes no mention in his

Given the exhaustive testing of the 48–215 both at Milford and in Australia, why was the instability of the car on rough roads not idenfied? It may have been significant that the prototype Holdens on test tiaround Melbourne had one occupant (the driver) and sandbags in the boot to simulate a fully laden car. Loffler says 'This problem was probably not fully understood by the drivers of the prototype cars' because the load also served to make the rear end of the car more stable. Russ Begg and his engineers thus may never have become aware of the car's tendency to oversteer on loose surfaces until after it was released to the public. 'Some owners kept a sandbag permanently in the boot to give better stability and a more comfortable ride', notes Loffler.

book of the upgrade, even though it seems certain that someone at GMH, probably his friend 'Wally' Wallace-Crabbe, would have mentioned the improvement. Clune was already enthusiastic about the Holden, based on his son's experience.

My son Tony owns a Holden, in which, in December 1952, he calmly drove off from Sydney to Perth, with some of his cobbers, to sail their boat in a regatta. They reached Perth in four days, clocking 2700 miles [4345 km], averaging thirty-four miles to the gallon, and returned in similar style, with no mishaps of any kind, except one puncture.

To me, this was a convincing demonstration of the quality of the all-Australian car, built in Australia to suit Australian conditions. I have driven imported cars for years, and I have certainly no reason to decry them, but the one I owned was rather heavy on petrol for the route I had in mind, where on some stretches petrol-pumps are very few and far between . . .

Tony's trip to Perth satisfied me that a Holden would do what the experts claim for it. Apart from that, I believe that the manufacture of motor-cars in Australia marks a turning point in the industrial history of our nation. It is a signpost of Australia's coming greatness as a full-developed community; as important perhaps as the introduction of the Merino sheep in Australia's earlier history.

Frank Clune secured a favourable arrangement when it came to taking delivery of his new Holden:

My friend, J.H. Horn, a director of General Motors-Holden's Ltd., and his chief of staff in the Public Relations Department, K. Wallace-Crabbe, O.B.E., arranged for me to see over the works at Fishermen's Bend—and especially to follow Miss Icy Blue along the assembly line.

Miss Icy Blue, as Clune dubbed his new car, was built in a day. GMH offered to service and clean the car on its journey and BP had supplied free COR petrol. Author and Holden traversed 16,822 miles (27,070 km) to arrive in Sydney on 12 June 1953.

The end of my road-test of the Australian-made car? Not quite!
 In July, I drove her out on a business-trip beyond Bourke and out to Paroo, a ten-days' trip.
 In August, I followed the Hume Highway from Sydney, through Canberra, to Melbourne. On arriving there, in her home town, the Holden had clocked 20,000 miles [32,190 km]—and at least 10,000 miles [16,090 km] of that on rough roads—within six months of her birth.

Even though a sense of obligation felt by the author towards GMH emerges in the text, it is difficult to quarrel with Clune's conclusions. The petrol may have been free but there can be no doubt that on several occasions the author appreciated the Holden's generous ground clearance of 8½ inches (216 mm).

Perhaps Frank Clune should have taken a caravan with him because a third concern, also related to the monocoque, was about the Holden's towing ability. Rumours spread that the car could not tow a heavy load without stretching its body. This last concern is a reminder that Australian automobility was still a work in progress heading into the 1950s. Loffler's image of the overladen Holden may remind us of the 'ancient Hudson' depicted by John Steinbeck in that early road novel, *The Grapes of Wrath*: the car as mistreated workhorse. And who was to know, in 1950 or 1953, what was the maximum weight that could be safely towed? There was abundant extemporisation and experimentation, as in a pioneer civilisation, and in terms of motoring culture that's exactly what Australia was. If during World War II cars could be laden down with primitive burners on the back to turn methane into fuel, why not load the poor beast of burden down to the point where its headlights are aimed at the Southern Cross? Clearly, many owners either never read their owners' manual or simply ignored it. But Australians were driving the road towards the age of mass motorisation; by the time Clune's *Land of Australia: Roamin' in a Holden* went on sale for Christmas 1953, we were almost on wheels.

Sixty horsepower worked wonders in the Holden, which was of course based on the Experimental Light Car, 195-Y-15. It seems probable that the decision to give 195-Y-15 an output of 60-brake horsepower was down to the Opel Super Six and Kapitän, both of which provided this number in much heavier cars.

Virtually since the start of motoring, engine power has risen steadily. In 2007 the Chevrolet Corvette Z06, GM's most powerful car to date, had 505 horsepower. But the power to weight ratio leap made by the Holden in 1948 took some catching. As late as 1955 plenty of cars weighing more than the 48–215 had less power, while most with 60 or even 70 horsepower were much heavier. The following table indicates the enormity of the Holden's edge in 1948. The table has been compiled from *The Autocar: Road Tests—1953* along with material from the Wachtler report and *The Autocar*'s 1951 test of the Holden.

	Cylinders	BHP	0–50 mph (0–80.5 km/h)	max speed (mph)	weight (lbs)
1948 Holden 48–215	6	60	13.3	80 (129 km/h)	2247 (1019 kg)
1948 Austin A40 Devon	4	40	22 (approx.)	68 (109 km/h)	2128 (965 kg)
1951 Ford Zephyr	6	68	13.5 (approx.)	80 (129 km/h)	2500 (1134 kg)
1952 Wolseley 4/44	4	46	19.6	70 (113 km/h)	2492 (1130 kg)
1953 Standard Vanguard Phase II	4	68	13.8	77 (124 km/h)	2828 (1283 kg)
1953 Sunbeam-Talbot 90 Mark IIA	4	70	14.4	81.4 (131 km/h)	3360 (1524 kg)

Chapter 9

Diamonds are a grille's best friend

In previous chapters we have seen the importance placed on styling in product differentiation by General Motors and how every new design had to be signed off by Harley Earl, whose authority spanned all divisions including GMH. Earl, appointed by Sloan himself in 1927, set the styling rules for GM, which were mostly followed by the other American manufacturers and sometimes by their British and continental European counterparts. 'Easter eggs done up in cellophane' was Pininfarina's lordly dismissal of American cars in 1948, but domestic consumers rushed to embrace the latest models. In the United States the annual model change rolled around every fall like an early secular Christmas. The nature of the industry with its huge economies of scale made it easy to apply annual cosmetic changes with an all-new body every three years or so. But the nascent Australian automotive industry could not afford the luxury of frequent change. The Holden shape

> 'Easter eggs done up in cellophane' was Pininfarina's lordly dismissal of American cars in 1948 but domestic consumers rushed to embrace the latest models.

that made its public debut on 29 November 1948 had to remain in production for the better part of eight years, and this at a time when styling arguably played the biggest role in the United States in automotive history—before or since.

Of course in Australia the early postwar years were heady, just as they were in the United States where buyers who were forking out $700 over the odds for a 1948 Chevrolet or $500 for its Pontiac cousin were actually buying a car with warmed-over 1942 styling. The annual model change must have seemed almost irrelevant when one's old car was almost worn out and there was the need to replace it. New cars of any kind were in short supply in Australia as in the United States (and the scarcity was even more extreme in Britain). A sellers' market prevailed everywhere.

But by 1950 supply in the United States had almost caught up with demand and the new-style postwar models were being produced in record-breaking numbers; once again, the lure of the annual change worked its charms in the world's largest consumer market, in contrast to Australia. The US market had reached saturation point by the late 1920s so many customers twenty years on were buying their third, fourth or fifth car. No statistics are available but it is probable that around half of all new Holden sales in the 1948–53 time frame were to people who had never previously owned a car. This was a Ford Model T situation: styling is almost irrelevant when set against the joy of radically enhanced personal mobility. In this sense Australia was at least twenty years behind the United States. When they did finally get a car in the family, Australians tended to hang onto it for rather longer than was the norm in the world capital of consumerism. After 1956 a new shape was introduced every three years or so and many Holden owners were happy to swap their old Holden Special for the latest one. As for the horsepower race which ran alongside the increasing extravagance of styling from the mid 1950s on, nothing even approximating this played out in Australia until 1962 when the first Valiant was introduced with 145-brake horsepower to the Holden's 75, and even then in a minor key as first Ford and then Holden responded. So it is a commonplace but inaccurate observation to say that Australian automotive trends have mirrored those of the United States. Australia has, at least as far as its cars are concerned, never been America writ small.

Don Loffler, Norm Darwin and other automotive historians and journalists have commented on Holden styling but without consideration of the industry as a whole. In truth, styling played little part in most Holden purchasing decisions not just in 1949–50 but right through the 1950s and into the 1960s. While there were always aspirational vehicles such as the Chevrolet Bel Air and the Ford Customline, the appearance, indeed the entire image of the Holden Special, satisfied the overwhelming majority of prospective customers; the latest automotive fashion just never mattered much in this laconic country. As for the specialist American automotive historians, C. Edson Armi and David Gartman, the word 'Australian' appears a handful of times in their combined total of 576 pages, when Hershey is quoted by Armi on designing the Holden. Interestingly, until now these two studies stand alone. So scholarly as opposed to journalistic discussion of American and Australian car styling remains in its infancy. In this chapter, my approach will be largely to 'read' the cars, which are in a sense the major primary documents in our possession.

The simple fact that Hershey was entrusted with the new styling for the first postwar Cadillac—GM's most prestigious brand—shows how much respect he enjoyed at General Motors; in any disagreement between pushy Hartnett and any of Harley Earl's people, it would be the latter who would usually enjoy support at the highest corporate levels. There does seem to have been one exception to this rule, and it was a fortunate one. Harley Earl had already approved a clay model containing an extension of the front fender into the door in the manner of the 1942 GM cars. Hartnett did not like it and urged Ed Riley to argue for a 'straight through fender' design. This latter would have added too much weight but Riley was able to convince Earl to compromise. 'Prior to this meeting', wrote George Quarry to Hartnett on 27 August 1945, 'our hope of discarding the downswept line had looked grim—the clay incorporating this feature having been approved, the wood model under instruction [*sic*] and the body draft in preparation'. Quarry continues:

> *Your constant requests, the reaction and support of the Vauxhall group, (especially Sir Charles Bartlett and David Jones) and constant repetition of the objection to the 'transient' styling culminated in a reasonably warm discussion over at Styling, following which Mr. Riley discussed with Mr. Earl, and wrote Mr. McCuen, on August 2nd, requesting radical revision of the styling, broadly along the following lines.*
>
> a) *Elimination of the extension of the front and rear fenders into the doors, even at the expense of lengthening the wheelbase.*
> b) *Complete elimination of the downswept crease line.*
> c) *Relief of the massive appearance of the front end.*
> d) *Incorporation in the front and styling of some distinctive motif, rather than the scaled down domestic appearance.*
>
> *. . . The important point is that present indications indicate that a compromise design will be reached, wherein the rear door will incorporate a small fender extension, while the front fender will finish forward of the cowl pillar. The point concerning design, manufacturing and service relative to this feature has been thoroughly checked, and everyone is satisfied.*

How right Hartnett was on this occasion because this fender-door fad vanished with the first all-new US postwar designs. Hartnett had evidently gone to great lengths to make his point, including 'your examples of the "5-guinea dress allowance"', as Quarry put it. Separate mudguards themselves began to seem antiquated by about the time the FJ facelift was introduced in October 1953. Had the Holden been required to soldier on until July 1956 with such protuberant mudguards, the advertising copywriters would have faced a huge challenge trying to convince potential customers that the car had 'beauty'.

In addition to being completed before work began on the first of General Motors' postwar Detroit creations (the 1948 Cadillac), the Holden also preceded the 'coming or going' Studebaker Champion and the gorgeous Cisitalia. The Studebaker gave Ford its packaging blueprint for the postwar Custom, while the Museum of Modern Art declared: 'The Cisitalia's body is slipped over its chassis like a dust jacket over a book.' Pininfarina placed himself at the opposite pole of design from Earl: 'In the name of aesthetic purity I declare war on superfluities and chrome fixings.'

In the styling studios of General Motors in Detroit the Holden was sandwiched between the carryover pre-war designs which were reintroduced as 1947 models and genuinely new designs. It was 'a cute little car' barely worth recollection for its designer, although perhaps this brevity of memory might have something to do with being overruled by Earl after the Hartnett–Riley campaign against the downswept fender line. Contrast Hershey's Holden comments with his praise of the 1955 Ford Thunderbird, which, as noted earlier, has been widely, although controversially, attributed to the same designer: it seems that others also make claim on that redoubtable classic, later to be one of the automotive stars of the magnificent 1972 movie *American Graffiti*.

It was as if the designers were finally being allowed to open their eyes to cars again after the war, and Hershey did his work on the Holden right at the start of this period in a limbo land with the future yet to arrive. Soon after 195Y25 was signed off by Harley Earl in 1945 a number of converging new styles dated it almost overnight. The available evidence suggests Earl had not clarified his own thinking about future directions when the Australian Car Program came his way. But with new design influences coming into play, such as the pivotal postwar Studebaker, the Holden nevertheless looked far more modern than the 1948 Chevrolet, which was essentially a 1942 model with a new, horizontally themed radiator grille. Arguably, in this respect (although probably in no other), the timing of its debut was not ideal: the Holden came a year or two too early to benefit from the full gamut of the early postwar thinking about style.

If the 1947 Studebaker was the first and among the most influential of the US postwar designs, the 1949 Ford V8 Custom, which featured 'three-box' styling (where the front box is the engine compartment enclosed by bonnet and wing panels, the central box is the passenger compartment and the third box is the usefully more spacious boot, with no separate mudguards or droopy tail to be seen) for the first time in a Ford Motor Company product, was a close second, and more important in the Australian context where Studebaker was only a minor player. The 1949 Ford, which was only the third all-new model since the Model T and effectively saved the company from impending bankruptcy, made its debut just months before the Holden, at a gala function in New York's Waldorf Astoria Hotel, where Chevrolet would soon show its new car, and was received with enormous enthusiasm. (The clay model of this Ford was actually baked in designer Richard Caleal's kitchen oven.)

Styling moves on

By 1950 the Holden's styling had fallen off the cusp of modernity in terms of international styling trends. For General Motors designers (who were by this time engaged in the 1952–53 models), it was a footnote in ancient history, and even the car-ravenous Australian public must have sensed that the Holden was already showing its age. Briefly, it had been fresher and more forward looking than the carried over pre-war American designs which sold in North America until well into 1949 and (in greatly restricted numbers, due to a lack of US currency) in Australia until 1950–51. But there was as much styling distance between the 1949 Ford Custom and the Holden as there had been between the 1948 Chevrolet and 'Australia's Own Car'; 1949 was a watershed styling year for Detroit and most of those designs had been started in 1946. If Ford's freshly baked 1949 Custom looked a little like Lou Thoms' fanciful sketch (circa 1944) of an updated 195-Y-15 complete with bullet-style tail lights (shown on page 10 of Don Loffler's *She's A Beauty!*) then Ford of England had something even more futuristic on the drawing board by this time. The Consul and Zephyr siblings made their debut at the 1950 Earls Court show in time for the 1951 season, but they contained deep design secrets.

The new British Fords had a strong American flavour and their genesis was clearly not in Dagenham but Detroit. In one way, it makes sense to describe the Ford Consul and Zephyr as the small Chevrolets that never were because this project may be said to have begun almost a decade earlier, not at Ford but at Chevrolet. Indeed, it was Frank Hershey who had developed the styling concept that was later reworked by Ford. At the same time as he developed a radical new look for Cadillac, Hershey applied the thinking to the mooted Chevrolet Cadet. Remember the time frame: immediately after the Holden, the designer finalised the 1948 Cadillac, while working on the experimental models. In May 1945 General Motors announced its plan to build a smaller Chevrolet. Was it significant that this timing places the decision smack in the middle of 195Y25? Did the Australian car program give GM executives the necessary brave pills to decide to build what would become the Cadet? Regardless, Frank Hershey had a hand in both Holden and Cadet. Work began on the small Chevrolet in mid 1945, at the height of the 195Y25's development. Hershey and chief assistant Ned Nickles sketched experimental Cadillacs and the Cadet along similar themes. Key styling elements were totally integrated front wings, wraparound front bumpers, partially enclosed wheels of small diameter, and a much lower and wider stance than even the 1948 Cadillac. Chrome strips from bumper to bumper and the small wheels made these cars look longer.

Beneath the Consul/Zephyr's radically 'straight-through' styling lay a number of mechanical innovations, but the most important of these reveals the hidden history of the aborted Cadet program. Earl MacPherson gave his name to a new type of front suspension, which was fitted to the English Fords. Before he went to Ford and wrote his name into history, MacPherson had been chief engineer of the Cadet. Frustrated by GM's announcement on 15 May 1947 that the car was 'indefinitely deferred', MacPherson was ready to accept an overture from Harold Youngren of Ford.

The Cadet was to have been a monocoque built on a 108-inch wheelbase and weighing 2000 pounds (907 kg). It was to use a new 2.0-litre six-cylinder engine. Other advanced features would include suspended pedals, a radical independent suspension and 12-inch wheels. The Cadet has already been looked at briefly in the previous chapter but now we see its connection with the Holden. It is impossible to believe that the Australian car program did not influence this concept.

Fascinatingly, the Cadet's real world influence came via the Consul/Zephyr, and the six-cylinder Zephyr may be seen as the strongest rival to the Holden from its arrival in Australia in 1952. The wheels were just 13 inches (330 mm) in diameter, compared with 15 inches (381 mm) for the Holden. The Zephyr rode on a 104-inch (2642 mm) wheelbase, just 1 inch (25 mm) longer than the Holden's.

Had the Australian car been styled in 1947–48 rather than two years earlier, it would probably have still looked contemporary by 1955. The most informative comparison here comes from within General Motors. The E-Series Vauxhalls, of similar configuration to the Holden but somewhat less roomy inside, made their debut in August 1951, and this shape would remain in production until 1957.

Had the Australian car been styled in 1947–48 rather than two years earlier, it would probably have still looked contemporary by 1955.

The most striking aspect of the 48–215's styling was the radiator grille, a lavish chrome affair with more than a passing resemblance to that of the expensive Buicks of the immediate postwar era. This 'face' of the Holden was surely consistent with the nationalistic pride many felt in the car; it was smiling, optimistic, well-fed.

Interestingly, the radiator grille was far more heavily chromed and bolder than the design for the 1949 Chevrolet, which had to take its lowly place in GM's North American domestic car line-up, beneath Pontiac, Oldsmobile, Buick and Cadillac (in ascending order).

Although the FJ Special boasted chrome tailfins, two-tone paintwork, garish Elascofab upholstery and the availability of a wide range of Nascar accessories, these changes were not sufficient to make it look modern. Frank Hershey's styling looked old well before the FJ was launched but by 1954 this was no longer merely a potential aesthetic issue. The fashionable new three-box designs did not just look sleeker but were also roomier. Bumpers aside, the widest part of the early Holdens was from mudguard to mudguard and the width between the doors was clearly less. Occupants sat higher off the floor and had less elbow room than would be possible in a current design. And because the upper line of the boot in a three-box design was straight rather than curved, there was more luggage space and a more practical shape to the compartment, meaning that not only more items could be accommodated but also larger ones. The vertically mounted spare wheel of the Holden further detracted from the boot's practicality. Certainly the Holden's superior ground clearance was still appreciated by many customers, but the rounded roofline, tall body, and two-piece windscreen defined this as a product of the 1940s. In 1948 that was what boots, rooflines, body proportions and windscreens were like when nearly all car designs had been carried over from 1939. The pre-war fashion was for rooflines to be high enough so that all occupants could wear hats. The 1951 Ford Consul and Zephyr models had curved windscreens, and from that time the old two-piece style began to look anachronistic.

Three-box designs quickly succeeded humpier predecessors from around 1952. A few newly launched mid 1950s cars, most notably the compact Jaguar saloons of late 1955, had curved rear styling for aesthetic reasons (sporty lines counting more at Jaguar than luggage space), but the Holden's lumpy, rounded rump was a constant reminder of its age, as was the overall height of the vehicle.

A goddess appears in Europe

If by the beginning of 1955 there was already plenty of evidence that inter-national car design had finally emerged from the shadow of World War II, the star exhibit of that year's Paris Salon seized the attention of the industry like no other postwar model before it. With the radical DS19, Citroën appeared to be showcasing at least one kind of automotive future.

The American cars had by this time all adopted low-slung, three-box styling. They were longer, lower and wider in dimensions. Bigger was generally seen as better, so in the General Motors range a Cadillac was considerably bigger than a Chevrolet, and had more chromework as well. Interior styling was also quite different from that of pre-war models. The visual differences between a 1955 Chevrolet and its 1939 forebear were enormous. And the newer model not only looked as if it came from a differ-ent era but it was powered accordingly with a high-compression overhead valve V8 engine. Naturally this type of motor was showcased in the Cadillac several years before the Chevrolet. That was in 1949. But by the middle of the decade, even the entry-level Chevrolet could be ordered with a powerful V8 engine which delivered a top speed of more than 100 miles per hour with sparkling acceleration.

US postwar prosperity was reflected in the products of Detroit. The ingrained Protestant ethic was also in evidence. (You couldn't guess the state of an individual's soul but his or her worldly wealth might provide a clue; work was virtuous and hard work generated wealth.) The annual model change brought ever more chromium plate and a welter of new colour combinations. More power, longer, lower, wider, more impress-your-neighbour capacity were the catchcries. For Detroit in general and General Motors in particular, excess was its own reward. The rest of the automotive world looked on, sometimes emulating, sometimes not. Where GM, Ford or Chrysler held a shareholding, then Detroit fashion found expression in European models, but there was no unrestrained rush towards what was often seen on the other side of the Atlantic as flashiness—sometimes in unconscious envy, I suspect, because throughout Europe petrol was dearer, taxes were higher, and road space was limited.

None of this American surge of the new prepared anyone for the seamless and insistent modernity of the Citroën DS, which invited the suggestion of *diesse* (French for 'goddess'). If the products of Detroit were inherently aggressive and thrusting, and would become more so throughout the decade, this new French car created a fresher, smoother 'streamlining' aesthetic, imbued with Bauhaus themes. Semiologist Roland Barthes seemed infatuated and devoted a whole essay, 'The New Citroën', to the DS. (For semiologists, sometimes seamless seems less but *is* more.)

For Detroit in general and General Motors in particular, excess was its own reward. The rest of the automotive world looked on, sometimes emulating, sometimes not.

> *There are in the D.S. the beginnings of a new phenomenology of assembling, as if one progressed from a world where elements are welded to a world where they are juxtaposed and held together by sole virtue of their wondrous shape . . .*
>
> *There is a return to a certain degree of streamlining, new, however, since it is less bulky, less incisive, more relaxed than that which one found in the first period of this fashion. Speed here is expressed by less aggressive, less athletic signs, as if it were evolving from a primitive to a classical form.*

The dichotomy invoked here implies a theoretical pincer grip of modernity in which the FJ Holden was caught. It lacked the exciting V8 performance and aggressive style of American cars, and beside the new Citroën even a two-toned FJ Special with Elascofab upholstery and a plethora of Nasco accessories looked quaintly old fashioned. But this pincer grip remained theoretical in 1955–56 because the Holden was, after all, *Australia's* own car, not the world's. If the Citroën DS19 was never going to be a top seller in Australia—the relatively high price alone would

The dichotomy invoked here implies a theoretical pincer grip of modernity in which the FJ Holden was caught. It lacked the exciting V8 performance and aggressive style of American cars, and beside the new Citroën even a two-toned FJ Special with Elascofab upholstery and a plethora of Nasco accessories looked quaintly old fashioned.

guarantee this—then neither were the latest American cars as typified by the 1955 Chevrolet V8. Price notwithstanding, few imported cars stood up to the durability and reliability standards set by Holden in those days. Nor were there widespread service networks to provide the frequent servicing required, with most 1950s cars requiring lubrication every 1600 kilometres or so.

Nineteen fifty-five may be seen as a key turning point in automotive design with, it may be argued, an increasing divergence between European and US practice. The radical Citroën also incorporated several important technological elements including the use of disc front brakes for the first time on a production car. The *Diesse* represented the highest European automotive aesthetic. Some months after the Paris Salon came the London Motor Show at Earls Court, where Jaguar's 2.4 Litre model was a highlight. Four years after the Ford Consul/Zephyr's introduction of three-box styling to Europe, Jaguar still went its own way. The 2.4 Litre was as curved and rounded as the Zephyr had been square, but no observer could have confused it with a pre-war design. The rounded guards and drooping boot expressed a sports car theme justified by the twin overhead camshaft engine proudly displayed beneath the bonnet. Jaguar was using its success in racing to give its sedans a unique character.

The Citroën and Jaguar were utterly different machines but both fused style and technology in a new way. One was intended to be a triumph of fashionable function. The other was about the fusion of beauty and performance in 'a special kind of motoring which no other car in the world can offer'. While the DS delivered phenomenal space in an interior dominated by plastic and cloth, the 2.4 Litre was a cramped, even claustrophobic, car which used leather and wood to give the sense of an expensive traditional English luxury model. The Jaguar's boot was at least as small as it looked, but the long bonnet conveyed the message its maker intended: bespoke power, 105 miles per hour (169 km/h) from a sports car engine. At both Citroën and Jaguar it seemed that neither designers nor engineers had considered what was

- **7 May 1945** World War II ends in Europe.

- **11 May 1945** The new postwar Armstrong Siddeleys are announced in *The Autocar*.

- **Also in May 1945** Chevrolet announces its plan to build a smaller Chevrolet.

- **1946** Studebaker introduces its radical postwar Champion.

- **15 May 1947** Chevrolet announces the 'indefinite' deferral of the Cadet program.

- **29 November 1948** Prime Minister Ben Chifley launches the Holden.

- **1950** One of the highlights of the Earls Court Motor Show is the Rover P4, deliberately styled from the 1947 Studebaker and thus one of the first English cars to incorporate postwar Detroit themes. Also at Earls Court that year, Ford of England shows its new Consul and Zephyr models, incorporating many elements originally intended for the stillborn Chevrolet Cadet.

happening in Detroit, except perhaps dismissively; one imagines they thought similarly to Battista Pininfarina about 'superfluous fixings'. In 1955 there was remarkable diversity in the European industry and it was by no means clear that the kind of sameness of basic design which was the eventual outcome of Sloan's famous product policy would prevail.

Chapter 10

The world catching up, 1955–64

In a sense the Holden was not only Larry Hartnett's mooted car 'between the two types' of large American and small British, it was also the car between two eras. Based on a 1938 prototype and developed in the mid 1940s, the 48–215 took the most advanced 1930s mass-production automotive thinking forward into the 1950s. In a sense it was the one shot in the locker. Australian economies of scale or, rather, the lack of them, would not facilitate frequent and extensive changes, meaning the familiar US annual model change was not on the agenda. Rather, what was good for the late 1940s would have to endure in the market at least seven years without a major rework, and even by 1956 it would not be viable to start with a clean sheet. This, then, is the context in which the Holden needs to be judged at least until 1960.

The overwhelmingly enthusiastic response to the Holden by Australian buyers and the positive reports it received not just locally but in the British specialist press suggests that the 48–215 and its successors could surely have succeeded in other markets, too. No other 1948 car, including the Volkswagen, had greater prospects for international success than the Holden. But

GMH's need to attend to its home market—and with demand so far in advance of supply—precluded any serious prospect of a major export program before 1954 when FJs were sent to New Zealand and other Pacific markets. There were other reasons, too. Vauxhall management would surely have been unenthusiastic about having to compete with Holden on British territory. It was not until the launch of the 1957 Vauxhall Velox and Cresta models that Luton had a car to equal or perhaps eclipse the Holden. Besides, GMH simply had no need to go beyond satisfying domestic demand and shipping a few thousand vehicles to British Commonwealth markets, mostly within comfortable geographical range.

Australians were so much in love with the Holden that GMH needed to do very little to retain not just easy market leadership but absolute dominance. From 1951 until the mid 1960s, no challenger even drew close. But where the qualities of the 48–215 and FJ models made them clearly superior—and especially in the Australian context—to all six-cylinder rivals, by 1956–57 this was not necessarily the case. Mostly, though, the public couldn't care less: the Holden was proven, it was 'Australia's Own Car'; we were used to it, warts and all. So even though the handbrake never worked as well as it should and the seats weren't that comfortable on long trips, such minor quibbles did not make many of us think seriously about another brand. Equally to the point was the Holden's continuing merits of lower initial price and operating cost, high resale value and ruggedness.

By the end of the first half of the 1950s, the Holden faced a different automotive world from that of 1948, but fortunately from GMH's point of view many of the changes seemed irrelevant to Australian motorists. The first model's neat, essentially conservative styling placed it almost perfectly at the midway point between the 1939 Chevrolet and the 1950 Ford Zephyr with rectalinear styling.

Heading into the mid 1950s, the Holden remained sharply competitive by any objective measure without even considering the emotional appeal it held for many buyers. But it was beginning to look dated even before the spring 1953 FJ facelift. With function predominating over form for Australian buyers—much the same as it had in the US before 1920—styling was not yet the priority it had become across the Pacific, where the market had long been 'saturated' and questions of reliability and suitability for local conditions were seldom raised; for many Australian buyers even well into the 1950s, the new Holden was their first car and for many others it was their first *new* car.

In 1953 there was nevertheless keen anticipation of a new model and perhaps a feeling that the next Holden would be more contemporary in style. Already the 1952 Vauxhall Velox (shown in late 1951), with its faired-in mudguards and generous use of chrome, looked more modern than the 48-215, and it showed how more overt Detroit styling themes could be applied to a smaller car than the domestic US models. Rumours developed that in 1954 Holden would release a new and slightly larger car, styled in the Chevrolet idiom. The only thing wrong with this story was the premature timing. The FE would not debut until July 1956. In October 1953, just three weeks before the FJ's launch, managing director Earl Daum tried to nip this thinking in the bud, denying 'reports that a new Holden car with a larger body, increased weight and power will be released early in the new year'. He added that it 'would be some years, if at all, before any radical changes would be made'.

During the life of the 48-215 there were two separate sedan models, but both were essentially functional (the second being the Business sedan aimed at fleet and taxi owners). There was no hint of Sloan's famous product policy where a broad range of cars catered 'for every purse and purpose'. The first step to increasing customer choice came with the creation of the Holden Special FJ and although this variant added little in the way of functional attributes, it did provide a hint of glamour, while enabling GMH somewhat misleadingly to advertise 'three different sedan models—the de luxe Special, the Business sedan and the economy model, Holden Standard'. It was as if long-time GM stylist Harley Earl had applied a signature to the Holden in the form of two minuscule chrome tailfins, not sculpted into those separate rear mudguards but merely *applied* to the rounded upper surface. The rather elegant, formal radiator grille of the original gave way to a toothy, flashier one. Two-tone paintwork was offered and, hey presto, Detroit parenthood became more visibly evident in the Holden. There were some mostly minor mechanical revisions beneath this new jewellery, but the most important change since 1948, the 'new suspension' had been slipped surreptitiously beneath the 48–215 in February 1953.

Just as the first Holden had arrived at the ideal time in Australian cultural history, arguably so did the FJ Special. More than 120,000 Holdens had been sold by October 1953 and Australia's drive towards mass motorisation was gathering speed. Many of those buyers would be looking to replace their car with something fresh, rather than simply replacing one plain, trusty Holden with an almost identical one. Back in the Model T era, Alfred P. Sloan Jr had identified the need for regular model changes in a saturated market. Essentially, what had happened in the United States in the mid to late 1920s was taking place in Australia a generation later, during the 1950s. In the United States, the Chevrolet buyer could aspire to a Pontiac, the Pontiac buyer to a Buick, and so on up to the Cadillac. At least in Australia there were now two clear tiers of Holdens (three if you count the Business sedan), albeit distinguished mainly by bright gestures rather than substance. The Special was no more powerful, spacious or agile than its cheaper sibling, but it did have leather upholstery and, later, fancy Elascofab vinyl in two-tone combinations

> The Special would offer Elascofab vinyl in two-tone combinations and with decorative buttons—the Australian automotive equivalent perhaps of blue suede shoes.

and with decorative buttons—the Australian automotive equivalent perhaps of blue suede shoes. Armrests on the front doors were standard and a cigarette lighter was fitted.

In 1955 when Elascofab upholstery was introduced as an optional extra on the Special it was seen by GMH's marketing people as more desirable and fashionable than the standard leather, and was described as 'fine quality restful upholstery'. The Holden Standard was trimmed in PVC (vinyl).

The gap between the outgoing 48–215 Holden sedan and a new FJ Special was similar to that between a Chevrolet and Pontiac, offering current owners (as well as first-time buyers) an incentive to purchase a new car. That simple model name, 'Special', was cleverly chosen. By implication the opposite of 'Special' was 'Standard' and, in the simplicity of 1950s marketing, this became the official name of what was essentially an FJ version of the original car, lacking additional chrome ornamentation even to the extent of a bonnet mascot. (The devaluation of the term 'standard' from benchmark to basic also created a corporate headache for the Standard Motor Corporation!)

However, GMH was going to need more than a model called Special to sustain its market dominance through to the arrival of the FE. Increasingly, the advertising emphasis was on value for money. Both the Standard (£1023) and Business (£1052) sedans cost £54 less than their predecessors, while the Special actually cost £2 less than the outgoing small 's' standard Holden. Don Loffler believes that 'value for money' brought a renewal of Holden waiting lists.

A second advertising theme was 'beauty', as if by trying to make a virtue out of the necessity of the same old body continuing from 1948 past the middle of the next decade GMH could head off any criticism;

in advertising you merely assert something to make it seem true. 'The Beautiful Holden—Australia's Own Car' was the heading for one full-page
example:

> *How naturally Holden fits into this typically Australian scene—sunshine, the wayside
> stall, gum trees in the background and the family group selecting choice fruit for their
> picnic meal.*
>
> *Holden has a special place in the hearts of most Australians for the beauty of its
> styling and for practical reasons, too.*

Here in the second paragraph is a neat reversal of reality. While its practicality was unchallenged, the Holden had never received much beyond faint
praise for its looks. Another advertisement cheekily claimed that 'Beauty is
Only One Reason for Holden Popularity'. A third declared that 'Holden's
beauty brings you pride and joy', and the opening line must surely have
made some readers laugh: 'It's a really *wonderful feeling* to own a car that's
widely admired for its beauty.' It would have been useful to provide some
evidence but none came. Instead, faith was placed in advertising. Holden ads
appeared in the *Australian Women's Weekly* and a three-car team with all-
female crews tackled the 1954 Redex. (Perhaps the copywriters would have
been better advised to take the approach Doyle, Dane Bernbach would later
use to great effect for the Volkswagen Beetle: a series of advertisements
parodied the car with themes such as 'Lemon' and 'The Only Beautiful
Picture of a Beetle'—with no car in shot!) The Beetle's success had to do with
its minimalism and to an extent the Holden's did too.

While the original Holden received strongly enthusiastic reviews, a
small number of criticisms were creeping into commentaries on the FJ. The
car's good engine performance and economy were acknowledged but no
longer in superlatives. As Tony Davis observes in *Spotlight on Holden
1948–1959*, 'the FJ still offered great value for money and had an unbeat-
able reputation for ruggedness'. When exports to New Zealand commenced
in November 1954 with an initial shipment of fifteen Standard models,

advertising tended to concentrate on this theme. General Motors of New Zealand promoted the Holden as: 'Australia's famous car for dependability and rugged transportation.' Styling is given just one short sentence—'At the same time it boasts most attractive lines.' New cars were prohibitively expensive in New Zealand and there were waiting lists. Arguably, the New Zealand market was even more car-starved in 1954 than Australia had been in 1948; styling was the least of buyers' concerns. The vehicle population was aged, and those in the market for a new car were principally concerned with the cost of ownership and vehicle durability.

The most important and longest 1954 road test was the 9600-mile (15,456 km) Redex Round Australia Trial, the second staging of what was seen as a definitive motoring event. Notwithstanding that a four-cylinder Peugeot 203 had won the 1953 Redex, more entrants in 1954 chose a Holden than any other model, in many cases presumably because this was the car they already owned. Of the 246 starters departing the Sydney Showground on 3 July 1954, 31 were FJ Holdens (three of which were entered for the *Woman's Weekly*). Other well represented makes included Peugeot, whose sales had jumped as a consequence of the previous year's victory, Standard with the rugged Vanguard, Ford with a mixture of V8s and Zephyrs, and Humber with the big, fast Super Snipe. Twenty-four of the FJs finished, but like every other car in the field they were embarrassingly upstaged by an ancient 1948 Ford V8 (nicknamed 'The Grey Ghost') driven by charismatic 'Gelignite' Jack Murray, who won the event without losing a single point. Gelignite Jack crossed the finishing line wearing a gorilla mask, a stick of 'jelly' within reach, as if to emphasise the ease and ludicrousness of his victory in an already old car of essentially pre-war design. A Peugeot 203 came second and a Holden third. GMH's marketing people presumably took some consolation from the fact that the attrition rate across the whole field was much higher than for Holdens. Twenty-four—more than two-thirds—of the FJs finished whereas only just under half the field (120) made it back to Sydney.

The hip pocket nerve factor

Don Loffler notes that just one month after the 1954 event GMH cut Holden prices to keep demand running high. It also amounted to a tacit acknowledgement that with every passing year, every Redex Trial, every round of new model launches, the Holden had to rely more on value for money and reputation than on any other merits to sustain loyalty. This was a bit like Ford's experience with the Model T once Sloan got his 'car for every purse and purpose' policy into place: buyers could pay a little more for the latest GM car or buy another example of Old Faithful. The days of a black market were a distant memory by late 1954. However, evidence of respect for the car comes from a quick comparison of resale values.

In November 1955 (according to the 15 November 1955 edition of *Australian Monthly Motor Manual* magazine), a 1950 Holden was still worth £630 but an Austin A70 of the same year had depreciated to £525. Or the used-car buyer might have preferred the once-grand Armstrong Siddeley, which was also worth just £525! Typically five-year-old cars cost about 60 to 70 per cent of their new price, while the Holden was above 75 per cent and the Armstrong Siddeley was among the worst performers at around 30 per cent.

The FJ Holden's failure to win the 1954 or 1955 Redex Trials did not seem to hinder its sales prospects, even though it gave Peugeot and Volkswagen a leg up the charts. Perhaps ruggedness was assumed as a Holden trait five years and more after the debut of the 48–215; besides, Possum Kipling had come very close to outright victory in 1953. And there was great interest in making the Australian car go faster. Magazine publishers knew that stories dedicated to this subject would help sales and there were quite a few stories of highly modified '100 mile per hour' (161 km/h) Holdens. Numerous small companies produced accessories designed to enhance the performance, appearance, handling or comfort of Holdens, and mid 1950s magazines contained advertisements for Lukey mufflers, twin or triple carburettor conversions and even fibreglass sports bodies. A subsidiary company of GMH, Nasco, produced a bewilderingly comprehensive range of 1950s-flavoured automotive accessories including a Venetian blind for the rear window, Coolaride cushion seat pad, chrome hood ornament and all-weather window shields. By 1955 the Holden had been the top-selling make for four years, remembering that there was just the one basic car in different variants where Ford, for example, had the Anglia, Prefect, Consul, Zephyr and Custom/Customline, which makes the Holden's dominance all the more impressive. There was a strong demand for Holden accessories. So by equipping one's FJ Special with a Lukey muffler, twin-carburettor conversion and perhaps a set of rear-wheel spats, it was *almost* possible to forget how similar it was to a 1948 model.

Detroit's priorities were evident in the FJ Special but in a muted way. By the time it was launched the new season 1954 models were on show, and with few exceptions they were bigger, chromier and significantly more powerful than their predecessors of 1949. An FJ might have kept performance company with a Chevy, but things would change in just twelve months when General Motors brought high performance to America's best-selling brand via a new V8 engine. The six-cylinder 'Stove Bolt' unit, little changed since 1937, was effectively replaced as Americans embraced V8 engines in their age of plenty. As recently as 1952, the Chevrolet had received damning praise as being the best choice for conservative drivers who rarely ventured beyond 60 miles per hour (97 km/h). Ford had long built V8 engines and the 1955 versions were competitive, but this was the first time the top-selling brand of the biggest automotive corporation in the world had offered a modern high-compression engine of this configuration.

The Chevrolet filled the same mainstream role in the United States market as the FJ Holden Special did in Australia. By 1955 the Ford Customline offered a modern high-powered V8 and was an aspirational vehicle for many Australian motorists. The Customline's performance, style and price defined it as a member of a much higher class than the now humble Holden. This was the next big step upmarket, and many a used Holden made way for a lusty chrome-laced new season's Customline.

So by 1955 the Holden not only looked old but its performance, while still class-leading (if only for about one more year), no longer represented

... it does serve to underline how advanced the Holden had been in 1948, what a triumph of engineering it had represented then, how worthy it was to have been Australia's first mass-produced car.

any kind of international benchmark worthy of special comment in the pages of British motoring journals. This may not have been relevant to buyers, but it does serve to underline how advanced the Holden had been in 1948, what a triumph of engineering it had represented then, how worthy it was to have been Australia's first mass-produced car. Even in 1955, very few cars still offered 80 miles per hour (128 km/h) top speed as well as the ability to return 30 miles (48 km) to the gallon, but plenty could approach 100 miles per hour (161 km/h) or sprint to 60 miles per hour (97 km/h) more swiftly than an FJ, even though few were available in Australia at less than double the Holden's price. Expectations of performance were changing, driven by Detroit. And fuel economy, never really an issue in the United States, was becoming less important to Australian motorists.

The FE makes its debut

It was indeed Detroit that drove the agenda for the FE Holden which finally went on sale in July 1956. Paradoxically, the FE was the first model to be styled in Australia, the work done by Alf Payze under the supervision of Glen Smith, who reported to Detroit. Where the original Holden had been midway between American and European cars not just in its size and general configuration but also in style, Payze appears to have taken many of his cues from the 1955 Chevrolet, even though that car's 'wraparound' windscreen feature lay three and a half years further into Holden's model calendar. Three-box styling, more extensive use of chrome, a curved windscreen and rear window, smaller diameter road wheels (down from 15 inches to 13) and the longer-wider-lower theme so favoured in the mid 1950s set the FE Holden dramatically apart from its 'Humpy' predecessors.

Accurate news of Holden's bold new styling preceded the official timing. Six weeks before GMH announced the FE, *Modern Motor* published leaked photos of incomplete FEs on the production line. More daringly, two journalists from the magazine took jobs at Holden's Fishermans Bend factory so that they could get a more thorough 'scoop' on the car. They smuggled a camera into the plant and took photographs of the finished FE. This was the most famous Australian motoring news story of the era and precipitated a lasting tradition of scoops at *Modern Motor*, not all of them as accurate as this one.

For three successive editions the FE Holden was the cover story, and this more than any other single piece of evidence conveys the significance of the 1956 model to the Australian car-buying public. When the FE went on sale in July, the magazine purchased its own example at full retail price. A road test duly appeared in the August edition: 'The car was waiting for me in a busy city street. Fighting my way to it through the admiring crowd, I finally slid in behind a handsome steering wheel with gull-wing spokes and a most decorative chrome-plated horn ring.' However, beneath its elegant new bodywork the FE Holden was remarkably like the 1948 model, using much of the same mechanical componentry. The engine had been reworked slightly to deliver a little more power and the gearing was different (thanks mainly to the use of the smaller diameter wheels). The FE also got a 12-volt electrical system, only a year or so after this feature was introduced on Chevrolets. With its longer wheelbase, wider tracks and revised suspension, the new model cornered better and was more stable at high speeds. A little more than an inch of ground clearance had been sacrificed, but at the official claim of 7.33 inches (186 mm), the Holden still cleared the road by more than most mid 1950s models. *The Autocar* was 'pleased to record . . . greatly improved handling qualities'. It also had a better steering system and smoother gearchange.

Because the new Holden was bigger with more room for passengers and luggage, it was also heavier, and every bit of the extra power was required to endow it with a similar level of performance to the 1948 model but with no chance of matching the old models' fuel economy. Testers mused over this aspect of the FE Holden but criticism was mainly muted; by 1956 Australian motoring priorities were admittedly different from those of 1948, with petrol rationing a faded memory and the price per gallon cheap by international standards. But by any empirical standards the FE Holden's performance–economy equation was markedly inferior to that of its predecessors—a significant step not sideways but backwards. 'The FJ had it all over its successor for top-gear punch and flexibility', claimed *Modern Motor*, 'and in the advertising blurbs on the FE "some owners" no longer reported "upwards of 30 m.p.g."'. The magazine was also able to report that at a steady 30 miles per hour (48 km/h) the car could achieve 30 miles per gallon, which contrasted with the original Holden's 37 miles per gallon at an average speed of 35 miles per hour (56 km/h). This fuel efficiency had been astonishing for a six-cylinder, six-seater car in 1948 and was a direct consequence of Russ Begg's tightly controlled engineering program which paid scrupulous attention to keeping the weight out of the car. But by the time the FE was under development, Begg was back in Detroit and no such guidelines applied. The later model weighed some 5 per cent more but its fuel economy declined by more than 10 per cent, so other aspects of its engineering also played a part—the tuning changes to the engine and the lower overall gearing key among these, as mentioned in the July 1958 issue of *Modern Motor*:

> . . . *not easy to see why the FE wasn't superior in the first place to the FJ in all departments. Output went up from 60 to 70 b.h.p., for a weight increase of only 1 cwt., giving the car a better power/weight ratio.*
>
> *Presumably the motor development brains fouled things up somewhere.*

So, in summary, while the 48–215 had delivered functional excellence without a great sense of fashion, the FE could be said to have almost reversed the process: it was a competent and rugged car of high style.

No longer, though, did the Holden eclipse all would-be rivals in almost every area of mechanical design. Indeed, the differences between the cars of the mid 1950s and those of the late 1940s were equivalent to the differences between the 1940s models and their 1939 predecessors; the march of automotive technology was rapid. In 1956 Ford introduced the Mark II Zephyr, which had significantly better performance than the FE with similar fuel economy. For 1957 Austin had a lusty A95 Westminster, which as well as having more engine power than the Holden also had a four-speed gearbox. Of course, both these models

> While the 48–215 had delivered functional excellence without a great sense of fashion, the FE could be said to have almost reversed the process: it was a competent and rugged car of high style.

were more expensive, but the Holden no longer stood alone. Among four-cylinder cars, the Peugeot 403 was far more refined and dynamically poised than the Holden. Its overall performance was of a similar order with superior fuel economy. And the French model offered far more comfortable seats in a richer feeling interior. So to some extent the FE Holden could be said to have traded on the reputation developed by its predecessors. Buying a Holden had become the Australian default position: this was Australia's *volkswagen* in the true sense of the term and with none of that nasty xenophobia and racism inherent in Hitler's use of *volk* and *volkisch*. It might have done well in other markets, too. *The Motor*, in its road test of an FE in the context of England's green and pleasant land, rated it rather highly:

> *There is no doubt that the Holden is a sensible, durable and practical car which, although produced specifically for one Continent, would find a ready market if ever it were made available throughout the world.*

Two developments in 1957 served to remind the Australian public and executives of rival companies that the homegrown Holden was absolutely the dominant brand in Australia. The first was the opening of the GMH proving ground at Lang Lang, south-east of Melbourne, and the second was the introduction of a station wagon version of the FE, known quaintly as the Station Sedan. By 1957 almost one in two new vehicles sold in Australia was produced by GMH and most were Holdens.

A lot more car for the money

In 1958 the FC model was introduced and this became the most popular Holden of the 1950s, achieving the highest market share. Its relationship to the FE was somewhat like that of the FJ to the 48–215—hardly a major revision, but a facelift with some extra features and improvements. GMH's engineers had revisited the engine tune and the FC proved slightly less thirsty, while offering modestly improved performance. Under the heading 'Smoother, Thriftier New Holden', *Modern Motor*'s Bryan Hanrahan began his test: 'Might sound like it, but there's nothing rude in saying the latest version of the FE Holden, the FC, is now as good a performer all round as the original FJ model.' *The Motor* tested an FC Special sedan in Britain, describing it as 'a roomy and easy-going "six" which is the best-selling car "Down Under"'. However, the magazine noted that: 'The measured figures for acceleration, maximum speed, top gear hill-climbing ability and fuel economy which appear on the date page are creditable rather than exceptional, and fall short of what recent 6-cylinder Vauxhalls have achieved.' In the conclusion, the road tester correctly analysed the 'single reason' for the Holden's continuing success:

> If there is any single reason for the Holden dominating Australia's motoring scene in a way for which it is hard to find a counterpart anywhere else in the free world, it must be that General Motors-Holden's Ltd. offer Australian customers a lot more car for their money than do other manufacturers. The one size of car on which they

concentrate obviously appeals to a great proportion of Australian motorists as providing a sensible combination of roominess and performance with moderate running costs. The practical advantages secured by developing one basic design for more than 10 years have, in Australia, obviously outweighed the commercial advantages which lead manufacturers elsewhere in the world to introduce new models with greater frequency.

There was no doubt GMH played its home-ground advantage to the full. Economies of scale had taken strong effect after 'more than 10 years' of the same basic design, and it still cost more to buy a Ford Zephyr, Vauxhall Velox or Standard Vanguard (now, at last, of monocoque construction and with an Italian-styled body), none of which offered greater space or would be as cheap to run. It was a kind of continuing victory by default. When you have a true *volkswagen*, most people need a compelling reason to put their money elsewhere. The FC Holden was a worthy car, essentially an FJ with more modern looks, superior accommodation for passengers and luggage, and better stability. It rates somewhere between average and creditable against other mainstream sedans that sold strongly on overseas markets, among these the Peugeot 403, Mercedes-Benz 220S, the Vauxhall Velox and Standard Vanguard. On mechanical design and performance/economy alone it was no longer advanced or even distinctive. But all challengers cost considerably more, while the FC Special was barely 10 per cent dearer than the Australian-manufactured 1.5-litre BMC twins, the Morris Major and Austin Lancer. The Lancer was rhymingly described as the 'family car answer' but BMC misunderstood the Australian question.

When you have a true *volkswagen*, most people need a compelling reason to put their money elsewhere.

Where it was possible at the time, and equally so with hindsight, to judge the FC Holden kindly, the same grace does not apply to its 1960 successor, the FB. If ever there was a 1950s car that was released in the wrong decade, this was the FB Holden. Even the name reveals an error of timing: GMH had planned to release it in 1959 but production was delayed. 'FB' was code for '1959'. A little extra power was squeezed out of what was by 1960 an old-fashioned engine, but overall performance was not improved and economy suffered. At the time of its introduction the magazine writers were positive, but their tone changed when the Ford Falcon was introduced. For example, in the April 1961 edition, *Modern Motor* declared the FB to be a 'slip-back' in some areas of design. *The Autocar* delivered faint praise with a caution:

> *While the car is restyled, the 'new look' cannot be described as radical, and there is obvious similarity between the 1960 Holden and the 1957 U.S. models from the parent G.M. plants . . .*
>
> *By completing production of the previous Holden before the Christmas holidays, G.M.-Holden start off a new year with a new model and with virtually no stocks left of the previous design. This may be important, for the Ford Motor Co. of Australia, Ltd., intend to market a six-cylinder 'all-Australian' car before the end of 1960; if this is offered at a similar price to the Holden, it could be a serious challenge.*

At the start of the new decade, then, the Holden was still the only locally manufactured six-cylinder car on offer and its value for money was still unquestionable at £1100 for the Special sedan. As for the BMC models mentioned above, these struggled to compete with the Volkswagen, successful here in the under-£1000 bracket. Buyers accepted the FB Holden, despite performance and economy being by now below average for the engine size. Its outright performance was almost identical to that of the 48–215, but the fifteen additional brake horsepower were required to shift its greater mass— up from 20 hundredweight to 22.25, a similar percentage increase to that of the maximum power output. While overall economy in the region of 30 miles per gallon was a much quoted 48–215 attribute, the FB owner did well to achieve 25. The Holden, despite its Special nameplate and extroverted two-toning, was a spartan car by comparison with almost any European car, lacking even a rudimentary heater as standard equipment. Although the

FB was signed off by Harley Earl's styling department, it was already old when new and derivative of the 1957 Chevrolet.

Design complacency sets in

While General Motors' cars in all other world markets faced strong competition, the Holden did not and this is the main reason why there was no significant advancement in design between 1948 and 1960. John Bagshaw, who worked in sales and marketing when the 48–215 was launched, served later as head of that department in the 1970s and returned in 1988 as managing director, told me that complacency set in within 'the first six months of Holden being such a market leader'.

The products of Detroit throughout the 1950s did not seek Bauhaus marks of approval and seemed at times to be parodic in their extremes, but at least they competed with each other. Battista Pininfarina might have been peering into a crystal ball when he launched his elegant new Cisitalia sports coupe in 1946, describing it as introducing modern 'Italian taste' and famously declaring his war in the name of 'aesthetic purity'.

Aesthetic purity or no, American buyers got much more performance, comfort and convenience beyond mere extra size in any 1959 or 1960 model than in its counterpart of ten years earlier. Power-assisted steering and brakes, automatic transmission and high performance were all givens of the typical 'Big Three' behemoths by the end of the first full postwar decade. Acceleration from zero to 60 miles per hour (97 km/h) took about ten seconds in a Chevrolet, Ford or Plymouth V8 and the top speed was upwards of 100 miles per hour (161 km/h), compared with seventeen seconds and 85 respectively in 1950. And such an apparently small but significant item as an electric windscreen wiper motor had been taken for granted for years, to the extent that the FB Holden was one of the last mass-produced cars in the world not to incorporate one. British Vauxhalls, as already noted, were livelier than the Holden by 1957, as was the Opel Kapitän. And buyers of these GM mid-sizers could specify two-pedal motoring, a luxury Australians would not get until 1961.

Ford Australia's managing director, Charlie Smith, had decided by 1956 that his company would have to embark on full local manufacture and the car chosen was the Zephyr. The plan was to introduce a facelifted version of the Mark II model in 1959 or 1960 to be manufactured in a brand new factory at Broadmeadows, north of Melbourne. But a trip to Dearborn, Michigan, to view the planned Australian Zephyr produced a change of mind. Smith was given a sneak preview of the still unreleased US Falcon, the first of the North American 'compact' models intended to end the dominance of the Volkswagen among smaller cars.

When Smith and his men viewed the sleek new Falcon they probably gave no thought to Holden's Lang Lang facility, but hindsight reports this as a major mistake, which will be analysed later in the narrative.

It was a sober group that met with our Canadian directors and decided that this vehicle looked like a real breakthrough in terms of an economical, well styled vehicle, and as such, recommended it to be adopted by Ford Australia as a locally manufactured product.

When the Ford Falcon was introduced in September 1960, the immediate strong demand suggested that some of the Holden's recent dominance was by default. The advent of a strikingly modern looking rival with superior performance and optional automatic transmission seemed to herald a new era in Australian motoring. Initially, Falcon sales were strong but problems quickly sullied the newcomer's reputation. This car which stood up satisfactorily to North American conditions was insufficiently robust to handle Australian suburban roads, which belied Ford Australia's claims to have undertaken exhaustive local tests. Charlie Smith would only have needed to drink a glass of Foster's Lager with his counterpart at GMH to have been able to guess this scenario. This tells us something about the insularity of the Ford approach to thinking globally compared with that of GM, at least during the Sloan heyday.

Will you still love me in 1964?

The 48–215 was not just the best car in the world for Australia, it was one of the best cars in the world, full stop. While the EH Holden, even with its vigorous new (149 and 179 cubic inch) engines, could no longer be called one of the best cars in the world, it was still probably the best car in the world for Australia.

> **The 48–215 was not just the best car in the world for Australia, it was one of the best cars in the world, full stop.**

Imagine if GMH had spent more money developing the car and less on styling changes, especially in the transition from FC to FB. But the entire organisation had become conservative in the post-Sloan era. Overzealous husbanding of 'the beans' had severe technological and safety implications, as seen in the Chevrolet Corvair episode. Fortunately, the Holden escaped most of this, although better brakes would have been appreciated, especially in 1963 when the available power was almost twice what it had been in 1948 in a car less than 30 per cent heavier. Then editor of *Wheels* magazine, Bill Tuckey, has dined out for decades on his memorable heading, 'Tear along the Dotted Line', the line being made by the tyres in the erratic emergency braking trajectory of an EH Holden. What had been murmurings in earlier road tests became protest. 'Australia's Own Car' was no longer quite the sacred cow it had been.

Complacency and conservatism caused GMH to squander much of its product potential in the late 1950s. The three most celebrated Holdens of the 1948–1965 period were the FJ, FC and EH. Had GMH foregone the FB makeover and instead uprated the FC with a higher level of equipment, better brakes, electric wipers and the 75-brake horsepower engine, such a vehicle could have been highly competitive until about 1962. More comfortable seats would have been easy. A temperature gauge rather than an 'idiot light' would have been appreciated, especially by country drivers. As for the brakes, I am not talking about the adoption of the still fairly new disc brake technology but a refinement of the existing drum system. European manufacturers such as Fiat and Peugeot did so well with this technology that they did not make the switch to discs until 1960 and 1967 respectively. Even Rolls-Royce did not equip its cars with disc brakes until 1965. But even in 1948 Holden drum brakes were the weak point in an excellent design. They did not improve through the following decade, meaning that they were marginal, giving average stopping distances. Directional stability was erratic—tear along the dotted line, indeed!—and fade was a problem.

Cylinder head improvements and a more efficient exhaust could easily have given the old engine an additional 10 horsepower over the FB's 75. But even 75 would have given the FC a lift in performance, improving acceleration and perhaps making a top speed of 86 or 87 miles per hour (138 or 140 km/h) achievable.

Such development work would have cost far less than the FB's new appearance. The FB, an unnecessary 5 inches (127 mm) longer for little extra interior space, brought another significant weight gain. If development work had begun on the EJ in 1957 when the proving ground was opened, GMH could probably have had the new 'red' engines ready for that model rather than its famous EH successor the flagship Premier Station Sedan version of which graces the cover of this book. But as it was, the FB-EK models represented a lot of marching in exaggerated form on the spot—a waste of time.

Lots has been written about the various Holden models and for our purposes a very quick overview will serve. The FB was viewed by many at the time of its launch as being, at best, only half a step or so forward. Its controversial 'dogleg' A-pillar, like most of its other styling themes, was pure 1957 Chevrolet but two and a half seasons late. There were still no electric wipers, still no option of an automatic transmission and, of course, the extra 5-brake horsepower vanished into the ether due to extra weight. Fuel consumption rose again to make this the thirstiest Holden to date.

The EK looked neater, had new acrylic lacquer (introduced partway through the FB's short cycle) and offered an automatic transmission option, but was old-fashioned even when launched late in 1961. A new car was sorely needed.

Modern Motor magazine believed it had this one covered—literally. The cover of the April 1961 edition showed a strange looking car circulating at the Lang Lang proving ground. Here indeed was stylist Alf Payze's version of the EJ. But the Americans refused to endorse the design and made changes especially around the front and rear. There was no denying that the production EJ looked much better than the Aussie prototype. But what followed was a loss of local autonomy. The facelifted EH was done in the United States, arriving in a packing crate. Pontiac chief stylist of the late 1950s, Joe Schemansky, was appointed director of design and the 1966 HR was his first effort.

But back to the EJ, which was certainly a big improvement. It was elegant in the contemporary fashion of the 1961–62 Chevrolets. Several inches of unnecessary length had vanished. The new Holden was lower, more comfortable and handled much better. There was an excitingly luxurious Premier variant, which carried a premium over the Special of about £300 at £420. It was the next step, after the Special and the Station Sedan, towards introducing Sloan's product policy to Holden. The Premier gave owners rich local cowhide and front bucket seats. There was deep carpet and a heater as standard equipment. Automatic transmission was standard and so was metallic paint. The steering wheel was white, just like on your neighbour's Mercedes. It was high fashion for Holden, a worthy contender for the garages of Toorak where it could take up custody alongside a Merc or Jag or maybe a Pontiac. Of course, the Premier was also heavier and its automatic transmission further taxed the 75 horses corralled in the grey engine. On outright performance it was no match for the 48–215 and used up to 50 per cent more fuel.

There is a positive lurking here. The EJ Premier still performed to a standard most customers were happy with. It could run to about 78 miles per hour (126 km/h) and cruise at close to 70 (112 km/h). You could accelerate quite smartly once you'd moved the weight away from a standing start. This tends to highlight the brilliance of the original Holden's performance. Let's look at it another way. Launched just after the Holden 48–215 was the Morris Oxford, an all-new British monocoque sedan. Its 1.5-litre four-cylinder engine delivered 41 horsepower. Compared with the Holden it was p-a-i-nfully slow. Now imagine a 1962 Oxford that was slower than the 1949 model. Inconceivable.

Holden had gained just 25 per cent more power in fourteen years, where most manufacturers had picked up more like 50 or 60 per cent.

Holden had gained just 25 per cent more power in fourteen years, where most manufacturers had picked up more like 50 or 60 per cent. The 1962 Morris Oxford produced 60 horsepower, just like the original Holden, but it was heavier and slower than the inaugural version of 'Australia's Own Car'. And the British Motor Corporation, which delivered the Oxford, had a new six-cylinder model for Australia—the Austin Freeway, launched three months before the EJ; the Freeway with its 'Blue Streak' sixpack could just keep pace with the EJ!

What this tells us is that the engineering brilliance which went into first the Experimental Light Car 195-Y–15 and then the Holden 48–215, especially in terms of the performance/economy equation, was the best in the world. The Holden was perhaps the finest example of Alfred P. Sloan Jr's vision for General Motors. It was a true *volkswagen*, conceived especially for Australia but good enough to sell anywhere.

The 1951 Ford Zephyr had 68 horsepower, but the 1962 Mark III model delivered 106 and the upmarket Zodiac 114. As for the prestige cars, most of which were slower than the original Holden, they had progressed even more dramatically. The 1949 Jaguar Mark V had 125 horsepower. The 1962 Mark X had 264. The much-mentioned Wright family's 1950 Armstrong Siddeley Whitley had 75, but the last ever Armstrong Siddeley, the Star Sapphire (discontinued in 1960), boasted 165. The world had moved on a long way. Mainstream cars had really only just eclipsed the 48–215's performance levels heading into the 1960s, but a standard Holden could no longer keep company with luxury models by the early 1950s.

As for the EJ Premier, it undoubtedly represented a new point in style and sophistication for what had started out as a simple utility car conceived in wartime. When the Holden came to market there were just one million cars on Australian roads. The two million mark was reached in 1956. The millionth Holden (a bronze EJ Premier sedan) passed down the line in October 1962, which indicates the enormity of the Holden's contribution to mass motorisation. Fittingly, number 1,000,000 was an EJ Premier.

How does the EH fit into our story? By spring 1963 when it went on sale, Australian buyers were already being spoiled for power with the lusty Chrysler Valiant. But the first all-new engines since 1948 gave the EH serious appeal. The standard 'red' six offered 100 horsepower to the Valiant's 145, but the larger capacity optional '179' made 115. In the real world there was little difference in performance between the Holden and the heavier Chrysler. Both were quick cars by 1963 standards.

The EH very nearly re-established the kind of supremacy the '48' model exhibited, although admittedly it was joined by the Valiant, if not quite the XM Falcon. In Premier guise, here was a truly desirable machine—quick, beautifully trimmed and finished, tough in the Holden way, spacious and the height of 1963 elegance. By this time, apart from the Premier, only very expensive cars used genuine hide. And, prudently, the car came with manual transmission (unavailable on the EJ Premier) as standard, so buyers didn't have to put up with the hiccoughing Hydra-Matic. Metallic paint—called 'iridescent' then—was still a distinguishing feature of Premiers; even the gold badging looked good, and who was going to complain about the famous '179' chequered flag badge, except when it went missing? Power-assisted steering had arrived on the options list. GMH was developing disc brakes for the front wheels but they would not be ready for another couple of years. And imagine if some of those hard-working engineers had considered the use of Michelin radial tyres on the Premier version. (It would have been easy enough to get hold of some sets and torture-test them on prototypes at the fantastic Lang Lang facility.) My point is that the EH Premier provided the basis for a car every bit as exceptional in 1963 as the '48' had been fifteen years earlier. A

The EH Premier provided the basis for a car every bit as exceptional in 1963 as the '48' had been fifteen years earlier.

disc-braked example with radials and power steering would have set Holden right in among the smaller capacity six-cylinder Mercedes and Jaguar models at half the price and considerably less than half the long-term running costs. (And if the engine of your Jag overheated to the point of destruction, you couldn't just replace it with a reconditioned unit from Repco, as you could with a Holden.) So the EH, especially the Premier manual version, represented a serious update of the original concept: functionally, it was superior to any comparably priced car on the Australian market.

Sadly though, it was mostly downhill after the EH. The 1965 HD, wholly styled in the United States, combined a wider body with the same tracks. It was over-bodied, ill-handling, heavier, thirstier, and on the story went. In terms of a chronological narrative, the HD constitutes a good place to stop, or at least to rest.

Important cars in the era of the early Holdens, 1946–55

- **1934 (but really 1945)** The Volkswagen Beetle takes over from the Model T as the world's *volkswagen*. Perhaps the Holden had similar potential? One difference was that, although the Volkswagen's styling changed little from the late 1940s until 1967, the technical features and equipment levels received steady improvements. Arguably, a 1961 Volkswagen represented a bigger step forward from its 1948 predecessor than the EK Holden did from the 48–215. The Morris Minor was another potential *volkswagen*. The 1961 Minor 1000, for example, was far superior to its 1948 predecessor, but greater changes might have kept it competitive internationally for longer.

- **1947** Chevrolet announces it will indefinitely suspend production of a smaller Chevrolet. The Cadet program began in 1945, just as the Holden was being completed. But it was a very different type of car. (Read: Ford Zephyr prototype.)

- **1948** The new Cadillac, styled by Frank Hershey, becomes one of the most influential automotive designs of its era. Oh yes, Frank also styled a 'cute little car' called the Holden.

- **1951** Ford of England releases its six-cylinder Zephyr. In many aspects it is similar to the Holden—engine size, performance, interior space, monocoque construction. But its 'straight-through' styling, low-slung body and small wheels reveal a different agenda. This car was to have been the Chevrolet Cadet, aborted in 1947. Some of the Zephyr's styling themes came from Frank Hershey's experimental models of 1945–46.

- **1955** The (1.5-litre) Peugeot 403 is introduced in Europe. This successor to the Redex-winning (1.2-litre) 203 is probably the best conventional sedan in the world at this time. Brilliant steering, handling and ride, astonishing ruggedness, an overdrive transmission and high cruising speed make it a favoured choice of enthusiasts. The 403 succeeds in Australia, too, from 1956, and marks the point at which in objective terms the Holden no longer seems the only viable mainstream car choice. But in conservative Australia, the 403 remains something of a fringe dweller. Sophisticated, poised and elegant as it is, you can't carry six occupants and tow a trailer as easily as you can in an FE Holden. The would-be revenge of the 'four'.

- **1955** The astonishing Citroën DS19 offers a different way forward. Like the Peugeot 403 it will be assembled in Australia, but it sells in a completely different class to the Holden. In 1955 it serves to show how old fashioned the FJ's styling has become.

Conclusion

The iconic status of the Holden in Australia is well acknowledged, but the historical significance of 'Australia's Own Car' can only be properly understood in the international context of General Motors as fashioned by Alfred P. Sloan Jr from the early 1920s through to the late 1940s. Unlike his chief rival Henry Ford, Sloan developed a product policy that did not devolve upon a 'one size fits all' approach. He understood that as initial demand for motor cars in the US became saturated and a majority of new car buyers sought replacement vehicles, the primitive Ford Model T would lose its appeal. Higher performance, a greater range of convenience features, and more aesthetic appeal would count for more than basic utility allied to a bargain basement price.

Equally importantly, Sloan understood that overseas markets were different, and that GM needed to participate multinationally through the General Motors Export Company (later renamed General Motors Overseas Operations) in order to maximise its success. The imperative was to respond to local demands: under Sloan, GM thought *locally* in order to act *globally*. This multinational process arguably had its real origins in the deal struck with Holden Motor Body Builders of Adelaide in 1923 to secure all production from its new Woodville plant for General Motors bodies (to be fitted

to imported chassis). Rather than start its own locally-based body manufacturer, General Motors Export Company preferred to use an existing
operator. Then in 1925 GM bought the British company, Vauxhall. In 1929
the corporation acquired Opel as its German subsidiary. Two years later GM
acquired the Holden company and General Motors-Holden's (GMH) was
formed. Where Vauxhall and Opel manufactured entire cars, GMH made
car bodies to be fitted to imported chassis.

Historians of the Holden and, indeed, those whose focus is General
Motors itself, have failed to grasp the importance of the Opel connection
to the future of GM. Even Henry Ashby Turner (*General Motors and the
Nazis*) does not explore the broader consequences for the corporation in
developing Opel to the extent it did in the 1930s, the question being outside
the scope of his study. Opel was unquestionably the greatest automotive
beneficiary of Nazi industrial policy. In 1933 Hitler removed sales tax from
new cars. At the time German motorisation was equivalent to that of the US
in 1911. Fordist mass production technology had only arrived in Germany
when General Motors acquired Opel, which already sold more cars on its
domestic market than any other manufacturer. Remarkable synergies
ensued. By 1936 Opel became the first mass producer of monocoque (one-
piece, meaning the chassis and the body were of integral construction) cars
in the world. This breakthrough technology offered great potential to make
stronger and lighter vehicles which performed better and used less fuel.

The key engineer in this process was Russell S. Begg who, by the outbreak
of World War II (and safely ensconced back in Detroit just weeks later), was
among the most widely experienced practitioners in the automotive world.
He was certainly foremost in the development of unitary construction. The
work he did in the 1930s was not emulated by many companies until after
World War II and the cars built in Detroit, especially those of GM, Ford
and Chrysler, continued to be large body-on-frame designs rather than
monocoques.

Vauxhall in Britain followed the Opel lead and in 1937 General Motors
Overseas Operations began its own experiments on monocoque vehicles

in Detroit. It was one of these experimental cars (Experimental Light Car 195-Y-15) that was later transformed into the Holden. The genius of Russell Begg was indispensable to the entire process, which began at Opel and culminated in the first Holden. Only General Motors could have given Australian its own car; only Russell Begg could have driven this process so expertly.

Hitler launched World War II in September 1939, earlier than would have been possible without the dramatic advance of the indigenous automotive industry, led by Opel. By this stage General Motors had lost control of its German subsidiary to the Nazis, writing it off as a tax loss in late 1942. But Opel made more trucks than any other company and before the end of the war Daimler-Benz would be compelled to produce Opel Blitz trucks under licence.

Historians have rarely paid much attention to the implications for the international automotive industry of World War II. That is largely because most scholars have approached such questions from a national perspective. It is widely understood how the domestic US industry grew phenomenally in the postwar years and how its vehicles reflected a new prosperity. Equally, the plight of postwar Britain, still in the grip of petrol rationing and with a desperate need to export 50 per cent of its automotive production, has been well documented. So, too, has the future of the Volkswagen. But the nexus between Opel in the 1930s and the development of the Australian car has been largely neglected by scholars. While historians of the Holden have tended to a nationalist approach without wishing to acknowledge the depth of US involvement, let alone the Opel legacy, students of General Motors have generally taken a perplexingly US-centric approach. Few seem aware that the growth of Opel during the Third Reich was exponential, and unparalled by any other major automotive brand in the world.

The first three major wars of the twentieth century (Boer, World War I, World War II)—increasingly dependent as each was on industrial capability —exerted a major influence on the automotive industry in Australia and the history of the Holden company. In the Boer War Holden built a strong reputation with the Australian government through its prompt supply of high-quality saddles. World War I imposed limits on shipping which led to the development of an indigenous body building industry with Holden, again, the major player. But it took World War II to provide the impetus for full automotive manufacture.

Even before the war in the Pacific had drawn to its close, the Australian Labor government was making overtures to the local industry to manufacture a car in Australia. A strong local automotive manufacturer was seen to be as important in the Australia of the late 1940s as it had been in Germany fifteen years earlier, and for essentially the same reason: only a strong automotive industry can be harnessed to national defence (or, in the case of Germany, attack); plants that manufacture cars in peacetime can make trucks, tanks, guns, aircraft engines and even aircraft for war.

The Curtin government turned first to General Motors-Holden's, partly perhaps because it was the market leader, but mainly because the managing director, Larry Hartnett, was well known in government circles and its director of ordnance. GMH had been Australia's largest manufacture of war materiel. Hartnett is widely credited as the father of the Holden but Sloan and his senior colleagues in General Motors Overseas Operations (GMOO) were already keen on the possibility of manufacturing entire cars in Australia. Hartnett went to New York to argue his case and the executive committee agreed.

Russ Begg was appointed chief engineer to adapt the experimental light car to meet a blueprint laid out by GMOO after reading Hartnett's 'wish list'. So, while the concept of a new car somewhere 'between the two types' of large American car and smaller English car was Hartnett's, the engineering was a dialectic of American and German but with significant Australian input. No other manufacturer in the world could have developed such a car in 1945. The very requirements for the Australian market—strength, durability, lightness, fuel economy and high performance—were uniquely fulfilled by Begg's decision to combine a powerful six-cylinder engine and a very light body. Even some of his senior colleagues were deeply sceptical but the approach turned out to be as successful as it was radical.

The Holden was the best car made anywhere in the world in 1948 when it came to meeting the unique demands of Australia. This was a very different machine from either an American Chevrolet or a German Opel. It was even different from the similar sized but heavier E-Series Vauxhall introduced three years later. When historians pass judgement on the Holden they usually make favourable comparisons with other cars available in Australia in the popular price classes. But, in fact, the Holden bears comparison with much more expensive models available elsewhere in the world at the time. The Holden's acceleration was superior to many sports cars but it used no more fuel than a typical four-cylinder car of the era. It had as much space for passengers as the larger Chevrolet and swifter acceleration.

The rigour with which Begg and his team (many of whom were young Australians seconded to Detroit) engineered the Holden was born of the philosophy inaugurated by Sloan in the 1920s. Under Sloan, enormous attention was paid to meeting the specific requirements of each market. General Motors differed from Ford in its overseas policy. Where Ford built assembly plants, GM bought indigenous companies and combined their local experience with American techniques; General Motors embedded itself into local automotive culture. This was the synergy that bred the Holden car: Detroit plus Germany plus Australia equals the best in the world—for Australia!

Before the advent of the Holden, Australian motorists had inclined towards American cars that were more rugged and durable, although throughout the 1930s a growing number of consumers chose cheaper and smaller British cars. Hartnett's concept of a dialectic between the US and Europe had actually been embodied at Opel under Begg's direction. But where Germany had its new *autobahnen*, Australia still made do with roads closer to those of the Model T Ford era in North America. So a far greater level of ruggedness was required of the Holden than for cars made for any other western country. In many ways, the Holden was not just a new car but a new *kind* of car, combining European fuel economy with American performance and space and Model T ruggedness.

The basic design of the Holden was so good that the car won effortless market leadership as soon as supply met demand. Even though only modest engineering progress was made between 1948 and 1963, the Holden remained Australia's top-selling car. Sloan, of course, was well out of the picture by the mid 1950s and the General Motors corporate culture changed to one of excessive cost consciousness and complacency. The Chevrolet Corvair fiasco, detailed by Ralph Nader and former General Motors senior executive John Z. De Lorean, speaks of a very different corporation from the one Sloan drove from strength to strength from the 1920s through to planning for the post World War II era of dramatic industrial expansion. When Corvair engineers pointed out the designed-in dangers (to apply the memorable sub-title of Nader's *Unsafe at Any Speed*) of the car, the corporation's most senior executives did not listen. As De Lorean chillingly recalls, it was only when family members of these same executives died in Corvair crashes that changes were belatedly made. Had Sloan still been at the helm, the Corvair would have been modified before going on sale. Fortunately for Australia, it was Sloan's culture of thoroughness that informed the design of the Holden.

Afterword

The great news is that anyone reading this book will know that the spirit which took Holden to such iconic status in the 1950s is well and truly back in the 21st century. The name itself has been less exported than perhaps it should have been, but look beneath many a Chevrolet or Pontiac badge and there sits a proudly Australian car. Export Holdens from Australia to the United States? The unthinkable became reality just a few years ago when one of the mightiest of all American names—Pontiac GTO—was applied to a mildly revised Holden Monaro. And in March 2007 the announcement came through that the Commodore SS was going to Detroit as the Pontiac G8. It has been a long drive from Alfred P. Sloan Jr's product policy of the 1920s through the surge of Opel during the 1930s and the dusty black 195-Y-15 Experimental Light Car. Today the EFIJY show car and the VE Commodore combine to hint at the most captivating story in the history of General Motors.

Acknowledgements

I start by thanking my wife Jennie Hawkes Wright for her encouragement to tackle a PhD on the subject of the Holden. The PhD, still incomplete at this time of writing, led to *Special*.

During the past five years I have been well taught by a number of historians at the University of Melbourne. Dr June Senyard suggested a logical framework for the thesis. Professor Alan Mayne, who has since escaped from Melbourne to Adelaide, was a very patient and wise supervisor. I benefited from a period spent with Professor Chips Sowerwine. In the latter years of the thesis it was Dr David Goodman who helped me sharpen my focus and at the same time see the larger historical picture. In 2006 I was a tutor in Dr Steven Welch's Total War in Europe course and he invited me to present a guest lecture, the research for which yielded rich material on Nazi Germany of immediate and profound relevance for my PhD and this book.

Marc McInnes, retired executive of Holden's Limited (formerly GMH), has been a sensational help to me. Perhaps no-one knows more about Holden culture than he, who worked first as an engineer and then in public relations during a career spanning more than four decades. Marc's own passionate interest in automotive history pushed and pulled me in assorted, surprising directions, and I thank him for his untiring interest. Don Loffler,

234

my fellow Holden historian, has also offered advice from which I have bene-fitted. Thank you also to veteran motoring journalist Peter Robinson and Armstrong Siddeley expert Robert Penn Bradly for their suggestions. My good friend and Citroën lover Geoff Webber sketched the *Diesse* but his repertoire appears to know no bounds.

Annette Barlow of Allen & Unwin met me back in the days of *Heart of the Lion*. It was she who had the confidence to commission me to write a second history of Holden. I feel blessed to have such an encouraging publisher.

Thank you to all these people and to my friends and colleagues who offered thoughts about the place of the Holden car in Australian culture, or who have shared relevant automotive memories with me.

Select Bibliography

Books and articles

Armi, Edson C., *The Art of American Car Design: The Profession and Personalities: 'Not Simple Like Simon'*, Pennsylvania State University Press, University Park, 1988.

Armstrong Siddeley: Gold Portfolio, Brooklands Books, Surrey, c1994.

Banham, Russ, *The Ford Century*, Workman Publishing Company, New York, 2002.

Barthes, Roland, *Mythologies*, Paladin, London, 1976.

Bayley, S., *Harley Earl and the Dream Machine*, Weidenfeld & Nicolson, London, 1983.

Berger, Michael, *The Automobile in American History and Culture: A Reference Guide*, Westport, Connecticut, 2001.

Blainey, Geoffrey, *The Tyranny of Distance: How Distance Shaped Australia's History*, Macmillan, London, 1968.

—— *The Steel Master: a Life of Essington Lewis*, Macmillan, Melbourne, 1971.

—— *Jumping Over the Wheel*, Allen & Unwin, Sydney, 1993.

—— *A Shorter History of Australia*, William Heinemann, Melbourne, 1994.

Bradly, Robert Penn, *Armstrong Siddeley: The Postwar Cars*, Motor Racing Publications, Kent, 1989.

Broomham, Rosemary, *On the Road: The NRMA's First Seventy-Five Years*, Allen & Unwin, Sydney, 1996.

Brown-May, Andrew, *Melbourne Street Life*, Australian Scholarly Publishing Limited, Melbourne, 1998.

Burgess-Wise, David, *Vauxhall: A Century in Motion, 1903–2003*, CW Publishing, Oxford, 2003.

Bushby, A.C., *The Holden Collection*, A.C. Busby, city unspecified, Australia, 1978.

Buttfield, Nancy, *So Great A Change*, Ure Smith, Sydney, 1979.

Carson, Richard Burns, *The Olympian Cars: The Great American Luxury Automobiles of the Twenties and Thirties*, Alfred A. Knopf, New York, 1976.

Chandler, A.D. Jr, *Managerial Innovation of General Motors*, Arno Press, New York, 1979.

The Changing Trend, General Motors-Holden's, Melbourne, 1936.

Cheney, S.A., *From Horse to Horsepower*, Rigby, Melbourne, 1965.

Clune, Frank, *Land of Australia: 'Roamin' in a Holden'*, Hawthorn Press, Melbourne, 1953.

Commonwealth of Australia Yearbooks 1910–1955.

Country Roads of Victoria Board 34th Annual Report, 1946–47.

—— 42nd annual report, 1955.

Cray, Ed, *Chrome Colossus: General Motors and Its Times*, McGraw-Hill, San Francisco, 1980.

Critchlow, Donald T., *Studebaker*, Indiana University Press, Indiana, 1996.

Daley, Frank, *The Holden Saga*, unpublished manuscript.

Damman, George H., *75 Years of Chevrolet*, Crestline Publishing Company, Osceola, 1986.

Darwin, Norm, *The History of Holden Since 1917*, E.L. Ford Publications Pty Ltd, Geelong, 1983.

—— *The History of Ford in Australia*, Eddie Ford Publications, Geelong, 1986.

—— *100 Years of GM in Australia*, H@ND Publishing, Geelong, 2001.

Davis, Pedr, *Wheels Across Australia,* Marque Publishing, Sydney, 1987.

Davis, Tony, *Spotlight on Holden 1948–1959*, Marque Publishing Company, Sydney, 1994.

Davis, Tony and Kennedy, Ewan, *The Holden Heritage,* Holden Ltd, Melbourne, 1998.

Davison, Graeme, *Car Wars,* Allen & Unwin, Sydney, 2004.

Doherty, K, 'When we caught a tiger', in *N.W. Tasmania Short Stories and Articles,*Tasmanian Fellowship of Australian Writers, North West Branch, Boat Harbour, 1977.

Donner, Frederic G., *The World-Wide Industrial Enterprise: Its Challenge and Promise* (McKinsey Foundation Lecture Series), McGraw-Hill Book Company, New York, 1967.

Dupain, Max, *Max Dupain's Australia*, Viking, Melbourne, 1986.

Easdown, Geoff, *A History of the Ford Motor Company in Australia,* Golden Press, Sydney, 1987.

Farber, David R. *Sloan Rules: Alfred P. Sloan and the Triumph of General Motors,* Chicago University Press, Chicago, 2002.

Finch, Christopher, *Highways to Heaven,* HarperCollins, New York, 1992.

Flammang, James M. and Lewis, David L. and the Auto Editors of Consumer Guide, *Ford Chronicle,* International Publications, Lincolnwood, 2000.

Flink, James J., *The Car Culture,* The MIT Press, Cambridge, Massachusetts, 1975.

—— *The Automobile Age,* The MIT Press, Cambridge, Massachusetts, 1990.

Gartman, David, *Auto Opium: A Social History of American Automobile Design,* Routledge, London, 1994.

GM: The First 75 Years of Transportation Products, Automobile Quarterly, Princeton, 1983.

GMH Annual Reports 1948–1965.

GMH internal document: 'Market, Product and Cost Data Related to Projected Car Manufacture in Australia: supporting data for presentation "Australian Post War Car Manufacturing Program", October 25, 1944', Planning and Development Staff, New York, December 1944.

General Motors New Australian Car: HOLDEN, GMH, Melbourne, 1948.

Gregor, Neil, *Daimler-Benz in the Third Reich,* Yale University Press, London, 1998.

The Gympie Times, Gympie City Centenary Booklet, The *Gympie Times,* Gympie, 2005.

Halberstam, David, *The Reckoning,* Morrow, New York, 1986.

—— *The Fifties,* Fawcett Columbine, New York, 1993.

Hartnett, Laurence. J. (with John Veitch), *Big Wheels and Little Wheels,* Lansdowne, Melbourne, 1964.

Holden: The First Twenty-Five Years, General Motors-Holden's, Melbourne, 1973.

Holden: 1948–1962, Brooklands Books, London, no year of publication provided.

Hopfinger, K.B., *Beyond Expectation: The Volkswagen Story,* G.T. Foulis and Company, London, 1954.

Jennings, Jan (ed.), *Roadside America: The Automobile in Design and Culture,* Iowa University Press, Ames, 1990.

Kay, Jane Holtz, *Asphalt Nation,* Random House, New York, 1977.

Keating, Michael, *The Australian Workforce 1910–11 to 1960–61,* The Australian National University, Canberra, 1973.

Kuhn, Arthur J., *GM Passes Ford, 1918–1938*, The Pennsylvania State University Press, University Park, 1986.

Lacey, Robert, *Ford: The Men and the Machine*, Little, Brown and Company, Boston, 1986.

Lacey, Robert, *Ford*, Little, Brown and Company, Boston, 1986.

Lackey, James H., *The Jordan Automobile*, McFarland & Company, Jefferson, 2005.

Lawler, Ray, *The Summer of the Seventeenth Doll*, Samuel French, London, 1957.

Lees, Stella and Senyard, June, *The 1950s: How Australia Became a Modern Society and Everyone got a House and Car*, Hyland House, Melbourne, 1987.

Lewandowski, Jürgen, *Opel: The Company, the Cars, the People*, SüdwestVerlang GmbH & Co, Münich, 1995.

Lewchuck, W, *American Technology and the British Vehicle Industry*, Cambridge University Press, Cambridge, 1987.

Lewis, D.L., and Goldstein, L. (eds.), *The Automobile in American Culture*, University of Michigan Press, Michigan, 1983.

Loffler, Don, *She's A Beauty!*, Wakefield Press, Adelaide, 2006.

—— *Still Holden Together*, Wakefield Press, Adelaide, 2000.

—— *The FJ Holden*, Wakefield Press, Adelaide, 2002.

Lowell, Robert, *Life Studies*, Faber & Faber, London, 1959.

Marchand, Roland, *Advertising the American Dream : Making Way for Modernity, 1920–1940*, University of California Press, Berkeley, c1985.

McCarty, J.W., 'Australian Capital Cities in the Nineteenth Century' in *Australian Economic Review*, 10.

McDonald, John, *A Ghost's Memoir: The Making of Alfred P. Sloan's 'My Years with General Motors'*, The MIT Press, Cambridge, Massachusetts, 2002.

McShane, C, *Down the Asphalt Path: The Automobile and the American City*, Columbia University Press, Columbia, 1994.

Nader, Ralph, *Unsafe at Any Speed: The Designed-In Dangers of the American Automobile*, Grossman Publishers, New York, 1965.

Nieuwenhuis, Paul and Wells, Peter, 'The all-steel body as a cornerstone to the foundations of the mass production car industry' in *Industrial and Corporate Change*, volume 16, Number 2, 183–211 <<http://icc.oxfordjournals.org>>.

O'Connell, Sean, *The Car in British Society: Class, Gender and Motoring 1896–1935*, Manchester University Press, Manchester, 1998.

One Hunded & Fifty Years of News From The Herald, Portside Editions, Melbourne, 1990.

Patton, Phil, *Bug*, Simon & Schuster, New York, 2002.

Pettifer, Julian and Turner, Nigel, *Automania: Man and the Motor Car*, Collins, London, 1984.

Platt, Maurice, *An Addiction to Automobiles*, Frederick Warne, London, 1980.

Reyner, Banham, *Los Angeles: The Architecture of Four Ecologies*, University of California Press, Berkeley, 2001.

Rich, Joe, *Portrait of a Technocratic Brigand*, Turton and Armstrong, Sydney, 1996.

Richardson, Kenneth, *The British Motor Industry 1896–1936*, Macmillan, London, 1977.

Sachs, Wolfgang, *For Love of the Automobile*, University of California Press, Berkeley, 1992.

Sedgwick, Michael, *Cars of the Thirties and Forties*, Colporteur Press, Sydney, 1979.

—— *Cars of the Fifties and Sixties*, Colporteur Press, Sydney, 1983.

Shuler, Terry with Borgeson, Griffin and Sloniger, Jerry, *The Origin and Evolution of the VW Beetle*, Automobile Quarterly Publications, Princeton, 1985.

Sloan, Alfred P. Jr (in collaboration with Boyden Sparkes), *Adventures of a White-Collar Man*, Doubleday, Doran & Company, New York, 1941.

—— *My Years with General Motors*, Doubleday & Company, New York, 1964.

Stein, Ralph, *The Automobile Book*, Paul Hamlyn, London, 1962.

Stubbs, Peter, *The Australian Motor Industry: A Study in Protection and Growth*, Institute of Applied Economic and Social Research, Cheshire, 1972.

Tuckey, Bill, *True Blue: 75 Years of Ford in Australia*, Focus Publishing, Sydney, 2000.

Turner, Henry Ashby, *General Motors and the Nazis: The Struggle for Control of Europe's Biggest Carmaker*, Yale University Press, New Haven, 2005.

Two Centuries of Australian Art, National Gallery of Victoria, Melbourne, 2003.

Victorian Railway Commission Report for the year ended 30th June 1948 in Victorian Parliamentary Papers 1947–1948, volume two.

Victorian Yearbooks 1910–1955

Von Frankenburg, Richard. *Porsche: The Man and His Cars*, G.T. Foulis & Co. Ltd, London, 1965.

Wachs, M. and Crawford, M, *The Car and the City*, University of Michigan Press, Ann Arbor, 1992.

Ward, James A., *The Fall of the Packard Motor Car Company*, Stanford University Press, Stanford, 1995.

Whitwell, Greg, *Making the Market*, McPhee Gribble, Melbourne, 1989.

Wik, Reynold M., *Henry Ford and Grass-roots America*, The University of Michigan Press, Ann Arbor, 1973.

Wright, J. Patrick, *On a Clear Day You Can See General Motors: John Z. De Lorean's Look Inside the Automotive Giant*, Wright Enterprises, Grosse Point, 1979.

Wright, John M., *Heart of the Lion*, Allen & Unwin, Sydney, 1998.

Wright, Richard A., 'The Sloan Years' in *Automotive News: GM 75th Anniversary Issue*, 16 September 1983.

Magazines

Australian Monthly Motor Manual, Wheels, Modern Motor, The Autocar, The Motor, People, Restored Cars, Australian Motorist, People, Pointers.

Brochures

The Changing Trend, GMH, Melbourne, 1936.

Opel brochures 1938–39.

Milford Proving Ground brochure.

Websites

adb.online.anu.edu.au

www.coachbuilt.com

www.autonews.net.au

Unpublished theses

Swan, Peter, *GMH and the Australian Automobile Industry: An Economic Perspective*, Monash University, 1971.

Warden, Alexander A, *The Personal and Administrative Career of Sir Laurence Hartnett and His Contributions to Australian Industry and Government*, The University of Tasmania, Hobart, 1973.

Archival Research

Holden archive, Mortlock Library of South Australian, State Library of South
    Australia, Adelaide.
Ford Australia archive, Ford Discovery Centre, Geelong.

Index